TRENDS IN POLICING

Interviews with POLICE LEADERS ACROSS THE GLOBE

TRENDS IN POLICING

Interviews with
POLICE LEADERS
ACROSS THE GLOBE

Dilip K. Das and Otwin Marenin

CRC Press
Taylor & Francis Group
Boca Raton London New York

CRC Press is an imprint of the
Taylor & Francis Group, an **Informa** business

CRC Press
Taylor & Francis Group
6000 Broken Sound Parkway NW, Suite 300
Boca Raton, FL 33487-2742

© 2009 by Taylor & Francis Group, LLC
CRC Press is an imprint of Taylor & Francis Group, an Informa business

Library of Congress Cataloging-in-Publication Data

Das, Dilip K., 1941-
    Trends in policing : interviews with police leaders across the globe / Dilip K. Das and Otwin Marenin.
        p. cm.
    Includes bibliographical references and index.
    ISBN 978-1-4200-7520-5
    1. Police--Cross-cultural studies. 2. Police administration--Cross-cultural studies. 3. Police-community relations--Cross-cultural studies. 4. Police chiefs--Interviews. I. Marenin, Otwin. II. Title.

HV7921.D38 2009
363.2--dc22   2008036396

Visit the Taylor & Francis Web site at
http://www.taylorandfrancis.com

and the CRC Press Web site at
http://www.crcpress.com

Table of Contents

Contributors

Bonnie (Yevonne) Armbruster has served, for the past four years, as the editor of the *Ohio Police Chief Magazine*, a publication of the Ohio Association of Chiefs of Police (OACP), in addition to editing the *Ohio Crime Prevention Digest*, a publication of the Ohio Crime Prevention Association (OCPA). She is the primary grant writer for the Law Enforcement Foundation, the fundraising arm of the OACP. Upon graduation from Michigan State University, Bonnie taught underprivileged at-risk children in suburban Detroit, Michigan, until she moved to Columbus, Ohio, where she taught in corporate settings before joining the OACP.

Police Colonel Dr. Jozsef Boda, PhD, assumed the position of director of the International Training Center, Ministry of Justice and Law Enforcement in July 1999. He holds a doctorate in military science (military intelligence) and a PhD in police peacekeeping. He has written many publications on various subjects concerning the military, intelligence issues, the role of the international civilian police in peacekeeping operations, police reforms, and the law enforcement system in Hungary.

Dr. Boda began his military career as Platoon and Company Commander and Chief of Staff of the Special Forces. In 1991 he joined the Hungarian National Police. From 1991 until 1997, he served as Deputy Commander of the Hungarian Special Police Force (Counter Terrorism Unit). In 1997, he was appointed as Hungarian Director of the International Law Enforcement Academy, Budapest, Hungary. Dr. Boda is also an active member of several professional societies in the realm of civic, public, and international affairs.

He has served with the United Nations Civilian Police (UNCIVPOL) on many missions: Cambodia (UNTAC), Mozambique (UNIMOZ), the Multinational Force and Observers in the Sinai Peninsula, Egypt, in Bosnia-Herzegovina (UNMIBH), and as a Senior Police Advisor to the United Nations Observers Mission in Georgia (UNOMIG). He was also a member of an expert group of the UN DPKO Strategic Generic Training Module, a police expert for the Geneva Center for Democratic Control of Armed Forces, and a member of the Police Working Group for the UN DPKO STM-3 Project. He is a member of the Governing Board of the European Police College (CEPOL) and its External Relations Working Group.

Ming-Chwang (Mark) Chen is a professor in the Department of Border Police, Central Police University, Taiwan, where he teaches courses in policing, administration, and management. He received his BA at the Central Police University, Taiwan, in 1976; his MA in police administration from the Graduate School, Central Police University, in 1981; and his PhD from the College of Criminal Justice, Sam Houston State University, Texas, in 1988. He joined the police in 1976 and worked in numerous positions and ranks. He has lectured widely in Taiwan and across the globe, and has published extensively, including a text on police administration, on policy issues in policing. Chen's interview was recorded by Cheng-feng Li, police captain, Secretary to President Ing-Dan Shieh of Central Police University.

Dr. Angela West Crews holds a bachelor's degree in psychology from Tusculum College (Tennessee), a master's degree in criminal justice and criminology from East Tennessee State University, and a PhD in criminology from Indiana University of Pennsylvania. Her master's thesis experimentally examined the accuracy and reliability of eyewitness identifications and her doctoral dissertation comparatively evaluated the effectiveness of HIV/AIDS education programs for male and female inmates in Pennsylvania prisons. She has over 14 years of undergraduate and graduate teaching experience, and has authored or coauthored numerous journal articles, book chapters, and grant proposals. Most recently, she has been interested in the measurement of concepts in law enforcement and correctional policy analysis and program evaluation, and in policies related to the release of ex-inmates into society. Her research interests are varied and involve all aspects of the criminal justice system, but share a policy analysis or program evaluation focus. Her areas of teaching include research methods and statistics, corrections, comparative justice systems, and criminological theory. She currently is an associate professor in the Criminal Justice Department, Marshall University, Huntington, West Virginia. She is active in the Academy of Criminal Justice Sciences as the chair of the Corrections Section, and in the American Society of Criminology. She also has served the profession in various capacities within the Southern Criminal Justice Association. She currently is writing a book chapter examining corrections from a critical perspective, and working with her husband, Dr. Gordon Crews, on two books relating to juvenile delinquency. In addition, the Crewses recently worked with the Joint Center on Violence and Victim Studies on a grant proposal to the U.S. Department of State to form collaborative partnerships with NGOs in Africa (Ghana and South Africa) to address the problem of human trafficking.

Dr. Gordon A. Crews is currently an associate professor in the Criminal Justice Department, Marshall University, Huntington, West Virginia. Prior to this position, he served as chair and associate professor of the

Department of Criminal Justice and Sociology at Cameron University in Lawton, Oklahoma. Since 1990, Dr. Crews has served as a faculty member and/or academic administrator at Roger Williams University (Rhode Island), Jacksonville State University (Alabama), Valdosta State University (Georgia), and the University of South Carolina Beaufort (South Carolina). He serves as executive counselor for the Juvenile Justice Section of the Academy of Criminal Justice Sciences and as former president and member of the board of directors for the Southern Criminal Justice Association. He earned a PhD in education/criminal justice, a graduate certificate in alcohol and drug studies, a Bachelor of Science degree in criminal justice and Master of Criminal Justice degree from the University of South Carolina. Prior to teaching, Dr. Crews worked in law enforcement as a bloodhound officer and trainer, field-training officer, and criminal investigator; in corrections as a training and accreditation manager; and in insurance fraud as an investigator.

His publications include journal articles dealing with school violence, occult/satanic involvement and youth, and various law enforcement and correctional issues. His books include *Faces of Violence in America* (1996), published by Simon & Schuster; *The Evolution of School Disturbance in America: Colonial Times to Modern Day* (1997), published by Praeger; *A History of Correctional Violence: An Examination of Reported Causes of Riots and Disturbances* (1998), published by the American Correctional Association; *Chasing Shadows: Confronting Juvenile Violence in America* (2001), published by Prentice Hall; *Living in Prison: A History of the Correctional System with an Insider's View* (2004), published by Greenwood Publishers; and *In the Margins: Special Populations and American Justice* (2008), published by Prentice Hall. His most recent book is entitled *Juvenile Delinquency and Violence: Examining International Police and Societal Response* (2009), published by Taylor & Francis. Dr. Crews' current research interests focus on an international comparison of police and societal response to individuals involved in alternative belief practices (e.g., Satanism, Wicca, Goth, etc.). Since 2000, he has conducted extensive field research in these areas across the United States, United Kingdom, Middle East, Netherlands, Central Europe, Scandinavia, and most recently in Turkey and Ghana.

Lucía Dammert is director, Program in Security and Citizenship, FLACSO (*Facultad Latinoamericana de Ciencias Sociales*), Santiago, Chile. She has a PhD from the University of Leiden, Holland, an MA in urban and regional planning (1997) and Certificate in Latin American Studies (1997) from the University of Pittsburgh, and a bachelor's degree in sociology from Universidad Nacional de Cuyo, Argentina. She has extensive academic and public policy experience throughout Latin America and has participated in several research projects sponsored by the Ebert Foundation, the Open Society Institute, United Nations Development Program, and the governments of

Argentina, Chile, and Peru. She has been consultant for the Inter-American Development Bank, the World Bank, the United Nations Development Program, and the European Commission, in countries such as Peru, Bolivia, Argentina, the Dominican Republic, El Salvador, Honduras, and Costa Rica, among others. Her most recent books are *Perspectivas y dilemas de las seguridad ciudadana en América Latina* (Quito, Flacso-Ecuador, 2007), *Seguridad y Violencia: Desafíos para la Ciudadanía* (editor with Liza Zuñiga, Santiago, Flacso-Chile, 2007), *Public Security and Police Reform in the Americas* (editor with John Bailey, University of Pittsburgh Press, 2006), *Seguridad y Reforma Policial en las Américas* (editor with John Bailey, México, Siglo XXI, 2005), *Seguridad Ciudadana: Experiencias y desafíos* (Valparaíso, URBAL, 2004), *La prevención del delito en Chile. Una visión de la comunidad* (coauthor with Alejandra Lúnecke, Santiago, Universidad de Chile, 2004).

Dr. Dilip Das served as police chief before joining academia. He is the founding president of International Police Executive Symposium, IPES, www.ipes.info, which brings police researchers and practitioners together to facilitate cross-cultural, international, and interdisciplinary exchanges for the enrichment of the profession. Professor Das also serves as the founding editor-in-chief of *Police Practice and Research: An International Journal* which is affiliated with IPES. His publications include more than 24 books and numerous articles. He is a professor of Criminal Justice and a human rights consultant to the United Nations.

Emilio E. Dellasoppa is professor at the State University of Rio de Janeiro. He was visiting researcher at the Núcleo de Estudos da Violência da Universidade de São Paulo and also at the Institute of Social Science of the University of Tokyo. His main areas of interest are urban violence and police institutions in Brazil. He is author of "Ao inimigo, nem justiça: political violence in Argentina 1943–1983," and of several papers and book chapters. Dr. Dellasoppa received an engineering degree from the University of La Plata (Argentina) and a PhD in political science from the University of São Paulo, Brazil.

John A. Eterno, PhD, is the associate dean and director of Graduate Studies in the Department of Criminal Justice at Molloy College in Rockville Centre, New York. He received his PhD in criminal justice from the University at Albany. He is also a retired captain from the New York City Police Department and is the managing editor of *Police Practice and Research: An International Journal.* His research interests include legal aspects of policing, violence, and aggression, and international perspectives of law enforcement. His book entitled *Policing within the Law: A Case Study of the New York City Police Department* was published in 2003 (Praeger). His recent peer reviewed publications can be seen in *Police Practice and Research: An International Journal,*

Justice Research and Policy, The International Journal of Police Science and Management, Policing: An International Journal of Police Strategies and Management, Women and Criminal Justice, Criminal Law Bulletin, and *Professional Issues in Criminal Justice.*

Robert F.J. Harnischmacher earned his Abitur in economic sciences at Kolleg Burg Eringerfeld in 1967. Throughout the course of his military service, he served as an instructor and authored close combat and self-defense learning material for special units of police (e.g., GSG 9 etc.), units of the military police (Feldjaeger of the German Bundeswehr), and units in foreign countries. He studied jurisprudence at the Westphalian Wilhelms University in Muenster. Currently he is the owner and managing director of the firm International Security and Media Consulting (ISMC) in Lippstadt, Germany. He has authored, edited, and coauthored a variety of publications on jurisprudence and law, and is an associate editor and contributor to the *World Police Encyclopedia.* He lectures at academies, technical high schools of public administration, national and international universities, at conferences and symposia and consults widely on security and intelligence matters.

Otwin Marenin is a professor in the Political Science Department/Criminal Justice at Washington State University. He received his BS from Northern Arizona University and his MA and PhD (in comparative politics) from the University of California Los Angeles. He has taught at Ahmadu Bello University and the University of Benin in Nigeria, and the Universities of Baltimore, California, Colorado, and Alaska-Fairbanks in the United States. His research and publications have focused on policing systems in Native American communities in the United States and on the origins and practices of policing in Africa, especially in Nigeria. More recently, he has done research and written on developments in international policing, transnational police assistance programs, and efforts to reform the policing systems in failed, transitional, and developing states. Recent publications include *Policing Change, Changing Police: International Perspectives* (editor), *Challenges of Policing Democracies* (co-editor Dilip Das), *Transforming the Police in Central and Eastern Europe* (co-editor Marina Caparini), and *Comparative Problems of Policing: Interviews with Police Leaders from Different Nations* (co-editor Dilip Das).

Darko Maver is a lawyer by profession and holds MA and PhD degrees. He is a full professor at the Faculty of Criminal Justice and Security at the University of Maribor, as well as at the Faculty of Law, University of Maribor and Faculty of Law, University of Ljubljana. He worked for 15 years at the Institute of Criminology at the Faculty of Ljubljana, was a director of the Criminal Police of Slovenia between 1990 and 1993, and later was responsible for international relations at the Ministry of the Interior of Slovenia. He was dean of the College of Police and Security Studies from 1998 to 2001. In 2003 he was Visiting Fulbright Scholar at Grand Valley State University, Grand Rapids, Michigan. He has published more than 150 articles and three books on criminal investigation, attended many international police and other conferences (including the Interpol General Assembly, United Nations conferences, IPES conferences, etc.), and has been a guest lecturer at Gong-An University in Beijing and the Faculty of Criminalistics at the University of Sarajevo.

Dr. Elizabeth H. McConnell has a bachelor's degree in criminal justice and a master's degree in sociology from Valdosta State University. Her PhD in criminal justice is from Sam Houston State University. She currently teaches at the University of Houston Clear Lake; however, she has chaired criminal justice departments at Charleston Southern University and the University of Houston Downtown. She has practical experience in corrections, having been a corrections officer, correctional counselor, and probation/parole officer. She has served on numerous university and professional committees and is an experienced evaluator of criminal justice degree programs. She is a champion of university globalization initiatives, such as study-abroad opportunities for students and faculty exchanges for scholars, both of which she has administered. Her research interests include fear of crime, youth gangs, and corrections. Her publications are diverse and include a coauthored book, book chapters, refereed journal articles, as well as several externally funded research grants. Her published work appears in *Prison Journal, Journal of Security Administration, The Gang Journal,* and *Youth and Society.* She is author of numerous book chapters and encyclopedic entries, and coauthor of *American Prisons: An Annotated Bibliography* (with Laura Moriarty), Greenwood Press.

Gorazd Meško, PhD, is an associate professor of criminology and dean at the Faculty of Criminal Justice and Security, University of Maribor, Slovenia. He teaches criminology and conducts research in the fields of crime prevention, victimology, and crime control policy. He is also an honorary visiting fellow at the Department of Criminology, University of Leicester, UK (2005–2008). He has (co)organized conferences on policing in Central and Eastern Europe in Ljubljana, Slovenia since 2000. He is a board member of GERN (the European Research Group on Social Norms, at http://www.gern-cnrs.com/gern/index.php?id=2&L=2). He has published extensively in fields of criminology, crime prevention, provision of safety, and criminal careers.

Dr. Andrew Millie is a lecturer in criminology and social policy in the Department of Social Sciences, Loughborough University, UK. His interview included in this volume was with the Commissioner of New South Wales Police. This was conducted in 2007 while he was a visiting fellow at the Australian Graduate School of Policing, Charles Sturt University, Manly, Australia. Dr. Millie has published across a range of criminological and policing issues. His areas of interest can be summarized as antisocial behavior, policing, the relationship between crime and the city, and sentencing and crime prevention. He is coeditor with Dilip K. Das of *Contemporary Issues in Law Enforcement and Policing*, published in 2008 by CRC Press. He is also author of *Anti-Social Behaviour*, forthcoming by the Open University Press.

Darryl Plecas holds the RCMP University Research Chair in the School of Criminology and Criminal Justice at the University of the Fraser Valley, British Columbia, Canada. He is the author or coauthor of more than 150 research reports, journal articles, and other works addressing a broad range of criminal justice issues. He received his BA and MA in criminology from Simon Fraser University and his EdD in higher education from the University of British Columbia.

Anthony L. Sciarabba is a research assistant in the Department of Criminal Justice at Molloy College in Rockville Centre, New York. He also serves as the associate managing editor of *Police Practice and Research: An International Journal*. Currently, he is involved in field research, evaluating a "Weed and Seed" initiative in Far Rockaway, New York, for the Community Capacity Development Office (United States Department of Justice).

Elrena van der Spuy is an associate professor at the Centre of Criminology situated within the Department of Public Law at the University of Cape Town. Over the years her research has focused on the history of the police in twentieth century South Africa, the influence of international ideas on the reform of the public police in South Africa, and on the trajectories of police reforms in Africa more generally.

Dr. Arvind Verma worked in the Indian Police Service for several years. He served as superintendent of police in the province of Bihar and occupied many senior administrative posts within the police organization. He received his doctorate in criminology from Simon Fraser University, Vancouver, Canada in 1996. His doctoral work was concerned with the development of new tools of information and data analysis using fuzzy logic, topology, and other "qualitative" mathematical techniques. His recent publications include the book *Indian Police: A Critical Evaluation*; and journal articles "State and Coercive Powers in India" and "Policing of Elections in India." Along with Kiran Bedi he has recently launched "Mission Safer India" (www.saferindia.com), an initiative to facilitate registration of crimes in the country.

Dominique Wisler has a background in philosophy (master of philosophy at the University of Fribourg) and political sciences (PhD at the University of Geneva). He was a visiting scholar at the University of Arizona in 1994 and a lecturer at the University of Geneva from 1995 to 1999. In 2000, he joined a consulting company specializing in strategic management and took part in police reorganization projects in various countries, including Switzerland, Bosnia and Herzegovina, Mozambique, and the Sudan. He served in 2005 and 2006 as senior advisor for the United Nations Development Program in Khartoum, Sudan. Dominique Wisler is also the founder of Coginta, Geneva, which advises police organizations and the development community. He is the author of several books, chapters, and articles in the field of policing, social movements, and the sociology of the state. His most recent publications include a book on the history of the Geneva constitution since 1847, published by Georg (2008), and a comparative book on policing in Swiss cantons (Haupt, Bern, 2007). He is currently preparing with Dilip K. Das an edited collection on terrorism, and another, with Ihekwoaba D. Onwudiwe, on comparative community policing.

Introduction

DILIP DAS AND OTWIN MARENIN

This is the second book in the series "Trends in Policing: Interviews with Police Leaders across the Globe." The first book has a slightly different title: *Comparative Problems of Policing: Interviews with Nineteen Police Leaders from Different Nations.* The suggested guidelines and questions for the interviewers are the same for both books, and for the third book, which we hope will be coming out later this year, the same set of materials is being used (see Appendix A).

This series was born out of a few strong convictions and a set of experiences. One of the convictions is that police leaders possess a plethora of rich experiences and practical and theoretical knowledge that can provide fascinating insights into the current state of policing across the world. We have defined the term *leader* in a somewhat loose sense. We have considered any police officer occupying a position in the top hierarchy of the police as a leader. He or she has knowledge of policy making, a position that enables him or her to view issues and events from the top, and has had several years in her or his policing career to speak on the various topics such as police administration, crime, public relations, future developments and so on with a degree of authority based on knowledge and experience. The 17 police practitioners interviewed for the book are leaders by the definition we have adopted for the purpose of the series.

Our second conviction is that collaboration between police practitioners and researchers (academics) is a rich avenue for acquiring knowledge and understanding of policing. Police leaders are busy professionals and they are also usually not accustomed to writing on their experiences even though, as part of their work, they will have reflected extensively on how to do policing. Interviews are a way to try to capture those reflections and understandings. Academics and researchers, on the other hand, are required to reflect and write. That is part of their job. It will be noted that an overwhelming number of the interviewers are researchers. However, we also do not consider it a deviation from our standards if interviews for the book have been conducted by a practitioner. In some countries (Hungary in this volume, for example) the tradition of police research and academic pursuits in policing are in their infancy. In such countries we consider it useful and beneficial to accept the assistance of a fellow practitioner for an interview.

It is our firm conviction that a synthesis of the views and judgments of practitioners and academics about developments in policing is a useful goal. In addition, the quality of policing can only benefit from such a synthesis of knowledge derived from diverse sources. Reading the interviews, we have been struck by how eloquent police leaders are when asked about their jobs; how much they have thought about how to deal with the practical problems and issues that confront their police organizations; how well they understand the political implications and impacts of their jobs; and how extensively they have been involved in transnational and international policing. Though all work in specific country and city settings, these leaders are well informed about what is happening in the world; they are true cosmopolitans.

The two editors of the series come from different experiential backgrounds. Otwin Marenin has traveled around the world doing field research in policing, in the course of which he has spoken to numerous police leaders. Based on his experiences he understands what a rich source of knowledge about policing they provide. Dilip Das was a police leader in India where police leaders do not enjoy the prestige and influence that are the prerogatives of the general administrators. He found it difficult to reconcile himself to the subordinate status of police leaders in the administrative hierarchy and system in India as he realized that they should be treated as second to none. This series is a vindication of the notion that police leaders must be treated with respect, dignity, and importance because of the complex human affairs they have to handle in their careers. They can be an enormous source of service to humanity. They are essential to the maintenance of the quality of life.

We also wish to thank the leaders who consented to give their time to sit down and answer the numerous questions directed at them. And we also wish to thank the interviewers, without whom books such as this one would not be possible. We also would add that we, the editors, having read the interviews carefully to prepare them for publication, have benefited tremendously by being the first (well, the second) readers to have access to the knowledge and insights offered by the police leaders interviewed. We hope that other readers will gain as much as we have.

Interview with Ken Moroney, Commissioner of New South Wales Police, Australia

INTERVIEWED BY ANDREW MILLIE

Background

At the end of August 2007 Ken Moroney retired from New South Wales Police after 42 years of service. During that time he witnessed, and was part of, some fundamental changes in Australian law enforcement. He rose from a 19-year-old probationary constable in 1965 to commissioner of police from 2002 to 2007, the highest position in the New South Wales Police. He also received various awards, including the Order of Australia, the Australian Police Medal, the National Medal, and an Olympic Commendation (see NSW Police, 2006). I was fortunate enough to interview him during his last month in office, and despite his obvious success, he came across quite humbly, keen to talk about the successes and strengths of others, particularly earlier commissioners Tony Lauer and John Avery, and his successor, Andrew Scipione.

The interview was conducted in the plush surrounds of the Commissioner's Office, high above Elizabeth Street in central Sydney—the kind of office you dream of, with panoramic views of the city. Also present was the chief of staff, Superintendent Mark Hutchings. Moroney had clearly been looking back at his career and was very honest in his answers. The interview took place on August 13, 2007.

Ken Moroney's Career

AM: I just want to start with some very general questions. I saw from your brief bio on the force Web site you've been in the police since 1965, is that right?

KM: Yes, I started at 19. There was nothing in our immediate family antecedents which led me to the New South Wales Police. My great, great grandfather had been a police officer in Ireland and he came from Freshford, which is near Limerick in Ireland, in the 1880s. He came here with his 14 children and his wife, settled here in Sydney. He didn't join the police force as it then was. So that's my only connection to police and policing, which is a very historical one.

AM: So what made you pick the police?

KM: I think it's the same thing that makes our recruits apply today, irrespective of the jurisdiction, irrespective of the country. I think the common things that police applicants, irrespective of age, have in common is that desire to have a fulfilling career. And I think more than that, it's about undertaking a career whereby you can, even at the most junior level within the organization, you can make a difference, and you can have an impact in the local community. Easier in rural Australia, than say metropolitan, CBD Australia, where I can, in the Sydney CBD, work, but I could live 100 kilometers away. So there's no connection between where you live and where you work, as opposed to, say, rural policing.

And of my 42 years I spent about 20 years in country New South Wales. And I know firsthand that there is an obvious connection between living and working in a rural location. Because you'll invariably find most, not all, but most police officers in those situations probably the president of the P & C,[1] president of the local every other thing, so there's that sort of unofficial "mayoral" type role. At 19 my great ambition was to be a sergeant in charge of a country town. I didn't set out to become the commissioner of police. That was just not part of my vocabulary. To be a sergeant in charge of a country town would just be the pinnacle of your career. And in part that was realized, albeit in my case for a relatively short period of time of about 6 years. But I reflect that, of all of my service to date, that period, that 20-year period was certainly the most satisfying and fulfilling period because of those connections between where you live and the community which you grew to know in a very intimate way.

AM: Which area was that?

KM: Oh, I worked initially in Lismore on the north coast of New South Wales, and then I worked in a number of smaller places in and around Lismore—a little community called Coraki, [a] very heavily populated Aboriginal town. And then variously in other smaller locations ... My next major rural posting was at West Wyalong in the southwest of the state.

I was brought back to Sydney [in 1986] by the then Commissioner of Police [John Avery]. I was back a year and then I was promoted. I went from the then rank structure of sergeant second class— sergeant today—to superintendent, which for its time was a huge accelerated promotion. Superintendents of police in 1987 were, by and large, in their late 50s; it was a promotion that was almost at the point of exit from the organization. So to have this 42-year-old who was unheard of, there were all of the usual comments, "the job was coming apart at the seams because somebody so young should be promoted." But I was appointed as the director of Police Recruit Education at the Police Academy at Goulburn, and I held that appointment for 4 years. And then John Avery appointed me as the chief of staff. I stayed with him for his last 6 months, and then I was the chief of staff to Commissioner Lauer. So that period, as I said, was the most enjoyable period; friendships made inside and outside the police are still the same friendships today.

AM: What would you consider to be some of the highlights in your career?

KM: I've had a number of jobs that have given me satisfaction: being the inaugural director of Police Recruit Education at the Academy, Goulburn, was a career highlight for me; being the deputy president of the Police Association at the same time as being in country New South Wales was fulfilling but it was physically a challenge. Other career highlights included involvement in the policing of the Olympics in 2000 under Commissioner Peter Ryan, his work at the Police Academy and work for the Police Association.

AM: That's a lot!

KM: It was physically a challenge and led me to a point of ill health, of trying to do so much at the one time, with the huge distances required. At that time I was travelling to and from the southwestern part of the state. And I'd always insist on, having been here for a day's work as the deputy president of the Police Association, of then still going home and doing 8-hour shifts.

Policing Philosophy and the Impact of Change

During the interview Moroney had a knack of preempting a lot of my questions. He talked at length about his personal policing philosophy and the impact of change. His philosophy could be summarized as an emphasis on proactive policing, and having an educated and professionalized police force. He also stressed the importance of having the right people in post, rather than simply, "more blue shirts and more blue shirts."

On Proactive Policing

KM: This morning among the executive we've been talking about the solvability of crime in New South Wales, and why it's perhaps not as high as some other states. I think there's a range of reasons for that. I think, variously, we count crime differently, which is never handy to try and get some comparative analysis, one state to the other. But certainly it is said of New South Wales that we have far more proactive crime prevention strategies and programs than other jurisdictions do in this country. So we're on the point now of saying, "do we need an equal balance of proactive or prevention programs," which obviously takes up a fair chunk of your policing resources, or do we reassess and simply say, "we've got to put more time and effort and energy—from the point of view of numbers of police, forensic capability, intelligence gathering, etc.—into reactive aspects of policing?" And that's the great challenge I think for police leaders today, particularly for the commissioner of police. I think the overwhelming majority of people want to see the police on the street, they want them out there, and I do understand that.

On the Impact of Technology

KM: We're looking at how we might reduce, an old terminology, how do we reduce red tape. And now there's not too much red tape in the organization *per se*, but new systems created to make the job easier have in fact made the job harder, for example, by the fact that so many police are off the street attending to our IT systems and processes that require detailed recording. So it seems to me that as technology has created a boon for us, in terms of how we store, maintain, and retrieve information, so then it's created a burden for us. Now I don't say "let's abandon computers and let's go back to the days of the quill and the pad," that's not going to happen. But it is that constant challenge of, how do you work in a modern IT age, with all the benefits that come from that age, and at the same time, how do you work through a range of systems, that the said IT system, created to be a boon, is in fact a burden?

On Police Recruitment

KM: I think the modern police leader today, when we talk about police numbers, will go to government and simply say, recruitment for the future has to be more than just more police numbers and more police numbers—or as we would say in this state, "more blue shirts and more blue shirts." But it is about the recruitment of the right mix of people, sworn and unsworn, police and civilian staff. It is about the recruitment of the right mix of people in terms of skill, background, qualification—both experiential and academic—

looking at the increased role that science is playing in policing, and I do regard policing as a science.

So how you recruit that right mix of people is not always attractive to governments. Governments of whatever political persuasion I think simply look at policing as "more blue shirts and more blue shirts." Whereas a modern, contemporary government wanting to invest in the future, that realizes an ongoing reduction in crime, realizing a reduction in the fear of crime, enhances visibility, police on the street, that reassures and equally deters at the same time, has to think about the policing agency of the future. And so the whole issue of research and development, the role of technology, the role of science, in all its manifestations and disciplines, I think becomes important for the modern police leader and the police organization of the future. It just can't be built around more police numbers and more police numbers, because as quickly as I recruit them and train them at the police academy, they seem to leave the academy and disappear into a great black hole quickly absorbed into the mainstream police force. And so it's been one of those things that I've sought to do over the last 5 years, is to recruit the right mix of people.

On an Educated and Professionalized Force

AM: With your background at Goulburn [Police Academy] I guess you see an educated police force as important, or professionalized?

KM: Absolutely, look, for a range of reasons. When I entered the New South Wales Police in 1965 my training was 5 weeks in duration. Contrast that to 1945 when Commissioner John Avery entered the police force, his training was of 2 weeks. Contrast that to today in 2007 where the training, inclusive of probation, is almost 2 years in duration. When I entered the police force there were basic fundamental requirements; you had to be a minimum height of 5 foot 9, you had to be a minimum weight of 10 stone 7, and you had to be 38 and a half inches around the chest. You did a basic fundamental test in mathematics and English (spelling). Now provided you met all those physical and educational requirements, and ideally you had what we then called the Intermediate Certificate—now the School Certificate—you were in. You were in. And, of course, provided you were of the right background and character, and all those other important aspects.

And again, we've moved forward enormously over that period of time, and a lot of that credit does belong to Commissioner John Avery, who wrote a book in about 1981, we affectionately refer to it as "The Little Red Book"—it's not "The Thoughts of Chairman Avery"—but ... [his] first thoughts about the importance of extending initial police recruit training, and linking it to tertiary qualifications. And it was probably regarded as ... rather radical, different, and "this will never happen." In 1987 I was appointed as the inaugural director of police recruit education and training at the Academy at Goulburn. My brief was to take it from what had blown out to be 12 weeks of training in 1987, to a fully accredited academic program. Now of course we heard things that "the sky would fall in and the world would end as we knew it and policing would be ruined." I remember clichés at the time, "there still needed to be room for the farmer's son in the New South Wales Police Force." It was as though we were excluding every human being on the face of the earth, and that wasn't the case at all. What we were seeking to do was the old adage of "a rising tide lifts all boats" philosophy. We were told that, by lifting the educational and academic standards of the program we wouldn't get recruits. And in fact history would now prove that that was clearly the opposite, where we lifted the standard. It wasn't education for education's sake, it was about lifting, through the various disciplines of the program, the study requirements of the program, understanding what is the role of police in a contemporary society like New South Wales. What does the community want of us, reactively and proactively? How do police become leaders in the community and lead greater change within the community? Or is it just about more laws, more laws, and more police and more police?

What [Avery] did then was, not only push from the bottom up at recruit level, he appointed Superintendent Patrick Ciocarelli, who sadly has passed away now, looking at executive development and leadership training. So it was very much a bottom-up and a top-down approach at the same time. Some would say, "well, what's going to happen to that big group in the middle?" He catered for that by addressing a whole range of what he loosely referred to as management and specialist skills training. It was a long investment in the future of our organization. So are we, 20 years on from PREP (the Police Recruit Education Program), the Executive Development Program, and the specialist middle-management training programs, are we different? Well the answer to that is simply "yes" in a range of demonstrable ways. I think Avery's other agenda was also built around the issue of professional standards, conduct, and integrity. Of providing thought and challenge for police, whether you're the most junior probationary constable, or the commissioner of police, or somewhere in between, about those ethical and moral dilemmas that will confront you from time to time, either individually or in groups, and to make you think. So 20 years on I think Avery's great legacy was not only the operational focus he had at the time, but [also] the strong push on educational standards.

And so the organization that I joined in 1965, where a handful in an organization of 6,000 might have had what we called the Intermediate Certificate. Beyond that the next tertiary qualification was called the Leaving Certificate, year 12. Maybe you could have counted those on ten fingers. University qualifications? You're kidding. Just not in the vocabulary. So from 1965 up to 1987 we saw this great quantum leap; 1987 to 2007 we've seen an even greater quantum leap. It's not unusual now to see vast numbers of police with master's degrees. Bachelor's degrees are just something that automatically happens now. And the number of police officers studying for PhDs? Now that was just unheard of, that would almost have been like some police heresy 20 years ago.

AM: Do you think the result has been better policing?

KM: Oh, you're probably asking the wrong person, I'm too biased. I suspect so, but that doesn't mean, we've discovered the Holy Grail of policing here in New South Wales. In my very biased way I believe I leave the organization 42 years on a better policeman, irrespective of my rank. Well you'd say, "that's obvious, it's 42 years more experience, you're a vastly different rank." I acknowledge all those things, but I think in terms of those day-to-day judgments and values that you have to have, and how you apply those values to your decision making. I see these things happening around me all of the time, really good police work, police officers out there being reactive, responding to crime, being proactive and preventing crime, working with various community groups—whether they're Aboriginal people, whether they're members of multicultural groups—and doing so many things that I'm sure variously they did 40 years ago, but not to the same scope that I see today.

On Other Changes: Women in Policing

AM: I guess another big change in those years would be the increase in women police officers.

KM: Oh, very much so. We were the first police force in the country to introduce women into policing in 1915, indeed one of the first police forces in the world to do that. Between 1915 and 1965 they'd grown from two to about 200 over that 50-year period. We now see their number at three and a half thousand. So there's been a huge explosion in female recruitment. And that's not only as a consequence of policy and affirmative action. You know, they've had a huge impact on our organization, and I mean that in a positive way. Certainly in the area of professional standards—no longer is this the blokey culture of 40 years ago. And the women have had a dramatic impact in the organization in terms of professional standards, impact on behavior, and ethical performance. They've had a huge impact out there in the operational environment as well, both in its specialist forms, child abuse investigation, etc., and in its generalist forms.

And so, some of my predecessors would probably roll in their grave today to see women, not only in charge of police stations, but women in charge of single unit police stations in rural New South Wales. That's something that, you know, a decade ago would probably have [been] just unimaginable. Women have had a huge impact on the organization and that, in part, came about because of a commitment one of my predecessors, Commissioner Tony Lauer, gave in about 1995 to increase the overall size of the police force, the overall size of the female population of the police force to 50%.

AM: OK.

KM: They said, "that's impossible, it could never happen." Well, now about a third of our operating strength are women. So it's something that, I don't know that it's a goal that's going to be achieved by 2010 or 2020, but the nature of our recruitment now is that the number of women in the organization is increasing more and more, and they're diversifying across a whole range of commands. And of our executive team, 3 of our 15 assistant commissioners are female. They haven't won those on the basis of being women, they've won them on the basis of skill and qualifications, and they just happen to be women. But they've had a dramatic impact. And perhaps the most dramatic impact was the appointment of the chief commissioner of the Victoria Police, Christine Nixon,[2] who we would proudly say "was home grown in New South Wales."

On Other Changes: Recruitment from Aboriginal and Multicultural Communities

AM: I'm interested in [the] recruitment of Aboriginal people within the police, does it happen very much, or is that something that you'd want to encourage?

KM: Yeah, look, the recruitment of Aboriginal people and people of diverse multicultural backgrounds is extremely important. An organization like the New South Wales Police has got to be reflective of the community that it serves, and this is a very diversified, multicultural community. And we've not had a huge problem in the recruiting of people from multicultural backgrounds, although we've experienced some difficulty in the recruitment of people from Asian backgrounds. I think there is perhaps an understandable historical mistrust of the police, more so based on the experience of parents and grandparents in home countries. I saw that as a great challenge and, in consultation with people from the Asian community, I said, "how do I get more young Asian people into our organization?" They said, "well you're appealing to the wrong group, you should be appealing to their grandparents." So we had a huge information day aimed at Asian grandparents that saw a reasonable increase in Asian recruits who had always considered medicine, law, finance as the real professions. So we just simply said we want you to consider ours as an equal. But other than that the recruitment of people from multicultural groups, from across Europe and other locations has been quite good.

The recruitment of Aboriginal people has not, until recent times, been as effective. I think there's one principal reason for that, or two. All of our training is centered at the Police Academy at Goulburn, which is 200 km south of Sydney. The predominant numbers of Aboriginal people of course come from the western part of the state which, compared to the south, is climatically different, very different,[3] and there is not a strong support base for them around Goulburn and its environs. The other thing we've found was that they had great difficulty in coping with the nature of the study program, even more so when there were small numbers. In mid-2006 we went and recruited 18 Aboriginal recruits, 16 completed their training at the Academy Goulburn and were attested in the class in January of 2007. The reason I believe that the number was quite high, was because there was a support environment, support network within themselves, they helped each other through. Our partners Charles Sturt University put them through a bridging program in terms of how to meet academic requirements, which is just as hard for the White Anglo-Saxon population here, as it is the Aboriginal population. So the bridging program, the support network created by having a much larger number of Aboriginal students has been quite successful.

But I've asked how we might enhance on that. One of the things I've asked is that we consider modeling what they've done in the state of Queensland [where] there are two police academies, one in Brisbane and the other in Townsville. And one of the primary roles—not the primary but one of the primary roles—of the Townsville academy in Queensland is to support people from the Aboriginal community, where there is a strong support network in place for them. We're looking at, with our university partner, how we might provide an annex of the police academy in western New South Wales. So that, you know, if [they're] from western, or far western New South Wales, bring them into central New South Wales, into Dubbo,[4] and provide them with some preliminary training which is all part of the accreditation process, familiarization, support network. And then at some point making the transition then into Goulburn, which I think will be far more effective.

AM: That will be interesting.

KM: Yeah, I think the mistake we've also made, whether it's Asian recruits, Aboriginal recruits, I think we've said, for all of the right reasons at the time, well once recruited, once trained, once attested, let's put them straight back into those communities. And that's been an experiment that's failed. Because that was, not understanding the culture from which they've come. Our Aboriginal probationary constables were treated quite harshly by some members of their own community who saw them, and to use their words, as "Uncle Toms." Members of the Asian community were looked upon by some of their people rather harshly as though you had betrayed the community. We've learnt from that. So it's a case of taking those recruits, those new probationary constables, and putting them through an induction process in another place and then, at the right time moving them back at their request, not at our insistence, but moving them back into those communities. And that's proving to be a far more successful strategy, which again goes to the important issue of support.

Theory and Practice

AM: Now, being an academic I'm very much interested in the links between theory, the stuff us criminologists come up with, and practice. Do you think the links between practice and theory are there, or is there a divide? Has the work of criminologists been useful to you?

KM: Look, 20 years ago I think the initial work done by John Avery and others was academic, or was seen as, "well that's a nice thing," you know, "it would look very nice on a qualification." I think 20 years on, clearly the role of criminologists, researchers, people who are part of the broader policing/law enforcement discipline, are making a huge impact on policing and police, at police tactics and police strategies. I think we've come to realize now that no one individual, or no one profession, or arm of the profession has all the answers. That at the end of the day, it is about a whole of government, a whole of community approach to issues.

Example 1: Policing to Match Local Issues

KM: Some popular media commentators might say [we need] a strict law enforcement approach, more police, stronger penalties by the courts, build more jails. In part, they may be *an* answer, but they are not *the* answer. So it's a case I think of, let us break away from that which we have done historically since 1788, where, if you're the commander here at King's Cross [in Sydney] you will police in the identical same way as the commander of Broken Hill [western New South Wales]. Now they're the two extremities of the state; and the commander in Albury in the south to Tweed Heads in the north—again the two extremities—you'll police in exactly the same way. Yet the policing requirements are radically different. If I said to the commander here at King's Cross, "what are you doing here to reduce, you know, stock theft?" he'd look at me as though I had two heads. Whereas, if I've said to the commander of Broken Hill, "what are your strategies to reduce the incidence of street level prostitution?" He'd look at me curiously too, because they're two different dynamics. Now obviously there are issues of prostitution in a far remote location like that, but not to the same magnitude. So I said to our commanders there are some inherent basic fundamentals of policing which I want you to meet wherever you work, but I want you to adapt your tactics and your strategies built around your local circumstances. And so, what's been important in that process then, is to have officers who are informed by the debate, in terms of operational outcomes [and] contemporary policing research done by police or academics that go to inform a system, what are the holistic approaches that we need to take?

Example 2: Northern Territory Child Sexual Abuse

KM: I read the approach to addressing the issue of child abuse and substance abuse in the Northern Territory of Australia is, "let's send in the army and let's send in police from all around Australia."[5] From this state we've committed 11 police officers to that operation, but not just any 11 police officers. I quite clearly set out that I needed people with a whole range of skills and qualifications, none the least of which was understanding the culture that they were going to work in. But I think the future of a community like the Northern Territory has to be more than just, "let's send in the army and lets send in more police." It is about how the agencies of government, and indeed the Aboriginal community itself, finds solutions to these problems that are going to be lasting and meaningful, and have some real impact. If it's only going to be, "well let's lock up the perpetrators in 2007," now I tend to believe history will repeat itself in another decade, or less than that. So it is about us saying to our commanders, "how do you address the issue?"

Example 3: Policing of Riots

KM: You know, in this state we have had three significant riots, one of them in Redfern, a heavily populated Aboriginal community, one in Macquarie Fields, which is an area of low socioeconomic capacity, ability, and one of course out at Cronulla.[6] I suppose on the world scale of riots, ours weren't riots, but they were riots nevertheless. Ours lasted hours and peace was restored. That doesn't excuse the behavior on any of those occasions. But how do you make sure there's not going to be another riot? Well, some might say, "well just put more police there, and the police that are there, get them to enforce the laws." Yes, that's important, but it is about saying to the commander, "I want you to work with the community, agencies of government, about how we're going to find some lasting solutions." How do you take a community like Macquarie Fields, where the average take home pay is about $300 a week and say to them, "you know, we're all going to build a great life here together," when their social circumstances is such that it is extremely difficult … Yet there are some of the finest people living there that you would ever wish to meet, and the same in Redfern as well. So how do you turn all that around? To their credit, the former commander of Redfern, now Assistant Commissioner Catherine Ahern—[who is now] in charge of our professional standards command—did that huge turnaround.

Interestingly, if you look at the issue that gave rise to the Macquarie Fields riot of January 2005, it was a very short police pursuit, short as in less than a kilometer, it lasted seconds, but resulted in the death of two young boys in a stolen car. And of course, in one sense the rest is history, the riot evolved from that. Almost 2 years to the day a similar police pursuit. A 13-year-old in a stolen car was killed, and he being allegedly involved in a whole series of crime. And my first reaction in January 2007 was, put the riot squad on standby, get out all of the riot shields, "here we go again," the same community. Yet this time nothing happened. What was the difference? More importantly, who was the difference? Two people, Superintendent Stuart Wilkins, the commander, and Father Chris Wiley who, working with the young people of this community, had done such a job to the point where this time the young people said, "the death of this 13-year-old is not the fault of the police, in one sense it's our fault. We saw this happening around us yet we did nothing as young people to stop another young person from committing crime and thereby and ultimately losing his life." But what they'd instilled in the community is a sense of pride, a sense of worth, a sense of value. In two years young people who, in January 2005, were throwing Molotov cocktails and bricks at the police, in January 2007 that didn't occur. Why? They'd been given training, education; out of that came self worth, also came jobs, apprenticeships.

In that sense you might say, "well where's that in the police textbook of leadership?" Oh well, it's probably spelled out in more eloquent academic terms than I can use, but it is about the commander of the day simply saying "how do I reduce crime in this community, when its whole social circumstance is such that, there is a perception of no hope, we just cannot get out of this cycle?" So, it's a case of those people working in that environment, instilling pride. I see police officers out in these communities running programs every morning which feed these kids on the way to school. It's had a tremendous impact. Did I tell them to cook barbeques for the kids? No, all I've said to them is, "your brief is to reduce crime, reduce the fear of crime, work with the community, work with the agencies of government, work with private enterprise, but that's your brief from me." And that's why circumstances worked in Macquarie Fields. If you applied it [elsewhere] it may not work.

Police Leadership

KM: The importance of leadership I think is about empowerment, where I empower the deputy commissioner for field operations, who empowers his region commanders, who empowers local area commanders, who empowers sergeants and constables to go out and do this level of work. Now, some might say, "well, do you pay a price for that?" Well I suppose if reducing crime is paying a price that's a good thing. But when you see crime going down there is the understandable political reaction and treasury reaction, "well, you obviously don't need as many police down there and obviously don't need as much money now." And you say, "well all right, I can take my foot off the brake, or do you want it to go back up?" So that's the great challenge: How do you maintain the huge infrastructure, and we have a 2.2 billion dollar budget for 19,200 personnel, and compete with 39 other CEOs at government level for more and more funding?

So where does the empowerment happen? One of the things I would dearly love to have seen—which will not happen before August 31st [when I retire]—is the establishment in this state of a police command college. I am a great advocate for a command college, I am a great fan of the Scottish Police College, and the English police college at Bramshill,[7] and the RCMP [Royal Canadian Mounted Police] college. I think they epitomize what a command is and ought to be about. The Scottish Police College is probably the pick of the three, although Bramshill and the Mounties might disagree with me.

How do I prevent another Redfern, another Cronulla, another Macquarie Fields? It is about preparing officers to take command, it is about succession planning as well, the command college. I don't know if it's about "crown princing," it's not about me touching someone on the shoulder and saying, "well congratulations, you're the next commissioner of police," or "you're the next deputy commissioner." I think it is about preparing the next pool of our police leadership group, and we're probably talking about the top two or three hundred police in the organization. Not everybody can be the commissioner, not everybody can be the deputy or the assistant commissioner, but good teams must have good leaders. And where our police leadership group, now and into the future, can be exposed to the best thinking that is around, and it goes back to your earlier question, what is the role of academics in police service delivery and police research? What is the role of models of best practice in police leadership from around the world? What works and what doesn't work? You know, what did we learn from, say, the Brixton riots? I suspect we looked at the Brixton riots of …

AM: 1981, I think it was.[8]

KM: Yeah, I think we probably looked at the Brixton riots as interested spectators, "that's over there, it'll never happen here." Now, we didn't have a Brixton riot to that magnitude but we had our own version of that three times. And so how do we prepare for those sorts of things? How do we learn from the best minds in counterterrorism, and not only in terms of response arrangements, but how do we learn in terms of what makes up the mind of a terrorist? You can fly from London to Sydney in 23 hours, you don't have to bring your bomb with you, you can engage in badness here and get on a plane and go to LA, 13 hours later. It's the speed of the modern world.

Transnational and International Policing

AM: That links me to the next question about transnational and international relations. How do you see New South Wales Police fitting into the global policing picture?

KM: Clearly there is a place for that, and that can only be a place that expands. I think the first thing we've got to enhance is how, as nine state and territory police agencies, while we discharge our individual state or territory responsibilities, how we work on a national basis. Because borders are only lines on a map, you know, movement across Australia doesn't require any passport or any border control.

I think secondly, is how this nation's police force works on a regional basis given the position that we are in the world, particularly with our neighbors to our immediate north. We've seen the unrest in the Pacific, in Fiji, in the Solomons, in Timor. What is our appreciation and understanding of that? What is our role as police in that?

And then I think it is then the third step of where this organization sits in terms of the global law enforcement community. We have strong working relationships with the FBI, with the Australian Federal Police, with the London Met., and the Scottish police. We had the usual, if I could describe it that way, the usual response arrangements in terms of crime, and organized crime. But certainly it's been the counterterrorism environment that has drawn us, as part of the bigger global police community. And so our ability and our capacity to gather, disseminate, and share intelligence becomes extremely important. When you look at the issues, as I understand them, surrounding 9/11, the inability of agencies to share information, was it born out of distrust, dislike, or plain ignorance? Well that's a bigger debate, but we saw the consequences of not sharing information. I think any police leader, any commissioner today, who doesn't ensure that you have a strong supportive network—not only a commissioner-to-commissioner basis, but equally command-to-command basis, sharing experience, knowledge, sharing of intelligence—then you're bound to repeat the mistakes of history. And so our strong relationship, particularly with North America, the UK and Europe, Western Europe in particular, has become extremely important. And I think if we build that base even further our relationship with the immediate environs, to our immediate north, with Indonesia, Singapore, and Japan, becomes increasingly important. What then the role of the Chinese? I think the one thing for us here in New South Wales, [is] not to suffer from cultural cringe, we're not the last colonial outpost anymore...

Learning from Other Leaders

At this point Ken Moroney returned to the subject of the proposed command college, clearly an important topic for him. He stated that, "if I leave a legacy in the organization, it is the realization of a command college, it is about preparedness for the future, [and] I do believe the command college will happen here, no doubt about that." He sees a need for "new and innovative contemporary leaders," and such leaders need "in their kitbag, tertiary qualifications [and] administrative experience." He also sees scope for taking officers out of the force for limited periods and, "putting them into private enterprise," in order to "expose them to a different skills level." But it is important also to learn from the history of leadership within the organization. Moroney recounted the experience of Tony Lauer when he became commissioner of New South Wales Police in 1991.

KM: On the day that he was sworn in as the commissioner Tony Lauer made a statement that's become quite legendary here now, and he said, "nothing has prepared me for this moment in time." And everybody looked at him, "what is he talking about?" You know, he'd been the deputy commissioner, he'd been an assistant commissioner for a number of years in significant portfolios of crime, internal affairs, operations, been the president of the police union for a number of years. "What does he mean?" You think you have a perception and understanding, until the day comes when you sit [behind the commissioner's desk] and your whole vision is different. Because there is that dawning realization that this is where the buck stops, right here.

That's been my good fortune, you know, to have gone to the FBI and done their programs there, where you listen to a [U.S.] sheriff, it might be the commissioner from the London Met., and you think, we've got the same problems in operations, in human resources, in trying to do so much more with so much less, trying to compete with the other agencies of government, we're all talking the same language. So the ability to exchange information and ideas becomes absolutely crucial. You know I've talked to Bill Bratton[9] a fair bit, "Bill you know we have an issue we've talked about here of late, stalking of women" and he'll e-mail, "why are you doing that program with Father Riley in Macquarie Fields, what's the benefit of it?" I think it is how you share that level of information with each other, and then you realize that the police world is really a very small thing.

Police Misconduct and the 1997 Wood Commission

The discussion shifted onto issues of police integrity. Moroney was very honest when it came to talking about the 1997 Wood Commission inquiry into police misconduct. It was he who raised the subject when considering the advances with DNA and forensic evidence.

KM: You know, I think forensic science is the greatest tool police ever had. It's had a playback effect for us in the reduction of complaints of police misconduct, fabrication of evidence, what one Royal Commissioner here called, "noble cause corruption." The police simply made up the brief, "we know you did it, so we'll build the brief of evidence around you and we'll convict you that way."

AM: Do you think the issues associated with the Royal Commission are certainly less now, or...?

KM: I can never be complacent. I can tell you, on December 8th, 1995, in the very early days of the Royal Commission all the senior police were called in one by one and gave evidence on oath. And we were asked of our perceptions of corruption. And I said, "yes, look it did exist, I'd seen it," But I thought, "look it's relatively low, you know, perhaps two out of ten." On December 8th, 1996, I was back there again talking about current and projected training for the police academy. I was then the assistant commissioner. The judge said to me, "there's something I want to ask." Here we are a year later and we'd seen all sorts of exposés and covert film, and I said, "oh obviously it's not a two, I don't think it's a ten, but it's not a two. It's far more serious than we've realized." You can never be complacent. I think we are different a decade on from Wood's Royal Commission.

AM: OK.

KM: Do we still have police officers engaged in criminal conduct, inappropriate conduct, misconduct, neglect of duty? Yes, yes, but what I've seen is a significant reduction in complaints, of what I will call serious criminal conduct. All misconduct is serious, but serious criminal misconduct. We've seen an increase in levels of complaint regarding rudeness, incivility, what I will broadly describe as customer service-type issues. We can resolve those things ... Forty-eight percent of our complaints now come from police officers themselves. That was unheard of a decade ago, it would have been in single figures. While there's been a positive trend down in the serious allegations, we've seen something that wasn't there, or certainly wasn't reported to be there, and that's the issue of substance abuse by some police officers. When I entered the police in 1965 alcohol was a big part of our culture, big part of the Australian culture, full stop. Now you hardly find alcohol is an issue in the organization. But what has emerged in some locations is illicit substance abuse by some police officers. So this becomes a new scourge that you've got to address, and you address it by adherence to our statement of values, adherence to your oath of office, rigid supervision, strong leadership. And part of the strong leadership is about taking strong punitive action. Now some might say, well some academics might say, you know, to bring about a greater level of behavior you ought not go down the path of punishment. But I have a difficulty in that I don't believe the general community is, as tolerant as the Aussie community is, I don't think they want their police officers out there, exercising the powers of a constable of police impaired by substances, legal or illegal. So I've had an absolute zero tolerance to illicit substance abuse.

So what has been the benefit of a reduction in complaints? It's been, among other things, affecting the professional standards of the organization, having a very strong working arrangement with the Police Integrity Commission and the Ombudsman for oversight and accountability and transparency. It's been similar to when we raised the educational standards. That attracted another level of recruit. As we then sought to lift the professional standards of the organization that too has attracted another level of recruit. If we've made enhancements to our policies of having more women in the organization, that's had another positive impact. So, what we say to our commanders is, "don't be frightened by innovation."

Ken Moroney's Legacy

AM: I was going to finish by asking you what you think your legacy has been. You've already said about the, hopefully, the command college, but …

KM: In one sense history will judge how effective I've been, both as a policeman and as the commissioner of police and I leave that history to others to write. But when I walk out this door on August 31st next, if I'm judged simply by, "whether we agree with him or not, he did the job to the best of his ability," is probably the legacy that one simply seeks to look for. I would hope though that I've been able to have some impact in police education and leadership training. I would hope that I've had some impact in the professional standards of the organization. I think equally, I hope that I've had some impact on restoring the faith of the police in themselves. That this is a profession, it's not a job; that this is an occupation and a profession of which you ought to be enormously proud. It's an organization rich in its history, proud of its traditions and we ought to celebrate that. It's about instilling in our people a faith and a confidence, particularly in the post-Royal Commission period, of having faith in themselves, in their capacity and their ability, to go out there and do a job. What has been the result and effect of that? Academics will probably have a different explanation as to why crime has gone down, heroine droughts, better employment. I'm sure all those things are relevant, but I'd also like to think that—notwithstanding those explanations—that it has been a strong commitment by the police in this state to both reactively and proactively focus on crime, because they felt that they were doing a worthwhile job. And that's had that great cascading effect.

At a time when police jurisdictions in the west of Australia have great difficulty in attracting recruits we've never experienced that difficulty. And I think it comes down to one issue, it has been about "the rising tide lifting the boat." What has been the rising tide? Professional standards, enhanced training, supervision, effective leadership, being concerned demonstrably so—about the issues impacting on the community, working with the community. I think that's had the big impact for us out there.

And paraphrase all of that, if I was 19 I'd do it all again. A lot smarter, but I'd do it all again! I would, I've loved coming to work. There are some [days] when you do, you pull out your hair and say, "how the hell did that happen? Why did that happen? Why didn't that happen?" But you've got to, I think, understand also, while you seek those explanations, a lot of people out there are trying very, very hard. And I think, in one sense the bigger our organization gets, the bigger, the more complex the issues become.

No, I'm satisfied with the job I've done. What I now seek to do is pass the baton to Andrew [Scipione]. He will take the organization in a similar, or maybe a different direction, and that will be OK. The last thing I will be is a critic from the sideline; he'll get none of that from me. I've had my opportunity, as I said, how well or how poorly I did is for others to judge. And now hopefully I've prepared Andrew to a point where he will take command, hopefully he'll sit in that seat [at the commissioner's desk] and never say, "nothing has prepared me for this moment in time." And while there will be the usual trepidations he's a man of enormous capacity and ability and intellect.

AM: Thank you very much.

KM: Ah, you're most welcome. I can sit here for hours and wax lyrical. But if you ask my predecessors, I don't think they'd be all that far different. I think the person I've modeled myself on is John Avery. I think history will come to show that he was probably the best commissioner we've ever had. He was the right man at the right time, and a man of tremendous capacity and ability. Avery really, really lifted the boat with the tide, and turned the boat right around. He'd probably shoot me for calling him old at 80, but yeah, just a very wise man, always a good judge of character you know, which is sort of, "I've watched you out here in the western part of New South Wales young fellow, you're coming to work for me now." That was a great benefit of seniority, as long as you're warm and vertical you all got promoted. But some of them were warm and vertical and near death. And that was a great thing of Avery's, to get rid of the seniority system, turn on the tap of merit, and simply take police out of comfort zones and take them out of positions where they would not have got into senior positions.

AM: It just seemed a bit of a gamble at the time?

KM: Ah yeah, my word, it was a huge gamble but you've got to have that sort of great foresight to keep the organization going. I keep coming back, it's got to be more than just more police and more police.

Bibliography

Avery, J. (1981). *Police - force or service?* Sydney: Butterworths.

NSW Police. (2006). *Focused on community partnership: annual report 2005–2006.* Parramatta: New South Wales Police.

Northern Territories Government. (2007, April 30). *Little children are sacred: Board of Inquiry into the Protection of Aboriginal Children from Sexual Abuse.* Darwin: Northern Territories Government.

Prenzler, T. (2004). Chief Commissioner Christine Nixon, Victoria: Australia's first female police chief. *Police Practice and Research,* 5(4/5), 301–315.

Scarman, Lord. (1981). *The Brixton disorders 10–12 April, 1981,* Cmnd. 8427. London: Her Majesty's Stationery Office.

Wood, J. (1997). *Royal commission into the New South Wales police service: Final report.* Sydney: Government of the State of NSW.

Endnotes

1. Parents and Citizens' Association: See http://www.pandc.org.au

2. See, for example, Prenzler (2004).
3. Goulburn can be really quite cold in the winter, as I [A.M.] discovered during a recent visit.
4. Charles Sturt University has a campus at Dubbo, as well as a presence at the NSW Police Collage at Goulburn. The university also has campuses elsewhere in the state, at Albury-Wodonga, Bathurst, Orange, and Wagga Wagga.
5. At the time of the interview this was a major operation to address child sexual abuse in Aboriginal communities. It followed the publication of the Northern Territory Board of Inquiry Report (Northern Territories Government, April 2007).
6. The Redfern riot occurred in 2004, and the Macquarie Fields and Cronulla riots in 2005. All are districts of Sydney.
7. Now part of the National Policing Improvement Agency.
8. The riots occurred during April 1981 (Scarman, 1981).
9. Currently police chief of the Los Angeles Police Department.

Interview with Additional Deputy Inspector General Md. Mazharul Hoque, Community Policing Pioneer of the Bangladesh Police Force

2

INTERVIEWED BY ANTHONY L. SCIARABBA

Background

Md. Mazharul Hoque was born in Bangladesh in 1961. Presently he is commandant of a police training center in Bangladesh that offers basic training to recruit constables and refresher courses to other ranks. After completing his postgraduate work in economics at the University of Dhaka, in 1988 he joined the Bangladesh Police Service, which is part of the broader civil service, as an assistant superintendent of police. He received his basic training from the Bangladesh Police Academy and also received foundation and orientation training from the Bangladesh Public Service Training Centre and Bangladesh Military Academy. He attended a number of training courses and seminars abroad covering various fields of policing, including community policing, with particular focus on the Koban system of Japan, and conflict management in the context of community policing. He is one of the forerunners of community policing in Bangladesh, which is now considered the dominant crime prevention strategy in the country. He participated in three UN peacekeeping operations in the former Yugoslavia, Bosnia and Herzegovina and in East Timor in various capacities, including as station commander and training manager. He has traveled to many countries in Asia, Europe, and America. He has held various senior management and command posts in the Bangladesh Police. His special interests include police training, strategic planning, police research, community oriented policing, and public order management.

The Bangladesh Police

The Bangladesh police force consists of approximately 125,000 personnel and is one of the largest police organizations in the world. The Bangladesh Police traces its roots back to ancient times and actually predates many Western civilizations. Its original mission was to collect intelligence throughout the country in order to maintain public order and quell antigovernment sentiment. The collection of such undercover information was made possible by the use of spies and undercover officers who managed to infiltrate many levels of government. As time went on, the Bangladesh Police continued its mission. In precolonial times, policing management duties were handed down by the sultans to officials with the rank of muhtasib (i.e., a supervisor who monitored public business and transactions), with daily police duties being performed by kotwals (officer-level personnel). The title of kotwals still holds a place in the current Bangladesh Police in that district police stations are referred to as Kotwali stations. Although a police force did exist in Bangladesh during these more historic periods, they were not professional in nature with regard to organizational structure.

The current structure and professional nature of the Bangladesh police force can be attributed to the British period. In 1765, during British rule, the police system was reformed in an effort to promote increased revenue for the government. The changes occurring during the period of British control were the most significant in the history of the Bangladesh police as well as the Bangladesh criminal justice system. In 1772, the British established both criminal and civil courts in Bangladesh. Additional changes by the British were established in 1792 in the form of police regulations, which subsequently were responsible for dividing the country up into police districts.

The largest and most significant British change came in 1861 when The Police Act was passed. This permitted the establishment of a structured police organization, which included the establishment of organizational levels (stations and districts), as well as an official chain of command (the police superintendent was now solely responsible and accountable for an entire district). Additional officer-level regulations and structures were established as well, including the formation of different units (armed and unarmed) as well as the development of an armed forces bureau responsible for more volatile situations. Additionally, special provisions for police training were outlined, including the formation of police colleges and training schools.

Further steps by the British to organize the police in Bangladesh came in 1902. These additional changes were aimed at increasing the bureaucratic nature of the police. This included the establishment and expansion of management positions (deputy inspector general and deputy superintendent). Also included in this round of organizational change were special provisions for police officers, including increased salaries and the development of criminal sanctions for police officers. Perhaps the most significant change in this latest legislation concerned the mission of the police in Bangladesh. A result of the Police Act of 1861 was the absence of a stated primary police mission. Following the changes enacted in 1902, the Bangladesh police were reorganized as an organization of force. Up until this time, the police were essentially service oriented in their mission.

Moving ahead to current times, Bangladesh has one centralized police force officially known as Bangladesh Police. It works under the administrative control of the Ministry of Home Affairs and is spread all over the country. The force enlists considerable numbers of good investigators and law enforcement officers. The police are highly integrated with the social fabric of the communities they serve. They enjoy a viable vertical as well as horizontal link with government and nongovernment organizations and members of the civil society. Additionally, there is a great amount of autonomy when it comes to policing in Bangladesh (http://www.police.gov.bd).

Today, the Bangladesh Police is headed by one inspector general of police, who is assisted by a number of additional inspector generals, deputy inspector generals, assistant inspector generals and other officers at police headquarters and in the field. Bangladesh is divided into six police ranges (areas based on population), with the average population of a single range consisting of approximately twenty million people. Each range is further divided into districts and each district is again divided into police stations. The most important unit in the police organization is the district, which is commanded and supervised by a senior superintendent of police. The average population of a district consists of about one million residents. A police station under its jurisdiction may have several police outposts, investigation centers, or police camps. While these additional police offices increase the effectiveness of the police, they are not considered separate police units. The average population within each police station jurisdiction is approximately 200,000 residents. In addition to the ranges and districts, Bangladesh has six metropolitan police units for the major cities. For example, Dhaka Metropolitan Police is the biggest unit of Bangladesh Police, consisting of 24,000 personnel (Hoque, 2008; Bangladesh Police, 2008).

The country of Bangladesh is located in southern Asia and is inhabited by 153,546,901 residents. It consists of approximately 144,000 square kilometers of land and water. The country is bordered by Burma and India. The southern part of the country is made up of many peninsulas and inlets (mouths of the Ganges). During the monsoon season, this area of the country is subjected to severe flooding that leads to the routine displacement of a substantial number of residents. Additionally, a little over 50% of the total land is arable, which creates the need for many citizens to live in areas that are hazardous to occupy.

The Interview

This interview was conducted on May 13, 2008 in the Hotel Netherlands in Cincinnati, Ohio during the 15th annual meeting of the International Police Executive Symposium (IPES).

AS: Can you tell me about yourself and how you entered the Bangladesh Police?

MH: I was born in Bangladesh and had primary schooling in the village schools and then had higher secondary education in Dhaka-Notre Dame College. I then obtained my master's degree in economics at the University of Dhaka. Following my graduate education, I sat for the Civil Service Examination, which is a nationwide competitive examination in Bangladesh for those seeking public service positions. I qualified for the position of assistant superintendent. This was where I made my entry into the Bangladesh Police. The position of assistant superintendent is comparable to a commissioned officer in the armed forces. After I was given the position of assistant superintendent, I was sent to the National Police Academy for training for one year plus an additional six months of on the job training. Following this, I went for additional administrative training for one year. I attended this training program with judiciary and customs officials. This is because the police command rank in Bangladesh is part of the broader civil service system. Continuing my training, I then attended the Bangladesh Military Academy for advanced military training. During this period, I was trained in explosives handling, program orientation, and administrative functions of the armed forces. During this period, I completed field training with paratroopers as well as more formal training within the Military Academy.

AS: Following your entry into the Bangladesh Police, you became very active in your country's peacekeeping missions. As Bangladesh is a significant contributor to peacekeeping missions throughout the world, can you describe your role in these missions?

MH: In 1988, I was sent to Bosnia on my first peacekeeping mission. During this period (1988–1989), I worked with the police training center and the police academy. This was a 10-month tour of duty. My duties consisted of looking after the police training programs, reviewing the design of such programs, and reviewing the curriculum of the training programs. On my second peacekeeping mission, I was sent to Yugoslavia. During this tour of duty, I was assigned the position of station commander of the United Nations Police Station in Croatia. In 2001, I was sent on my third peacekeeping mission, this time to East Timor. My responsibilities during this tour were, again, training and education oriented. I was the head of academics for the police college in East Timor.

AS: Following the conclusion of your third peacekeeping mission to East Timor, you returned to Bangladesh and your position in the Bangladesh Police. Can you describe your return to your home country?

MH: After returning to Bangladesh, I served with the Dhaka Metropolitan Police Department at the rank of assistant superintendent. I then specialized in police training because of my extensive peacekeeping experience. My primary job was training and program monitoring. I took what I learned overseas while peacekeeping back to my country and the Bangladesh Police.

AS: Following your return to the Bangladesh Police, you developed a strong interest in community policing. Can you explain this interest and your role in the development of community policing in Bangladesh?

MH: I was among the few who helped start community policing initiatives in Bangladesh. This began with survey research and experiments in 1992. In the following years, community oriented policing was on its way to becoming the dominant policing strategy in Bangladesh. But this was not an easy task. In 1993, I conducted a survey research project among the street-level police officers in Bangladesh, which assessed their knowledge of community oriented policing. The results indicated that 93% of the officers were unfamiliar with the concept. Following this, we started a campaign designed to popularize the concept of community oriented policing and to get the message out that this could be a good tool for the police and greatly assist us in our crime prevention duties. We undertook neighborhood projects involving community oriented policing techniques and strategies. Two years after the initial survey, street-level police officers were again surveyed to assess their knowledge of community oriented policing. This time, the results showed that 60% of the officers had heard of community oriented policing. Today, if you were to ask a police officer in Bangladesh about community oriented policing, they can provide you some understanding of its basic concepts. This is success.

AS: You mention that experiments took place during the development phases of implementing community policing in Bangladesh. Can you provide some insight into this stage of implementation and what you discovered?

MH: We found success in implementing community policing by approaching neighborhood residents immediately after a serious crime was committed. People become traumatized and feel vulnerable and there is an overall sense of insecurity. In some areas, we found it was better to approach the locals at these times, immediately after the commission of a serious crime. We told residents that we will come to you to discuss your problems and how we can work together to solve any criminal issues you are experiencing in your neighborhood. We had to go to them. We believe trust is very important and if you do this, trust is built.

A good example of this occurred recently in the city of Dhaka where there was a very sensitive case. We experienced a double murder; a mother and daughter were killed by their maid servant. Following this incident, we distributed a questionnaire asking residents for the particulars [descriptions] of the maid servant or other domestic helps. From the 600 questionnaires sent out, 12 were returned. I firmly believe that this low response rate was due to the possibility that they distrust the police.

AS: Following such serious cases, have you seen a difference in the acceptance of community policing among the community?

MH: Today, we have rallies [peaceful community gatherings] and community gatherings. So, the communities are responding positively. The chief of police is very active in organizing such rallies. We know that these events are a success because of the attendance numbers. These are usually very big gatherings and feature entertainment. So, there is a great level of community outreach involved.

AS: Since there is acceptance of community policing among many citizens in Bangladesh, how is the concept viewed by street-level police officers?

MH: What street-level police see as a result of community policing initiatives is "extra hands" patrolling the neighborhoods with them. Local police, while they do not know all of the intricacies of community policing, understand this as an important neighborhood policy.

The idea of "extra hands" carries over to the business sector of the country as well. For instance, I integrated a pocket of industrial guards with the Bangladesh Police to maximize the police presence and secure the industry. I had only 24 police personnel at the time in my substation. So, in one shift, you would have four to five officers on duty. As this industrial area was quite large in size, I made plans to integrate the guards with the police network. At the time, there were 350 guards in this area. This made sense as the Bangladesh Police already performed guard duties of their own, patrolling the roads and areas around industry. After a plan was made, there was an agreement between the police and the guards to create a joint patrol. This new force grew from two distinct forces to a joint-operations force consisting of 375 police personnel. This was made possible by reevaluating the situation at hand.

There is historical precedence for doing this in Bangladesh. When the British used to control the area, they would elect qualified citizens and issue them a police card for 7 days. This card would grant them police duties. After 7 days, they would return the card and receive their salary. They were getting paid for part-time policing. The Police Act of 1861 kept this provision for special police, which includes temporary part-time police officers.

AS: While this outlines the situation in more urban areas in Bangladesh, more rural areas are subject to differences. In Bangladesh, there is a great difference between metropolitan and rural areas. With this in mind, can you further elaborate on the task of introducing community policing to more urbanized areas?

MH: The urban metropolitan city is home to more formal justice. Many of the residents do come from smaller villages. So, they bring their beliefs and traditions with them. This is both an advantage and disadvantage. While this creates a sense of community among some residents, in some cases, residents are isolated from one another depending on where they came from. This tends to create situations which are responsible for the formation of criminal gangs. This also creates another problem among these gangs. Since they are from the villages, their traditional upbringing allows these groups to be well organized.

We also tried to introduce community policing to upper-middle-class areas in Dhaka. We found that residents in this area were more concerned with the traffic situation rather than policing. Most of them own cars and want to be comfortable on the road with their cars. Also, many of these residents have their own security guards that are responsible for guarding their homes and property. They simply are not interested in aspects of informal justice and community policing strategies as they rely heavily on more formal justice. I personally tried to bring community policing to the more affluent areas of the city, but they were not interested. We tried by asking to be invited to community meetings to introduce ourselves and discuss community policing. We had to be more proactive than usual. We had to go to their meetings once a month to discuss any crime problems they were having. We had to take a very proactive role.

Apart from the few affluent pockets, most city residents responded positively to these calls for community policing. Someone who is a high official does not usually come to the police station. But when you invite such a person to talk about his neighborhood, you find that all of these officials, including retired generals, will attend and discuss these issues. So, people are, by and large, positive about cooperating with the police in order to prevent crime.

AS: In order to place the discussion of the need of community policing in larger cities in context, what can be said about the crime situation within these cities?

MH: In Bangladesh, you can differentiate between two distinct periods of time. In the 1980s, the government was military based. During this period, the main focus of the police was to enforce violations against order rather than more general crime issues. During the 1990s, Bangladesh had elected governments in place. So, the focus of the police shifted. But if you were to look at the statistics, we can see that crime has been relatively constant. While statistics can provide some insight, other mechanisms are at work, including the underreporting of crime and the reliance on more informal justice which is commonplace in more rural areas and villages.

AS: You mention the villages of Bangladesh and the use of more informal justice. Can you provide some insight into how these areas operate with regard to policing and criminal justice?

MH: Social control and community-level justice play an enormous role in rural areas in Bangladesh. In these areas, there is something of an avoidance of the formal justice system and the police. In Bangladesh, the villages operate this way. A self-controlled village is not like an island; they don't live and function in isolation. For example, 10 villages know me by name. Everyone is like a relative to each other. Those of my father's age are like my uncles and those who are of my brother's age are like my brothers. The villages also know your family members as well. With about 1,000 residents living in each village, each person knows who you are and what you do.

Communities in Bangladesh solve the minor problems themselves. We conducted a study for the United Nations Development Programme (UNDP) and found that upwards of 75% of minor crimes occurring in these areas are resolved by community justice without police involvement. The villages have community justice groups, which are headed by local prominent leaders or village headmen. Policing of the community by the community is a tradition in Bangladesh. Also, villages punishing criminals is very common and, as such, the villages know exactly how to carry out justice. If someone does commit a minor offense (minor assault, battery, petty thefts), the community justice group will often order payback as well as an apology for committing the offense. Because of the close nature of the village residents, shame plays a key role and acts as a preventive means.

AS: Since shame does play a major role in the community justice process, is there any attempt to reintegrate the offender back into the community?

MH: Time is a good healer. Over time, as one's behavior improves, people tend to forget. Since you are dealing with a more family/relative style community, reintegration is simplified. But it all depends on the behavior afterwards. If someone is caught committing a minor offense and is a first-time offender, additional circumstances are taken into account, including possible excuses. All of these facts are viewed in a holistic manner. But there are shameless people, and for these people, the society realizes that informal justice does not work. The criminal would then find his way into the formal criminal justice system. The village will hand him over to the police.

AS: This is how the village handles minor offenses. Can you provide some insight into what happens when a village resident commits a more serious offense?

MH: Grave crimes and offenses demand police action. This is understood by the local leader of the village. The villages know their limits and when they need to go to the police. There are attempts to cross this limit, but these are very isolated incidents.

AS: With such a strong emphasis placed on community justice, what role do the police have in these smaller villages?

MH: The role of the police is very feral in the broader perspective. A village may see a police officer one time in an entire year. This is because there is no need for regular police patrol. One of the major tasks of the village police is to collect information from the village. Even if the village is located very far from the police station, once a month, the station commander calls all of the village police and obtains any information that may be needed. The village police act as a source of intelligence for the station commander. This is the most effective source of intelligence.

In the early days (1870–1960), the village police were concerned with making arrests. This was a single police officer dragging the offender to the police station. This is a similar system to the Japanese Koban system which also uses a single officer. However, the Bangladesh system predates the Japanese Koban system.

AS: You have shed insight into the development of community policing in Bangladesh. In addition to this, what do you see as the most important changes that have happened in policing over the course of your career?

MH: My personal belief is that society is changing faster than the police. For example, we had industrial police in the 1960s. Industry requires a lot of protection in Bangladesh, more than the average. That was the feeling in the 1960s. Today, our industry workforce consists of over 8 million people. The police force could not keep up with this growth. This is because of the competitive nature of business.

AS: As you noted, the inability of the police to keep up with the growth of business and industry is a weakness of the organization. In addition to this, your position allows you to gauge the strengths and weaknesses of the Bangladesh Police. Can you explain some of these strengths and weaknesses?

MH: My personal view is that the size of the organization is a major weakness. It is too big in my view. With over 125,000 personnel, I wonder if a smaller organization may be more effective. The principle of management is that the larger an organization becomes, the less efficient it becomes. However, this remains an unexplored opportunity. Some strengths of the Bangladesh Police can be found in the personnel. The current generation looks more competent, more honest, and more dedicated. They have a great opportunity to make positive changes every day.

Concerning weaknesses, one area that we need to improve is our technology and scientific capabilities. The rate of the modernization of technology is weak. Also, we need to expand the scientific investigation process and crime scene investigation needs to be more professional. Another area we need to improve upon is our effective skills when dealing with gender issues, vulnerable groups, and victimology. Good human relations need to be improved. This "human side" is a common weakness in most of the force. Those who can overcome it can make their force more effective and can better meet the needs and expectations of the people. This can make a more effective police force.

AS: As you discussed, many organizations have both strengths and weaknesses. In order to effectively measure such aspects, many police departments situated around the world use various management programs. If you can, please explain how the Bangladesh Police gauge the effectiveness of their policing strategies?

MH: The crime situation in Bangladesh is presented at regularly held crime conferences held every 3 months which are attended by the chief of police and all commanders. Here, the crime situation is analyzed. This is routine practice in the Bangladesh Police and was in place when I joined the force.

AS: Is there accountability for ineffective police strategies and practices?

MH: There is accountability. The community leaders meet once a month in every police station. Accountability arises out of these meetings. Community leaders would raise an issue that is occurring in their neighborhood. By the time the next meeting takes place, and if the same issue is raised, the commander will be held accountable and can be punished. But punishment is not based on hearsay. Formal investigations must reveal evidence. But the main point of these meetings is that the locals point to the problems, the problems are pinpointed, and the problems are then raised at these monthly police-community meetings.

AS: As a police executive, are you satisfied with the successes of the Bangladesh Police?

MH: I am personally satisfied with the success of the Bangladesh Police. But no organization can ever fulfill all of the dreams of its entire staff. But given the situations that exist in my country with regard to social, political, and economic aspects, I think the Bangladesh Police force is making very positive steps. Day by day, it is improving, so, I am satisfied.

AS: Are you satisfied with the rate of this success?

MH: The rate of success has varied over time, sometimes it goes slow and sometimes fast. This rate depends on many other factors, including politics. The country is moving toward national elections, so the rate of success does vary. But success is dependent on the will of the government.

AS: One apparently successful policing strategy is community policing. As a police executive, how much of the Bangladesh policing strategy is rooted in theories regarding policing? In other words, where does practice meet research?

MH: When we started community policing in the early 1990s, we started broken windows policing as well. These were separate experiments that took place in separate parts of the country. The community policing strategy was finally accepted in 1996. Community policing took the front seat and broken windows faded. However, the basic concepts of broken windows policing are understood by the officers. In reality, we are doing it. Our policing strategies continuously change. For instance, the implementation of community policing in Bangladesh is relatively new, and today, it is the dominant policing strategy in the country.

AS: As there is a connection between practice and research, do the Bangladesh Police work with neighboring universities and research institutes in order to create effective police policy?

MH: We have just started this collaboration. Currently, we have a National Training Board (NTB) in place in the Ministry of Home Affairs. This is very newly formed. I believe the first steps have been made and the next steps would include moving toward additional education for police officers. The National Police Academy of Bangladesh has affiliated itself with the local university, which will be offering degrees to police officers in criminology, criminal justice, criminalistics, and police science while they complete their police academy training. For example, the investigators are required to go through a 3-year training program (1 year in the police academy and 2 years on the job training). So, these 3 years are structured in a way in which the officer can obtain a college degree. This is still in the beginning stages and we will see in the next 5 to 10 years the effectiveness of this program.

AS: You highlighted some of the activities of the Police Academy. As commandant of police training, what can you tell me about your police training program?

MH: Looking back 20 years, the street-level police officers didn't have to be very qualified. They did not require a high school degree. Many of them could just write their names. Since 1990, the minimum education requirement is not only a high school degree, but a secondary school certificate [an examination that is given following ten years of education]. This adds up to 10 years of schooling. So, this is a positive change which has created a more qualified police force. We have very qualified people from different disciplines, including physicians and engineers. At the training center that I am responsible for, I train police constables. Before 1990, our focus was on physical capabilities. Today, the focus is on education and mental development.

In addition, the curriculum is continuously updated and this change is dependent upon our police officers who travel abroad, including personnel who go on peacekeeping missions. One part of the curriculum that has been updated is crime scene management. My research has found that 1 in every 100 constables was aware of the basic principles of crime scene management and techniques some years ago. Today, all constables are trained in crime scene management. Additionally, they are all trained in computer operations. They are being exposed to initiatives and training programs which were unthinkable before.

AS: You mention that police training in Bangladesh is advancing. You also mention that the police are improving their effective skills to better deal with all kinds of residents. With this in mind, what can you say about the social service functions of the Bangladesh Police?

MH: Traditionally, Bangladesh society is not very formal. Social stratification is present, however, but overall, society remains informal. So, when a community is experiencing problems or a natural disaster, there is never a problem of finding people to come and assist. This includes, in addition to the police, military, political leaders, nongovernment organizations, and private citizens. The police respond to the needs of the society. Apart from the policing mission, the police always respond to the expectations of the people of Bangladesh.

AS: We talked about the fact that many aspects of the Bangladesh Police are advancing with time. However, corruption within the government remains an issue. In January 2007, planned elections were suspended due to corruption issues. As a police executive, can you explain the problem of corruption with regard to the Bangladesh Police?

MH: Since the early 1990s, I see society making progress in terms of nearly everything, including infant mortality, mass education, literacy, and life expectancy. But I don't believe that Bangladesh can be a champion of corruption. When such a viable state is making progress in nearly all areas, the belief that Bangladesh suffers from corruption is weak. If a society makes progress, why should it go backwards in one area? I personally do not agree with this.

Corruption is an established segment of the police literature, so it does occur in many places. But I do believe we are improving every day. It is getting better every day. Police headquarters has an intelligence unit. Every day, the chief of police knows what is happening anywhere in the country, from activities in the police academy to activities in the individual districts. Because of the mechanisms of monitoring and the goodwill of the new generation of police, we are improving. Everyone is in favor of this change.

AS: In addition to corruption, another very important issue in policing is terrorism. Following the terrorist incidents of September 11, 2001, what changes, if any, have been made to policing in Bangladesh?

MH: Police training has changed as far as response units and police intelligence is concerned. This new training has already helped us. Very recently in 2005 we had a terrorist group placing explosives around densely populated areas throughout the country. Many people were injured and some were killed. Eventually, the plot was unearthed and a large number of the terrorists were arrested, sent to prison, and for some, executed. This action by the police, enhanced by our training, gave the message that the Bangladesh Police is capable of handling such incidents.

The population itself is what's important. The success of the police is dependent upon the support of the people. The citizens of Bangladesh do not endorse fundamentalism and extremism. Because of the closeness of the Bangladesh society, the citizens do not believe in revolutions or the revolutionaries. This is because they know them personally. The same is true for fundamentalist outfits. This is also due to religion as well. Every Friday, we all go to the mosque and pray. This creates a very close relationship with each other. Additionally, the success of these groups depends on the strength of the government's grip. I can personally say that in Bangladesh, there is no area in which the government's grip is loose.

AS: We have discussed issues of police strategy, training, and pertinent current policing issues, among other topics. Therefore, an appropriate way of concluding this interview is to ask you, as a police leader, what is your vision of the Bangladesh Police in the near future?

MH: There are many dimensions. This includes education, skills-based training, and technology-based policy. We have a hold in all of these areas. For instance, we have started technology-based policing in the cities, which includes the use of mobile phones. We have developed our own criminal behavior software program as well and all personnel are trained in its use. This software was the result of a collaborative effort by many members of the Bangladesh Police. Technology has become a blessing and we have embraced that as it is most important. Increased orientation with computers among the ranks is also embraced. Perhaps after a few years, a proportion of the police force will be computer literate. The importance of technology-based policy is seen in other areas of our society. A few examples include our airport, which is now fully computerized. Another example is our fully functional DNA laboratory. All of these are new innovations occurring within the last few years. We are aware that we are making strides.

We have an idea of the global standards of policing and we have a vision to catch up with the rest of the world. Perhaps not at more advanced levels, but equivalent to other countries similar to Bangladesh. Keeping this in mind, we are modernizing. Currently, we are updating our police training curriculum, which is expected to be in place in the next 3 months. In the meantime, we are starting new programs, such as the initiative of retraining the older members of the Bangladesh Police by giving them new looks and visions of policing.

We are trying our best. And it is not that we are an isolated society, we are part of the global village and we have international exposure. We know where we are and where we need to go and I firmly believe that we are on the right track. It is only a matter of time.

AS: Thank you for your time.

Conclusion

Additional Deputy Inspector General Md. Mazharul Hoque is a distinguished police executive in Bangladesh and a valued member of his society. With leaders like him, the Bangladesh Police will continue to achieve success and continue to advance in many individual parts of their organization. The rates of this success and advancement are greatly increased by many factors, including a new generation of highly skilled police officers, a training program that is sensitive to the demands of societal progression in areas such as technology and police research, and dedicated, sincere individuals.

Glossary

Additional Deputy Inspector General: The fourth highest rank in the Bangladesh Police.

National Training Board (NTB): Consists of Dhaka University vice chancellors, secretary to the State, the chief of police, and private citizens. The NTB originated from the Police Reform Program and receives most of its funding from British, U.S., Japanese, and German aid programs.

United Nations Development Programme (UNDP): The United Nations global development network is an organization advocating for change and connecting countries to knowledge, experience and resources to help people build a better life (http://www.undp.org).

References

Bangladesh Police. (2008). Historical profile obtained from http://www.police.gov.bd.

Hoque, Md. (2008). Organizational Profile: Bangladesh Police. *Unpublished paper.*

Interview with Dr. José Mariano Beltrame, Security Secretary, State of Rio de Janeiro, Brazil

3

INTERVIEWED BY EMILIO E. DELLASOPPA

TRANSLATION BY REGINA AZEVEDO
AND DANIEL GRUNMANN

This interview offers us the views of Dr. José Mariano Beltrame, current secretary of security of the State of Rio de Janeiro, on several aspects of police enforcement in Brazil. Coming from the Federal Police of Brazil, Dr. Beltrame analyzes the changes being experimented with in the profession, his professional experience, the relations between academic analysis and police practices, his visions of the principal issues and of the results obtained, as well as his opinions on possible future developments and on how to continue improving police enforcement techniques.

The interview took place on July 16, 2007 in his office in Rio de Janeiro.

Introduction

The security secretary of the State of Rio de Janeiro, Dr. José Mariano Benincá Beltrame is a federal police deputy, born on May 13, 1957 in the city of Santa Maria, Rio Grande do Sul.

Dr. Beltrame has a law degree from the Federal University of Santa Maria/ Rio Grande do Sul, as well as degrees in business and public administration from the Federal University of Rio Grande do Sul. He specialized in strategic intelligence in the Universo University/Rio de Janeiro and in the Escola Superior de Guerra.[1] At the War College, Dr. Beltrame attended courses on public security intelligence offered by the National Department of Public Security and courses on data analysis of police intelligence.

Dr. Beltrame joined the Department of Federal Police in 1981 as a federal police officer, acting mainly in the area of drug repression and police intelligence, and combating organized crime in various states of the federation. Deployed to the Federal Police Bureau of Rio de Janeiro as federal police deputy, he was the coordinator of *Missão Suporte*,[2] chief of the intelligence service and chief of the police liaison office with Interpol. He also coordinated the security of the 75th Interpol General Assembly, which took place in the city of Rio de Janeiro in 2006, besides being an instructor and lecturer in the postgraduate course on intelligence and public security offered by the Federal University of Mato Grosso.

The Interview

EED: Dr. Beltrame, to start this interview and better situate our readers, please describe your professional experience.

JMB: I joined the Federal Police through a competitive examination process and in 1981 I took office in Porto Alegre, Rio Grande do Sul. Since then I have been always engaged in developing activities related to police intelligence. Gradually, I developed interests in this area, and I can say that from the beginning of the 1990s we started taking actions towards a new direction of police investigation. We had always felt the necessity of utilizing technology because, up until then, the police had a tradition of almost exclusively using force and the discretionary power of *Delegados*.[3] During the authoritarian regime, for example, police would make use of search and arrest warrants freely. With the Constitution of 1988 everything changed, and clearly the paradigms of police investigation had to be changed as well. Then, the necessity of using technology, of analyzing data, cross checking information, using other sources of information, and wire tapping phone lines—which the Constitution allows with judicial authorization—became obvious. This was an important turning point in police work, entering the technological world, a net of relations characterized by a series of new attitudes and points of view.

Since 1992, or 1993, we started to create several state-of-the-art systems of police investigation, which today are the basis for the Federal Police's routine investigations. Today, thank God, we have all this equipment installed at the Secretaria.[4] Last Thursday (July 12, 2007) we inaugurated our Intelligence Center and from there we intend to always better the quality of our police investigation.

My path with the police, from this initial moment, took me around Brazil, conducting specific investigations related to organized crime and drug trafficking. In other words, I developed temporary activities on the border of Mato Grosso do Sul, as well as in the northeast of the country, in Brasilia, in Recife, in the interior of São Paulo, and here in Rio de Janeiro. I came to Rio de Janeiro precisely to work in a big center of intelligence at the Federal Police, which was created by the present national secretary of public security, Federal Police *Delegado* Luis Fernando Correa, who had begun this entire process during the 1990s in Porto Alegre. I always worked in this area. When he installed this system here in Rio de Janeiro, in 2003, he called me to work with him. I worked on what is known at the Federal Police as "Rio Support." Afterwards, Deputy Correa went to the National Office of Public Security in Brasilia, and I remained in Rio, developing a series of activities. Investigation involves a crazy rhythm that we all come to experience, and I am still here today after what has been almost 4 years.

EED: You are now facing a new challenge as the secretary of security of the State of the Rio de Janeiro. Beginning with questions related to the police profession, what have been the most important changes in the profession? You mentioned some, fundamentally connected with the incorporation of technology. Based on your experience, which changes have been the most important to the police—in terms of philosophies, organizational structure, specializations, politics and programs, equipment and personnel? Also, analyzing not only the Federal Police in general, but also your own experience around the country, how have these changes affected, if at all, our 27 Civil Police State units and 27 Military Police State units? And can this fragmentation be considered favorable, or not, towards the changes that we have been experiencing?

JMB: First of all, in my opinion, the military and civil police urgently need to go through a process of renovation. Both entities are very obsolete and in need of modernization. I do not think this should be taken as mere criticism. I think it is the duty of the state to invest in such modernization. Basically, both the military and civil police are badly in need of better salaries. A police officer cannot transmit dignity if dignity was not given to him or her. We also need better equipment.

EED: Would a better salary be a more urgent matter for the military police?

JMB: I think so, because of its environment. A civil police officer works behind a counter while a military police officer is on the streets, open to an environment that is not the same for the civil police. Both lines of work are essential and extremely important, but the military police is the one that receives the first impact. These officers need more dignity and that can be obtained with a better salary, better work conditions, and better equipment. The vehicles used by our officers, for example, often do not work properly; they break down, putting our officers in a shameful situation. The third important point is training. I'm not saying our police force is not prepared. I think that for the reality it lives in, our police force is quite prepared. However, its training should be improved constantly. In many cases it is better to buy a computer and to teach

EED: an officer how to use it properly than to simply buy more vehicles and weapons.

EED: The second item would be equipment?

JMB: Yes. Better salaries, equipment, and also the way the police force is seen by the people. People should be able to see a police officer and feel safe. It is definitely a long road ahead, a break away from a strong historic paradigm, but I can honestly say that we are already taking the first steps to change this perception. Why? First of all, I do believe this government will improve the police's salaries. Second, the Pan-American Games brought more vehicles and equipment such as nonlethal weapons. Officers have been trained on how to use such guns and, in order to diminish the use of firearm weapons, we will add a kit of nonlethal weapons to each police vehicle. Again, it is a hard and long road because the state is in a very difficult financial situation, but there will be no hope for our police if we do not meet these three items.

EED: Which changes do you see, between the beginning of the 1990s and today, regarding external conditions, basically those related to people, communities, legal resources, minorities' issues, and the relationship with political power?

JMB: In my opinion, both society and the police are still heavily imbued with traces from the 1960s and 1970s.

EED: Authoritarian traces?

JMB: Authoritarian traces.

EED: But why only in the 1970s? Is it not a historic tradition in Brazil? We could remember the Ordenações Filipinas.[5]

JMB: Exactly. It comes from the empire. Dom João VI established the police forces.[6] But I believe our police have changed greatly since then. We took a very important step thanks to two factors. First of all, the constitutional process that ended with the 1988 Federal Constitution, and second, the effect it had on the police and on training in its academies and schools. They all had to adapt and effectively disguise their pattern of exclusive use of force. For example, today in Rio de Janeiro, I would say that we are working with three approaches. First of all, we are taking a conscientious attitude, which consequently, is a courageous attitude, and in third place a transparent attitude. We are only missing the press coming with us on our operations, and that is something I cannot do without putting their lives in danger. In the past years, police information was not published. Proof of this would be when we forwarded in advance the coroner's report to the leader of a human rights organization, with the objective of relieving him of any apprehension. And the forensic report is a document that is normally not provided to the press. It is not sufficient to have the legislation; we need to show that we want to be transparent.

EED: Is it possible that Brazilian society has not changed these concepts of authoritarianism?

JMB: I think this is very dangerous. When I see, here in Rio de Janeiro, demands to bring the army, I think that what the Brazilian people think of is the use of force and not the true solution to the problem. I think that the society still associates the presence of the state to the use of force. Many people applaud when a tank is placed in front of the Copacabana Palace or when a machine gun is pointed at the Rocinha *favela* [slum], as if it was the solution. I find that horrifying, I think that society has to realize that public security is the last element that comprises the concept of citizenship. Before security there are a series of social and public policies that need to exist and security is one of them. The problem is that, for decades, the other public policies were nonexistent, and today public security is seen as the most important one.

EED: I have been teaching at the Dom Joao VI Academy, to the future higher rank military police officers. Two things have surprised me. First, our future officers do not study strategy; basic concepts of military strategy are not even considered. Second, it is my opinion that these officers take from Brazilian society a mentality that validates the use of force, which they then apply to their profession.

JMB: This is evident in all Latin America. I believe we are going to change. But what is intended here is the beginning of a process. People think this is a poetic, a philosophic idea. We need to tell people that the more we hide the dirt under the carpet, the worse this situation will become.

Recently, I saw a study stating that 25% of the teenage girls living at *Favela de Jacare* are pregnant. Where is the future for these unborn kids? Who are the fathers? How will these kids be prepared for the labor market? Who are the mothers? In what conditions will these kids be born and raised? And, where will they live? If these questions are not addressed, we will possibly have 25% more graves on top of the hill of poor houses already existing there.[7] We cannot close our eyes to this situation. I am aware that combating it the way we have been is not the solution, but only the beginning. In addition, we need public and social action. I think that Rio de Janeiro will be taking a strong step in that direction. We hope the four million reais that we will receive because of the PAC (Growth Acceleration Project) will also help us deal with this situation. There are projects for Manguinhos and Rocinha *favelas,* but there are no solutions without the creation of job programs and the generation of income.

EED: I arrived in Brazil in 1979. Since then, in my opinion, the situation has only been getting worse. Another area where the state has progressively lost control is the prison system.

JMB: What happened here, in my point of view, is that the issue of public security has not been of interest for the politicians. Our federal capital moved from Rio de Janeiro to Brasilia, and with that change we lost investments such as the stock market. Rio de Janeiro became a place for other activities. Our state governments only fought against the federal government. I think that here people still consider Rio the capital, despite everything. Since then we have had disastrous governments.

EED: So, in your opinion, one of the roots of the problem lies in an inaccurate evaluation by the political leadership on the question of public security?

JMB: Yes, without a doubt. There was a disordered occupation of the land, and complacency from some politicians regarding this process: They would go to these places, only bringing water and electricity, and no other form of infrastructure. We need to change this attitude. Security now comes in only after *all* control has been lost, after families have been separated, after the father has lost his job. When we no longer have the minimal conditions of citizenship and, because of disorganized growth, it is impossible to provide public transportation, day care, libraries, parks, schools, etc., when the situation has become chaotic, we call for public security.

I will give you an example: Last week we had a problem in Vigario Geral *favela*. A patrol car had stopped at a traffic signal behind a car when five people, dressed only in shorts, crossed the street, each of them carrying a rifle. What can we do in such a situation? If the police were to pursue them, these men would mix with the rest of the crowd, and the resulting crossfire would only raise criticism about the inefficiency and ineptitude of our police force. If the police did nothing, the people say, "See, right in front of their faces and they did nothing." Here is where we reach a point of confusion, where we have lost the reference for what to do. Society today seems to be in this situation: if the police take action, it is the wrong action; if they do not take action, it does not help either. Why is this? Because society has lost any reference. Everything today is centered on the *Complexo do Alemão.*[8] People believe that the Office of Public Security is the *Complexo do Alemão.* The case of the *Complexo do Alemão* is only a small part of the problem detected by our intelligence work. What about the rest of our work? We fight for an increase in the number of police officers, for open and competitive examinations, and for the new IML.[9] Newspaper cutouts from 1996 show how bad the situation of the IML was even then, but no one did anything. Why?

EED: Then, how do you see the relation between the politicians and the police? I will dare you with a question. Some time ago, a civil police officer told me that the police had lost its autonomy and that its main task—based on the association of the police with certain politicians—was limited to protecting the voting districts of those politicians. How would you respond to that statement?

JMB: I could say that, today, with me, that does not happen. I made changes in 90% of the police stations and no one dared to ask me to place a *Delegado* connected to a politician in a certain place. We made changes in 23 battalions, and again nothing happened. To be completely objective, it happened once. A person came and asked, "Why did you change my commander and my *Delegado*?" I told him, "I took out your men and replaced them with mine." For this reason, the civil police officer who made that remark some time ago was not completely mistaken but we will break this paradigm, at least that is the idea and that is what has been done. However, this is still not the solution. Why? Because the root of the problem is still there. So, what should we do? Keep on working; deploying people, and supervising the internal affairs departments.

EED: Many years ago, when Dr. Hélio Luz was the chief of civil police and General Cerqueira was the secretary, this very process took place, but it was then reversed, with grievous consequences, after he left office. Do you think you will be able to implement it this time?

JMB: I believe in two things: First, in the steady change that to this day our governor is enacting; and second, in the fact that I do not have any political pretenses that would take me away from my principles. If I cannot work with some small form of autonomy, I will quit. Because we cannot submit to the demands such as "Place this guy here and place that guy there." So, I think that although we made some progress, we did not do anything amazing. What was the great victory? It was that we did our homework.

EED: How would you compare the situation in the state of Rio de Janeiro in the early 1990s to 2006–2007?

JMB: I believe we have today a *Secretaria de Seguranca* (Department of Security) that has total freedom of action. There is no viable way to take such difficult and important steps without having freedom of action. One of the most important qualities of Governor Cabral is that he values decentralization and demands results. He gives us room to do things our way but he demands results.

EED: Please talk about your philosophies regarding police enforcement. What should be the role police play in society? What should be their functions and duties?

JMB: My dream is to have a communitarian police, one that is completely integrated in society and has a heightened sociability. It is the old system known in the South as "Pedro & Paulo" and here it is known as "Cosme & Damião."[10] I think this should be the police. It is the long arm of the state, around the corner, where the police officer knows all the residents, their lives, and their routines. It is not enough to simply put the officer there; the people have to believe in the officer through his or her actions. We are undoubtedly far from it. Personally, I think it is something we need to pursue or else we will not be able to resolve the issue.

EED: Would that be a "communitarian police" or a return to an old form of police enforcement used a long time ago in Brazil?

JMB: The police could reach that level. It would gradually become communitarian as it builds upon its sociability. I could even apply this type of police enforcement with one stationary officer, as long as there is interaction with the community. Today, for example, at the *Complexo do Alemão* there is a GPAE.[11] But it is not the state that is there. That territory does not belong to the state. We have a police officer there who, in order to stay, either submits to corruption or else leaves.

EED: When you say that the Complexo do Alemão does not belong to the state, you are stating that roughly 125,000 people in the city of Rio de Janeiro do not live under the control of the state.

JMB: There are places that we visited, like Areal and Matinha,[12] where we had not entered in the last 3 years. We could talk for hours, but this did not just happen in 2007. It is a product of decades of disorganized land occupation and of lack of state power. Who is responsible now? Public security. Then we go back to the beginning of this interview. There are voices in society that preach the use of force as the solution to our problems. They say, "Call the Army." Humanitarian concepts have fallen behind; one needs only to check the polls. I believe our work is very important in this sense and I hope that, in the future, more people will have the same lucidity.

EED: Relating to the tasks of the police, what should be their specific functions and what should be left to other institutions?

JMB: In my understanding, the essential task of the police should be prevention—the anticipation of any type of trauma that could be generated against citizens.

EED: Which are the organizational structures that work, and which do not?

JMB: I would say that today we have an intelligence organization that works very well and that it is better than ever before. And after the operation at the *Complexo do Alemão*, we saw a sign of the possibility of integrating the federal, military and civil police. The execution of that operation by three police institutions was an important step toward the integration of the police forces. There were problems—more than 1,300 police were operating in an area with more than 100,000 inhabitants—but I believe the entire operation was very positive.

EED: And which are the organizational structures that do not work?

JMB: In my opinion, the operation of logistics does not work. Logistics in police work comply with very crude standards set by a bureaucracy. The internal bureaucracy disturbs the development and execution of actions, postponing decisions that could have been taken more quickly. The communication system is not good. The administration of processes, the management aspect, needs to be improved. This is also being achieved through the Fundação Getúlio Vargas.[13]

EED: How are the relations with other Brazilian criminal justice institutions?

JMB: The relations with the judicial, as well as with the Public Ministry, are excellent. For example, we have in our custody 220,000 guns that are kept in a place without security and, in my opinion, create a health hazard. I will destroy these guns in a public square. For that, I need help from the Court of Justice and from the Public Ministry, to show that our policies intend to end this situation in Rio de Janeiro. We confiscate 15,000 guns per year, a number that never goes down. There is no reason for us to carry such an arsenal under our responsibility. However, all this cannot be done without the authorization from the Court of Justice and from the Public Ministry. I believe both institutions will be reasonable, and that maybe we can destroy this arsenal before the end of the Pan-American Games.

EED: Is there anything usable in this arsenal?

JMB: That is another issue. I would like to recycle some of the guns, but there is a federal law that will not allow it. There is a way around it, but the process is very long and I would rather have these guns destroyed than to wait for legislation to be changed in the National Congress.

There is an important point I should bring up concerning relations with other institutions. We created the GGI (Group of Integrated Management) here. The GGI includes several institutions: Revenue Service, East Military Command, Public Prosecution, Court of Justice, and all the police forces. This group meets informally every 2 weeks to exchange experiences. What did we accomplish with these meetings? Look, for example, at the operation *Tio*

Patinhas (Uncle Scrooge), against the installation of slot machines. I wanted to blast this operation on my first week at the *Secretaria de Seguranca*. But after studying the legislation, I learned that once you apprehend slot machines, they should remain in the custody of the police. I also noticed that many police headquarters were packed with these machines, and would be like that until the end of the investigation. Then, through the GGI, the Revenue Service gave me the following idea: The Revenue Service seizes the machines, and the police accompany their agents. However, it is the Revenue Service that keeps the machines under its custody for up to 30 days. If the owner does not come forward to reclaim them, these machines can be auctioned, given up, or destroyed. We will destroy, at the *Praca da Apoteose,*[14] 5000 machines. This way the police don't have to wait until the end of the operation to dismantle the machines. Every time the Intelligence Unit spots a place with a significant number of machines, we work in coordination with the Revenue Service. Also, at the beginning, we did not have a place to store the machines for 30 days. Through the GGI, the Navy offered a place to keep the machines. It is this exchange with other GGI institutions that has given us some space to breathe and face the problems. In some cases, we take the hardware of these machines and build computers that are later donated to poor communities. After that, I destroy what is left of the machines.

Another case solved through the GGI was the problem of the Forest Battalion of the Military Police. Motor-cross bikes were needed for certain places that were difficult to access. How did we get the motorcycles? In one of the GGI meetings, in that exchange of information, the Revenue Service told us that in Foz do Iguacu, they had apprehended a contraband of 16 motor-cross bikes. This week I handed out 12 of those motorcycles to the Forest Battalion and 4 to the Office of the Environment.

EED: Creativity and professionalism may yield solutions that not long ago were unthinkable. What would be the most important problem the police force faces today?

JMB: I think that would be the cells of violence. I believe we have entered another phase.

EED: What do you call "cells of violence"?

JMB: The drug traffic. And why do I consider the drug traffic a cell of violence? Because these people use the geographic configuration of Rio de Janeiro to establish themselves in certain places that make it possible to buy drugs anywhere in the city. In other cities, the search for drug dealers should be done in specific places; in Rio de Janeiro you will find drugs being offered everywhere. Another important point

is the topography of Rio de Janeiro: It facilitates not only the distribution of drugs, but also the robbing of people on their way out
of banks, the theft of mobile phones, cars, etc. In Tijuca (a middle-
class neighborhood in the northern area of Rio de Janeiro) we have
nine hills that are there at the mercy of these criminals.

EED: And there is still the issue of recruitment of human resources by
traffickers.

JMB: Exactly. But that is outside the reach of public security. The residents
who live on those hills do not want criminals there. So, what are
the necessary conditions for these criminals to establish themselves? They use violence and intimidation. The drug dealers are
the ones who brought the use of rifles to this city, not the military police. For example, today I cannot authorize helicopters to
fly over dangerous areas in order to avoid them being damaged or
knocked down by rifle bullets. There is a possibility for the police
to acquire armored helicopters but we need to evaluate this purchase in terms of availability of resources. Today we need quite a
few things. If I buy an armored helicopter, I can be misunderstood.
People can say, "You are supporting the violence." But that would
be the wrong supposition. An armored helicopter would keep my
men alive as well as keep it from falling upon and killing innocent
civilians in such cramped urban areas.

Going back to the initial problem. How does the traffic establish
itself on the hills? By force. The drug dealers hide themselves and
their guns in the workers' houses, and people cannot talk, because
the law of silence rules. At the *Complexo do Alemão* there are clan-
destine cemeteries where drug traffickers hold their execution tri-
bunal. There are mothers, whose kids are buried there, who cannot
cry for their losses; they cannot bury the dead properly, nor come
to the police station to say that their kids were killed and vanished
in what is called the "microwave oven."[15]

These cells of violence, in my opinion, should be wiped out,
because it is from there that comes all commands for "low crime"
as we call it here—crimes such as extortion by phone, the mobile
phone scam, bank exit robberies, car theft, motorcycle theft, passersby crime, etc.

Why did I decide to prioritize this operation? Simply because
I do not have the means to place a police officer in every corner.
There are 759 *favelas* in Rio de Janeiro. No police force in the world
is large enough to control all this. So, what to do? Besides, from
these 759 *favelas*, 358 already have an established and active drug
traffic. In the other *favelas*, traffic is present but has not established
itself completely. In which of these 358 are we going to act? The

main drug gang is the Red Command in the *Complexo do Alemão*.[16] Sixty-five percent of crimes are thought to have been committed by the Red Command. So, we started our operation up there and during 59 days we dismantled many barriers that were implemented by the traffickers. These barriers were used to stop residents to get to their homes using their own cars. These people would have to park their cars at the barriers and go to their houses on foot.

A group of mothers came to complain that, because of this operation at the *Complexo do Alemão*, their kids could not go to school. I told them, "I would rather have my child stay out of school for a year, and to have his or her school protected by the state, than to send him or her to a school where drug dealers patrol the streets carrying rifles. Because by controlling the schools, the traffic can use those spaces in any way it wants." We are at a crossroads now. The situation in Rio de Janeiro is not good but if we keep quiet, accepting the situation, the operation we did today where 70 people died will be for nothing. In 2 years, another 150 people will be killed, and the "microwave oven" will keep working, as well as the traffickers' control of the schools and the regions. There was one mother who bought a TV set in a big store, took 3 hours to have her credit approved but when she gave the delivery address, the worker at the store said, "We do not deliver at that address." It is not possible to keep a situation where traffickers control a territory that should be under the control of the state.

EED: Taking this situation under consideration, I would like you to analyze the relation between "theory and practice" on the issue of the control of violence and police enforcement; and between "the academy and the police institution."

JMB: First of all, I would like to highlight that I am in favor of disarmament. When we openly destroy guns, we want to emphasize this point. But I also would like to make another point: there are many controversial issues such as legal age, disarmament, and abortion. These issues should be openly and intensely discussed in society. Talking about disarmament, there are a number of topics to consider: Why disarm? Who will be disarmed? How will that happen? Also, it will not help to just change the legal age limit. What we need is to analyze whether, after we put a 15-year-old or a 30-year-old in jail, that person will be able to adjust to society again. If I send a 40-year-old man to Bangu [a high security prison complex in Rio de Janeiro], in what sociable condition will he leave that place? We really need more and broader discussions on this and other important issues.

Another question that needs an answer: If the drug traffic is at the *Complexo do Alemão*, why do those communities, with more than 120,000 people, not get organized and push the traffic away? Because of what is called passive corruption. The institutions that work inside the *Complexo do Alemão* are quite passive in confronting drug traffickers. There are social workers, and members of NGOs, who know who is the leader in the drug traffic in that area, where he or she lives, where he keeps the guns, who works for him, and, maybe, they even saw one load of drugs and guns brought into their *favela*. But if you ask these social workers and NGO members why they did not let the police know about it, they will say, "We were doing our work here and the traffic is doing its work there." This behavior is very strong inside Brazilian society. For a lot of people the end of the criminal activity will mean the end of a job. The Federal Public Prosecution is already working on this problem. It is supervising research and who, where, how, why people are acting this way.

I will give an example: I received representatives from eight communities from *Complexo do Alemão*. Eight representatives. Six of them were acting in a very similar way, while the other two were acting completely different. Those two were showing a much broader eloquence and they were also very well dressed. All had similar complaints. However, the two eloquent ones would complain about police enforcement and how they could not develop social work. They were representatives of nongovernmental organizations. Their views were completely different from the other six associations represented in the delegation. I think the Public Prosecution Service will act and many things will come to the surface during this process. I hope the service will separate what is a serious work from what is not. I have known that some organizations help with doctors and medicine but these same doctors will also cure an outlaw who was shot. We have already too many things which are mixed up, and a certain amount of promiscuity, which makes it so important to give continuity to some social work.

EED: Would active police officers be able to learn from the theoreticians (academic theory) and vice versa?

JMB: That would be the ideal scenario. In my opinion, theoretical knowledge would help our officers a great deal. If they had more access to this information, they would be able to learn more from their actions. This also applies to the theoreticians. Scholars should be inside the police academies and battalions, teaching through classes, courses, workshops, seminars, forums, roundtable discussions, visits, and even study trips. For example, during my visit to Colombia, I was fascinated by the workshops they were developing. However, it should be noted that in Bogota there are 5,800,000

people and 20,000 police officers. Here we have almost 11 million
people and 38,000 police officers. A theoretician will see a lot of
police in Colombia, and at the same time the police there see a lot
of social policies from the government.

EED: How are relations with human rights organizations?

JMB: Amnesty International was here, asking many questions. I received
them. According to our transparency policy, there was no reason
not to. Their reports will help us if they are associated with actions
to implement the contents of the reports. The collection of data
only is not sufficient by itself. In the Amazon, for example, there are
apparently 12,000 nongovernmental institutions. If they are there
to help the environment, great! Regarding the human rights folks,
here in Brazil, they are focused on the *Complexo do Alemão* operation. But, what was the reaction of these organizations concerning
the men who killed João Hélio?[17] And in the case of the *pit-boys 18*
who beat the cleaning lady? What about the case of the two officers
who were executed inside a parked vehicle? In my opinion, human
rights should be for everyone; because it is too easy to be a specta-
tor and choose which cases to work on, ones that will get media
attention. It cannot be that simple. I believe the human rights work
is very important but it cannot be only for chosen cases.

EED: Last question, did the event on September 11 affect your work?

JMB: No. Not my work. What I can say about September 11 is that it helped
to organize groups to combat some supposedly terrorist actions.
Because of the Pan-American Games, we have groups that specialized in terrorism attacks.

EED: Your conclusion?

JMB: I would like to point that we have possibilities for the General Office
of Security of the State of Rio de Janeiro. We mean to change a
few of its structures, give better salaries, bring more technology—
the Pan-American Games already helped us tremendously with
it—and bring in more officers. Also, we need to reestablish police
specialization—today, in Rio de Janeiro, we do not have specialized
criminal police—as well as technical (scientific) police, who would
be more capable of preserving crime scenes. Another important
point is to use more diverse methods of transportation for police,
such as utilizing motorcycles, for example, because it does not help
to have an armored vehicle filled with police officers stuck in a traffic jam. And, there is a fundamental need to improve police intelligence so that this entire process will be smoother. That is extremely
important. Also, if I had any political interests, for example, I would
not have stayed for 2 months at the *Complexo do Alemão* working
on the intelligence aspect: observing who comes in, who goes out,

school schedules, car movements, who are the drug dealers, how they behave, where they live, how they do the dealings, how the society works there. While the media kept criticizing me, I always knew the moment to act.

EED: But you were also praised.

JMB: Yes. But there is no reason to get emotional about it. It is part of the job. Today we are here; tomorrow we will be someplace else. These are the rules of the game.

EED: Thank you.

Endnotes

1. The school is the Brazilian institution for higher studies of war.
2. "Support Mission" was a special group of federal police agents under Dr. Beltrame's command. It was created to improve the impact of crime enforcement in Rio de Janeiro state. Its work, mainly based on intelligence coordination, was considered very successful.
3. In the Brazilian civil police structure, the precinct chief must be a *Delegado*. The *Delegado* must be graduated in law and pass through an examination process.
4. Unless noted, the *Secretaria* is the Department of Security of the State of Rio de Janeiro.
5. Portuguese laws were enforced in Brazil during the colonial period. First, the *Ordenações Manuelinas*, from 1521 to 1603, and then the *Ordenações Filipinas*. This code was promulgated by Philip II of Spain on August 15, 1603. It was recognized by João IV of Portugal in 1643, and remained in force even after the independence of Brazil in 1822. The Philippine Laws (*Ordenações Filipinas*) as to civil law, remained in force in Brazil until 1917.
6. The Portuguese Emperor Dom João VI created the Brazilian police in 1806.
7. In Rio de Janeiro, almost all the slums (*favelas*) go up the steep hills around which the city developed.
8. A big complex of slums, with more than 120,000 inhabitants, in the Northern Area of Rio de Janeiro, where a big police operation against drugs traffic was launched for about 2 months.
9. IML stands for the *Instituto Médico Legal*, where autopsies are conducted for the purpose of investigation.
10. Policing by two police officers who have developed good relations with the neighborhood.
11. GPAE—*Grupamento de Policiamento em Áreas Especiais* (Task Group for Policing in Special Areas)—is a division of the military police intended to work under the communitarian police concept, minimizing bureaucracy, on a 24-7 basis.
12. Two areas in the *Complexo do Alemão* which have been controlled by drug traffickers for a long time.
13. Fundação Getúlio Vargas is a higher education institute, focusing on teaching and research in law, economics, and administration.

14. A large square at the *Sambódromo*, the place for Rio de Janeiro's annual Samba Schools Parade during Carnival.
15. A pile of rubber tires into which the victims are placed and put to fire with gasoline.
16. Drug traffic in Rio de Janeiro is controlled by several gangs. The most important are the *Comando Vermelho* (CV), the *Terceiro Comando* (TC), and the *Amigos dos Amigos* (ADA).
17. This refers to the death of a 6-year-old boy dragged through Rio's streets, which horrified Brazil. The João Hélio tragedy happened on February 7, 2007, a little after 9:00 p.m. Rose Vieites, his mother, was driving her car, after going to church, on her way to meet her husband for a late dinner. With her were her 13-year-old daughter Aline, a lady friend and her little son. Two gunmen approached the vehicle when she stopped at a red light and ordered all of them out. Everybody obeyed promptly, but the boy took longer to comply because he was strapped in a car seat. The mother rushed to help him, but while she was taking him out the robbers drove away at high speed while she ran after them screaming that the boy was hanging from the car still half strapped to the seat. He would be dragged for over 4 miles. The police say that two youngsters, Diego da Silva, 18, and E. (a minor), have confessed to the crime, telling details of what they did and showing very little emotion. They have also implicated two other youths. (José Wilson Miranda. *Brazil Magazine*, February 10, 2007; also see http://www. brazzilmag.com/content/view/7885/54/ (2/10/2007).
18. Young males from the middle and upper classes, usually practitioners of martial arts, frequently involved in gang fights and aggression in night clubs and on beaches. These boys are called "pit-boys" after the Pit Bull dog, popular with these young and irresponsible owners, who see these dogs as a symbol of machismo.

Interview with Dr. Bev Busson, Commissioner (Retired), Royal Canadian Mounted Police

4

INTERVIEWED BY DARRYL PLECAS

Background

Dr. Busson has a very special place in the history of policing in Canada. She started her 30-year career in the first recruit class of women to be hired by the Royal Canadian Mounted Police and ultimately rose to lead the force as its first female commissioner before her retirement in 2007. Along the way she had many firsts. She was the first woman to become a commissioned officer, the first to be appointed as a criminal operations officer, the first to become a commanding officer, the first to become a deputy commissioner, and the first woman to head up the Organized Crime Agency of British Columbia. She has been a driving force in many significant firsts in policing in Canada, including the development of an integrated model of policing, the development of university accredited in-service police training, the creation of university research chairs in policing, and the introduction of crime reduction. She retired as one of Canada's most distinguished and respected police leaders ever. This interview was conducted just following her retirement and subsequent appointment to the National Security Council. She continues to serve the RCMP as an advisor on leadership and change management issues.

The Interview

DP: When was the first time you said to yourself, maybe I'd like to be a police officer?

BB: You know I have to confess this; it was the very day that they said they would be taking women in the RCMP. It was the early 1970s and I was happily studying to be a teacher and I hadn't really caught onto this sort of women's equality thing. I was working with special needs kids, it was a summer job and I had just written my exams in May. I was graduating and actually had signed on to teach at the local high school. I didn't question why there weren't yet women in the RCMP. I had a couple of school friends who wanted to join the force and I remember thinking to myself a couple times, if I was a guy I too would join the RCMP. I remember the moment they announced on the radio that they were taking women in the force, and it was like somebody had hit me with a poker. That morning I drove to the local RCMP detachment to apply. There was a young RCMP officer coming in the back door for the day shift and I came in the front door and went up to the front counter and told him I wanted to apply and he said, "For what?" I said, "For the RCMP" and he said, "We don't take women in the RCMP yet." From that moment on I knew it was what I wanted to do. During that time, especially in Canada's Maritimes, women in other police forces were not doing a lot of street work, certainly in the Halifax-Dartmouth region. If anything they were matrons and those kinds of things. I remember I heard the news clip say this was regular members of the RCMP doing the same work as men in the field and I just found that so seducing.

DP: That application to join the RCMP certainly worked—it landed you in the first class of women hired on as RCMP officers. But that proved to be the first of many firsts—a lot of important firsts for someone with a reputation of never really trying for promotion.

BB: I've never been competitive with other people; I've always competed with myself. I don't have to be the best, I just have to be the best I can be and be happy with what I'm doing. I've never really been ambitious to rank but ambitious to meet my own levels of success and it certainly seems to work for me. I've always seen police work as an avenue for making a difference and when you're on the street that's fairly easy. As you move up the ranks and become part of the management team and then the leadership team, if you keep focused on what you're there for, to make a difference, it becomes easy to see what needs to be done.

DP: How typical do you think that is of police leaders? When I think of people I know who are at the top, generally speaking they seem different than police officers. Oddly enough they are more likely to be people who don't aspire to be at the top. Would you say that?

BB: Yes, I think that's true. As you ask me the question I'm sort of scanning the people I know, my colleagues, and I would say that the vast majority of them are working to do their best rather than just being ambitious to get to a place in history. In most cases it tends to be people that have just wanted to make a difference, to really contribute. I think it's no accident that a lot of people are in leadership positions because it is a calling of service. People who are overly

ambitious for the wrong reasons don't get there because you really
have to be prepared to give a lot of yourself.

DP: One of the things you are famous for is your leadership style. It was captured at one function recently when someone said you rose above
everyone in rank but never put yourself ahead of anyone. That is so
characteristic of a servant leader. You're there to help everyone else.
Do you want to comment on that?

BB: Maybe it's my upbringing too, but I've always strived to not forget where I
came from and what my roots are. Just because you have an important job, it doesn't make you an important person. You're just fortunate and lucky to be in a place where you can do the things that
you want to do. It doesn't give you some God-given right to feel
more important or more special than anybody else. It's not a roy-
alty appointment. You happened to be in the right place and have
done the right things and now have the opportunity to make these
kinds of contributions.

DP: One of the things we always hear about in policing, because of its command
and control history and rank structure, is that top-down "I'm the
boss" thinking is inevitable. You do it because I told you so, because
I'm more senior to you in rank. What do you think about that?

BB: Every police leader ought to be able to look back on what it felt like and
what made it really possible for them to do a good job. As you move
forward, I think it's really incumbent on folks like myself to continue to look back to investigate our life as a constable, a corporal,
and a sergeant as we move forward. What was it about the people
I worked for that made me rise to those occasions? That's what I've
always tried to emulate rather than, well I'm here now and you have
to listen to me just because I have the jewelry on my shoulder.

DP: Is there any one part of your career that you would say proved to be the
most fun?

BB: I have to say I think the most fun was the 8 years I spent as a detective in
Kelowna, British Columbia. There were about 12 of us in a nonspe-
cialized section. There were some with more training in homicides
and more training in different things but when something big happened everybody worked together and it was a great team. Nobody
competed and everybody worked very closely together. We solved
a lot of crimes and we had a lot of successes together. People came
and went but we always brought people into a very cohesive team—
it was just amazing.

At the same time, I can't say that I can think of a job that *wasn't*
satisfying. Being an administrative officer wasn't my favorite thing
to do, but I made it satisfying by finding avenues to be fairly involved
in various operational issues. Even being the commissioner for the

months that I was in Ottawa, which initially was not my first choice of things to do, proved very satisfying once I set my pace and realized that there was room at national headquarters, even for a short period of time, for the kind of leadership, the only kind of leadership, I know. I didn't just enjoy it; I have to say I really enjoyed it.

DP: In terms of emphases in policing, we seem to have emphasized a number of approaches over the years. Moving through community policing to problem-oriented policing, to comprehensive policing and crime reduction, we seem to have struggled with all of them. What are your thoughts about that?

BB: First, I've always believed that the police and the community need to be on the same page. You can't act in isolation—if you do, effectiveness will dwindle away to nothing. But it isn't just the community-police relationship that's an issue. I also think one of the reasons policing has found itself on the treadmill over the years is because we haven't been able to get different parts of the justice system working together. We use the words "justice system," but there is no system. Each group acts independently and each part of society has its little teeth that don't tie into the other cogs in the wheel and everyone is on their own little treadmill going nowhere because the cogs aren't touching. Every once in awhile we catch a cog and so you get community policing. You catch another cog and there's a protocol with the medical profession around how you deal with drug-addicted people. You catch another cog and you're able to deal with sexual assaults of children. But it's never been built as a well-oiled machine. I like a crime reduction approach because it respects the importance of community and problem-oriented policing, and gives special partnership attention to bringing all stakeholders, in and outside the criminal justice system, together towards creating a well-oiled, integrated machine.

DP: It always seems that police never have enough money or resources. How big of an issue was that for you?

BB: It was and is an issue; we need more resources to work better, but it is not the real problem. The problem is we're dealing with the same offenders over and over again, and that's a *waste* of money and resources. The frustration is there will never be enough police officers to get it right if the rest of society isn't going to play. If we don't build a social structure where these folks have some level of support during their struggle to become citizens again, then no matter how many people you get to solve crime, it's always going to get worse.

DP: Let me ask you about the relationship between theory and practice. I know you have an appreciation of that because you led the charge in bringing academia closer to policing in BC and there are all kinds of innovations there that are firsts in the world. What can you tell us about the place of academia in the world of policing?

BB: I've always followed the philosophy that policing really is a profession. I think it dawned on me when I was going to law school that police are not absolute experts on what they do. Putting the theory to practice and seeing that work is what makes you an expert and the mesh between those two things has never really been solidified in a lot of cases. You get people that learn on the job and are amazing police officers who never studied theory or had any kind of academic training. When you get somebody in academia who is able to support what people have had a gut feeling around for a long time with either research or comment, then both things tend to reinstill for me the fact that there is of course the practitioner side—but it really is a profession and both sides together make an absolute complement to the work that gets done.

DP: Looking at where policing is going, are there things that you think are central issues that need to be addressed?

BB: One thing that has concerned me is all the talk around policing and politics. Policing doesn't belong in politics and politics certainly doesn't belong in policing. You see it in the microcosm of Greater Vancouver, for example, whether we're going to have the RCMP or a municipal force police a particular jurisdiction, and of course it becomes municipal politics and then the province gets involved in those kinds of conversations and it also becomes provincial politics. You also have a lot of municipalities wanting to tell their police chief what to do, so you've got politics interfering with policing. There needs to be a communication back and forth but you can't have the politicians telling the police who to arrest, what investigations to do, when to do them, when not to do them.

DP: As you are very much aware, the person who replaced you as commissioner of RCMP is a civilian (the first time ever that a civilian has been appointed to that position). What are your thoughts on that?

BB: I made it very clear when I was commissioner that I really hoped the next commissioner would be a police officer. I believe that due to the dangerous work and the need to understand the dedication and risk taking in the policing profession, that the commissioner *should* be a police officer. Leadership in an organization such as the RCMP requires a high level of confidence from those being led. I understand that the new commissioner has created an "associate commissioner" position which is filled by a very capable police officer … this is working to fill the gap, but it is not the best model. Having said that, I know the new commissioner and if it had to be a civilian, I was confident that he would be someone who would do some very good things.

DP: Do you find that there tends to be more of a focus on things other than the effectiveness of police in reducing crime? I don't mean this as a criticism of the current commissioner, but one of the things that struck me in my first meeting with him was that it seemed like his focus was on things other than the matter of reducing crime. It was all these other kinds of issues and I thought maybe that's just the job—maybe you spend all of your time thinking about issues related to government.

BB: What it is that seems to happen, is all the other people that you're associated with and answerable to have that as their main mantra. It's hard to have any other kind of conversation. You start to talk about crime reduction and how important those kinds of things are and you can all of a sudden see their heads going ... what is that going to do for the political issues? That's another reason why I think it's so important for the commissioner to be a police officer because yes you have to worry about budgets and yes at the end of the day there is a Canadian agenda that has policing in it, but it's not a government agenda, it's not a party agenda, it's a larger societal agenda and it's hard to make that differentiation.

DP: Do you think police in Canada have more challenges than police in other industrialized countries?

BB: I suspect we do, especially when you consider the level of judicial scrutiny in our justice system. It seems to me that it's very difficult to get cases through our system. The levels of disclosure, the packages you have to put together for search warrants ... it's more expensive, it's more labor intensive, and at the end of the day there seem to be so many roadblocks to getting evidence in. It often seems to be that the police are on trial. All of that tends to make Canadian policing very difficult. They have that in the United States. But at the end of the day at least in the United States, if they get it in, people go to jail. There is a sentencing product. There is accountability. I'm sure it's difficult to make a case in the United States but here it's *incredibly* difficult to make a case.

DP: Do you think there is good cooperation among police forces around the world? Now I know it depends which countries you're talking about, but I guess I am asking your opinion from what you know about what that used to be like.

BB: I believe it's better than it used to be. I think other countries are beginning to work together because the world has gotten so global with international crime and organized crime. If you're going to play in that field, you have to build the relationships, and it is relational, it's not institutional. It depends on who's in charge, who's the leader in such and such police department, and of course, what their political regime is. It's very difficult to have full disclosure with certain countries because of their human rights records and their levels of corruption within their police forces. But again it's back to who is in charge and the trust that's built up between departments. I like to think Canada is a real leader in things like symposiums and other forums for getting people together.

DP: You've had a very distinguished career, you've received the highest awards in policing and the Order of British Columbia, which is the highest honor a British Columbian can get. Are there things about your career that you're most proud of?

BB: I guess the Order of BC is the highlight. Not just because I got it for the things I've done for policing, but it was actually something that was held and compared to other British Columbians doing other things and that made me feel really good about policing. I felt that the value of doing police work was good enough to be held in esteem among all the other amazing things that British Columbians have done across the province. It's actually the first Order of BC that was given to a police officer and that made me more proud than anything and I thought it really was a compliment to policing, not just to me, but to policing as a profession.

DP: One last question—you know the purpose of this book is to give people an opportunity to hear from police leaders, but one of the other main things is to capture what is it that makes these people outstanding leaders. You've had lots of recognition that would tell us that you're an outstanding leader but what would you say the requisites are of a good leader?

BB: I think one of them is being fairly confident that you know what you're doing and also that in any one of the specialist groups you're working with, that there's people in there that know way more than you do. You need to be able to tap into that and allow that to be the focus. Again, it's important to find the formula that allows those people to feel invigorated and energized and happy about coming to work every day. If you can get that to happen then you get amazing results.

DP: Thank you for taking the time to talk to us.

Interview with Felipe Harboe Bascuñan, Undersecretary of the Interior, Government of Chile

5

INTERVIEWED BY LUCÍA DAMMERT

Introduction

The Chilean democratic process has, interestingly, been different from those of the rest of Latin America. After a bloody military dictatorship that lasted 17 years, democracy was established and consolidated both economically and socially. Regarding public security, Chile has also experienced an increase in crime in the last decade, although this has been on a much smaller scale than in other Latin American countries. Chile is also different in that its police force is generally perceived as both efficient and honorable. Many questions can be asked about the progress made with security policies and the challenges these policies face, especially those connected to the police in Chile. These questions were posed to Felipe Harboe Bascuñan, a young lawyer with a relevant government career in the area of public safety. After 4 years as undersecretary of the Chilean police force, Harboe was appointed undersecretary of the interior towards the end of President Lagos' administration, with President Bachelet reappointing him to the position. The interview took place in Santiago in October 2007.

The undersecretary of the interior is, without doubt, the government official who coordinates and carries out the country's public safety policies. From this point of view, experience in the development of civilian leadership during democratic consolidation is central to the understanding of the Chilean process, as well as to discovering helpful information that may be useful for other countries in similar situations.

The aim of this interview is to initiate an exchange between the academic and political points of view, with emphasis on the experience of the latter. The text touches on the need to consolidate civilian leadership, allowing for security policies, especially those connected to the police, to be developed. This should be put into context; faced with the question of whether it "is more difficult to be a police officer today than 20 years ago," the undersecretary begins with this interesting and stimulating comment: "It is much more difficult, because nowadays citizens are aware that they have a right to be safe. This wasn't considered a right before, but now people demand to live in a safe environment. However, what is more important is that citizens are not demanding quantity but quality, that is to say, service, opportunity and problem-solving."

This change in public attitudes undoubtedly places greater demands on the Chilean police force, topics that will be dealt with later on.

The Democratic Path to Public Safety

LD: The Chilean process has most definitely been marked by Pinochet's military dictatorship (1973–1990), during which the armed forces and the police were at the center of political decision making. Additionally, it is a period marked by their participation in the daily "disappearing" of citizens, as well as other human rights violations. How would you describe the democratic process in terms of public safety and the role of the police?

FHB: Under President Aylwin's government (1990–1994), the main aim during these first 4 years of democracy was to establish dialogue as a means of solving conflicts. We are talking about politicians who didn't communicate, were incapable of being understood and who, each time there was any kind of problem, questioned the current political regime. As a result, emphasis was put on the need to establish basic conditions for national safety and especially on breaking up groups considered subversive.

LD: What about public safety?

FHB: At this stage, there were no reliable statistics about or technology used to document police procedures. Police headquarters had their own processes, independent of government efforts. However, the government's main aim was precisely that—to incorporate civilian control into the force, taking sufficient care to avoid breaking up the organization.

LD: You are suggesting, then, that this first government stands out for its use of political dialogue.

FHB: Undoubtedly. And the government of President Frei (1994–2000) stands out for its social dialogue, which aimed to improve economic conditions, especially those of workers. Regarding safety policies, paramilitary groups were reduced to a minimum. As a consequence, the groups left behind—a minority—began to fall directly into crime, offering their knowledge of gun-handling, structure, and operations to small-scale drug traffickers. When you look at the small-scale drug trafficking networks at that time, mainly in the north of the country and in some parts of the metropolitan region, you can see that the structure of the cells and safe houses is very similar to the structure previously used by military groups. Thus, as a more critical analysis of security began, police headquarters began taking notice of certain information. Concerning the less obvious statistics, these didn't exactly become more transparent, but I would say that little by little more information became available. Some kind of exchange of information started between the government and the police. Additionally, the police began communicating and coordinating various procedures among themselves, which was unheard of before. The public safety problems at that time were mainly connected to the proliferation of small-scale drug trafficking in the north of the country and thefts in lower-class areas.

LD: After these two periods, what changes do you think were fundamental?

FHB: Later, emphasis was placed on improving the quality of statistical information and on setting up programs aimed not only at controlling crime, but also at crime prevention. Police participation in and coordination of this process grew from day to day. Additionally, the National Policy for Public Safety was drawn up to reflect agreement among the different sectors and institutions on the strategies and policies that were to be adopted. Finally, during President Bachelet's government (2006–2010), the National Strategy for Public Security is being established. This involves the first government effort to coordinate the different programs of prevention and control, as well as the creation of quantitative measures to reduce crime during Bachelet's time in office.

Public Confidence and Professionalism

LD: Chile is unique in Latin America in that it enjoys high levels of public confidence in the police. Nevertheless, one of the main questions in the region is, how has this been achieved?

FHB: There is a part of the process of democratic consolidation in Chile that is not well-known and that has hardly been analyzed: the process of police socialization. The police were the visible face of repression during the military dictatorship (1973–1990). With the arrival of democracy, a process began to involve them more in the community, mainly through a change of image, so much so that their emblematic black and white uniforms during the military government were replaced by green and white ones in the democracy, thus changing their corporate image. Second, a process began to present police officers as people who cooperate with the people, playing an essentially protective role. Thus, the change in concept, from the disciplinary police officer to the committed, protective police officer, was key to changing their image and means that the institution enjoys high levels of citizen and civic respect. In the same way, I think that, during democracy, when certain natural catastrophes happen, such as earthquakes and floods, police participation has played a key role in helping the most destitute and vulnerable and these images have been widely spread by the media, making a very strong impression on the population.

LD: This strategy seems to have been successful, but was this the answer to an academic research question or to a practical police need instead?

FHB: It seems to me that, at first, it was the answer to the practical needs of police headquarters, faced with a country whose political and social structure completely changed. There was no other option; the police couldn't be uninvolved in this process of change, because their non-participation would have contradicted the whole aim of the process itself. I think that, with the subsequent arrival of police chiefs with greater vision and links to democratic governments, a new police vision emerged which, based on international experience, consolidated the people's perception of the police as trustworthy.

LD: Within the framework of public confidence, the police have developed different initiatives. In your opinion, what are the three most emblematic?

FHB: The first is the program to prevent traffic accidents[1]—"The Police: Your Highway Friends"—which was set up when the processes of community integration and socialization were just beginning, with the aim of preventing traffic accidents and, at the same time, educating the population. Thus, the police as a protective, educating, and educated force appears; that is to say, with model police officers and exemplary conduct. The second program that has been developed, based on community presence, is the Block Plan, whose aim—or let's say principle at least—is to create better relations between the police and their neighbors. The third is the creation of the community police officer—a police officer specialized in community organization, neighborhood watch, and social prevention. This complements the Block Plan and meets the community's demands, both those linked to the police force itself and those channeled through the administrative bodies, which exist according to the specific situation.

LD: And what has been the main impact of each of these programs?

FHB: The initial aim was to consolidate the image of police officers as an example of good conduct and I think that this was achieved through the first program. As far as the Block Plan is concerned, I would say that in the communities with the necessary human resources, logistics, infrastructure, and technology, good results have been achieved. We can see that in 6 out of every 10 communities with these resources and where this plan has been implemented, the numbers of victims has decreased. It's true though that this may not be entirely due to the plan, since it's very difficult to directly link its enforcement to a reduction in the number of victims. In the communities where this program doesn't exist, especially in large cities, there are still flaws. The number of victims isn't necessarily directly related to this plan and the capacity and influence of community police in such large environments, with such large populations and important levels of urban segregation, have not yet had the expected results. Finally, I think that the community policing program has been the most successful, creating close links between the police and the community. Undoubtedly, certain aspects of this relationship have been strengthened. Nowadays we can see that, in the rendering of public accounts for example, where the community doesn't necessarily question police work, the real figures showing improvement in victimization levels or police programs are not questioned. Rather, the community becomes a partner in helping the police obtain information and carry out projects and recreational activities. This has generated new customs, which partly explains the population's positive perception of the police.

LD: Prevention is undoubtedly important, but what is your opinion of the reform of police intelligence and control in the last 20 years?

FHB: I think that the process of police reform has been extremely interesting. As I say, to go from a dictatorial political regime to a democratic regime, the inflexibility of a director general to a system where flexibility exists, from subordination, strictly speaking, to a civilian world with a political class that understands more and more about public security matters, with greater civilian expertise and a powerful social evolution regarding the degree to which citizens' rights can be exercised, has also entailed—or should have entailed—the improvement of intelligence systems. Dictatorship intelligence is completely different to intelligence in a democracy; while the first has no legal limitations and doesn't respect basic rights, in the second the latter are fundamental. However, in a country that's gone through a process as traumatic as ours, information or intelligence activity is regarded with distrust. This has meant that the police have had to adapt their procedures to fit the new democratic structure.

LD: In this process, it stands out that the police, unlike many of the world's forces, are still a military body. What are the advantages of this situation?

FHB: I think that discipline, such as internal discipline, respect for police chiefs and even how quickly orders are met, is a very relevant part of police action. The fact that Chile has a nationally united police force, which also happens to be military, disciplined and with its own hierarchy, are factors that allow for a unique police strategy and deployment, as well as permitting that training be exactly the same throughout the country. These things make it easier to apply public safety policies.

LD: But doesn't the presence of military characteristics mean that the police are essentially a military force?

FHB: In effect, the Chilean police force is a body that was created in 1927 as part of the army, specializing in protection and national security. It was born as a branch of the army and then became a separate, autonomous organization. Those who study at the different police schools are civilians and don't belong to or have a history in the armed forces, nor do they carry out army functions. Their training is military to ensure greater levels of discipline and a hierarchy in police command, among other important things.

LD: As well as these characteristics, the police force's training is essential to make sure it is a professional body. What kind of training does the force provide?

FHB: We must make the distinction between the Chilean police force's two different ranks: that of officer, which is a rank to which you must apply, after having studied for four years in the Chilean Police Academy. Graduates become second lieutenants and their career development takes them through the rank of second lieutenant, lieutenant, captain, major, lieutenant colonel, colonel, and eventually general. In the ranks of noncommissioned officers—in other words, the police operations division—applicants apply and study for one year, graduate as police officers and then become second corporals, then first corporals. At this point, they require further training at the Academy for Non-Commissioned Officers, where they spend one more year before they can rise to the rank of second sergeant, first sergeant, noncommissioned officer and noncommissioned major.

LD: Is the duration of this training process considered part of the police force's success?

FHB: Yes. So much so that although officers have much more training and are therefore prepared with high-level positions in mind, in the case of the noncommissioned officers, priority is mainly given to operational and doctrinal training. And resuming their studies during their career is aimed precisely at updating their knowledge. Notwithstanding, in 2004, a retraining center was created. The aim was to take a large number of police officers off the street and enroll them in a 3-week course to teach them about the new legislation that was being created regarding police powers, given that in Chile there exists an important array of specialized laws that the police must know about.

LD: All of this and, in general, the changes in the police force involve important public spending commitments, as well as sustained political support. What has this process been like in Chile?

FHB: From 1990 to the present day, police resources have increased between 40% and 45%. This is the real increase that the police force, which will have a total of 42,000 employees by mid-2007, has experienced. In addition, in the same period, the budget assigned to the police more than tripled to more than $350 million from a total of $940 million assigned to security in general. We're talking about an increase of nearly 12% just on the previous year. These budget increases aren't necessarily only related to operational or personnel matters. Many times, modernization, technology, and repairs of equipment or systems that are clearly deficient—for example, the communication system, among others—are also considered.

The Police and Justice System Reform

LD: In Latin America, justice systems are characterized by their slowness, inefficiency, and high levels of corruption. Faced with this situation, several of the region's countries have developed reforms of the criminal process that can briefly be described as changing from an inquisitive and written model to an adversarial and oral one. In Chile, this process has meant a real change in the way criminal processes are carried out, which has undoubtedly had an important impact on police procedure and work.[2]

FHB: This process of changing the code of criminal procedure creates an intermediate figure: the district attorney, who normally has plenty of legal experience but little direct experience working with and relating to the police. Additionally, the investigating judges are in charge of authorizing the measures taken by the police and therefore need the police to be much more prepared.

LD: From your point of view, what are the challenges of this new process for the police?

FHB: The challenges are multiple, but the main one is the need to adapt intelligence. The social evolution of Chile and the existence of problems linked to groups that define themselves as "against the system" mean that the police need to recognize that intelligence should adapt to needs and not vice versa. Therefore, one of the main challenges is to make intelligence processes more professional, therefore solving problems at different levels. Consequently, it's important to understand that the ways police work in a democracy are different, since they require a greater capacity for information analysis, using new technology as a management tool. And regarding internal structure, I think that it's become necessary to copy international examples, making those in charge of police intelligence capable of receiving partial sets of information from different specialized groups, analyzing it and processing it so that it's useful to every specialized body. At the moment, however, intelligence is just one of many areas and general control of all the information is lacking.

LD: And this also has to do with the district attorney's job?

FHB: Yes, it has to do with the work of the district attorneys and the work of the government as a whole. I think that the government should, little by little, abandon its fear of using information within a democratic state and that the National Intelligence Agency [the public institution in charge of coordinating intelligence] should be further developed so that it has greater operational and coordination faculties regarding related police entities, because intelligence is very relevant for criminal activity, as is information to maintain a country's national security.

LD: This important change in the justice system meant that police resources were perceived as insufficient. What is the government's position on decreasing the amount of months spent on training in order to increase the number of officers on the streets?

FHB: We believe that if we have a police force that the population is proud of, it's because its members are well prepared. Despite the greater political or social pressure that may exist to increase the number of employees, this increase must be implemented gradually in order to guarantee that the graduates have the same preparation and the same qualifications, that they adhere to the same doctrine and have the same principles and values. During President Lagos' government (2000–2006), I was undersecretary of the police for 4 years and the police force gained 2,970 employees in that time, which met the goal set out by the government to increase the force by 990 per year. During President Bachelet's government (2006–2010), an effort will be made to increase the number of additional police officers from the previous figure to 6000, at a rate of 1500 per year. This means that everybody who graduates, including the extra 1500 who graduate each year, has exactly the same level of preparation, which guarantees good service and that a good job is done, with prestige and efficiency maintained. This decision was also based on a previous negative experience, since during the 1980s (the military dictatorship), when the military, security forces of dubious legal origin, and the police coexisted, the government, with its biased interpretation of its job to maintain national security tried to remove a large number of police in 6 months. In truth, the process was relatively ill-fated, since it ended in serious accusations of corruption, which tarnished the police's image and caused the very police to ask for this type of procedure to be ended.

Investigation and Planning

LD: Decisions about the duties and strategy to be implemented by the police in Latin America have not been supported by studies or analysis. Additionally, there is little collaboration with related academic research institutions. In this sense, do you think that the police and the government have been able to establish areas of research and development that strengthen police strategy?

FHB: Very few. I think that there have been some interesting attempts, such as the crime prediction model, which is being developed with public funds and with the permanent collaboration and support of the police. But even so, it's in its early stages and I believe that the police acceptance of civilian development and technology is relatively new. But since they have opened up to these, they will also have to start accepting, little by little, innovation and other developments. I think that the government hasn't been visionary regarding the subject, since the processes of innovation and development of the police or armed forces are still kept separate, when they are both essential and have the potential to support innovation and development as has been demonstrated internationally.

LD: And within the force, which entity is in charge of planning and investigation and what are its aims?

FHB: The police planning and development board is in charge of these tasks. This is the part of the force that can remove itself from the day-to-day control of public order and national security to plan development strategies, as well as generating innovative procedures, technology, and processes. I think that we have adopted a new out-look during the last few years, which has made this entity not only a board that puts together projects and obtains public financing for them, but which is also capable of designing internal development processes that allow for the improvement of management control, effectiveness, efficiency and control, and, of course, the extent to which policies or plans are implemented. Is this board in charge of developing the Block Plan? Definitely. The Block Plan was developed by them and the General Inspector's Office, which is in charge of making sure that internal rules and processes are complied with. I think that's where the ideas defining the strategies developed in the last few years come from, although support and contributions have also come from the civilian sphere.

Leadership and Civilian Control: Advances and Challenges

LD: If you had to choose, what would you say are the four main challenges facing political security policies in Chile?

FHB: The first challenge is to establish security as a state policy and to make people, particularly those in positions of power, both public and private, understand that security is a national matter that should be incorporated into the concept of citizenship as a whole and pri-oritized. However, at the same time, there needs to be sufficient stability, as well as an understanding that, while some processes are aimed at the mid- and short-term, many initiatives are long-term. Second, regarding security, an institution should be created through which the initiatives that are being undertaken are for-malized, for example, formalizing or creating an official institution that allows public and private cooperation, two sectors tradition-ally separate, or cooperation between the production, business, and government sectors. A matter as important as security is relevant to trade, industry, and urban development, among other things. We get to a point where the police in general are needed, particularly for matters of public and private cooperation. Third, the media should be involved in this challenge, since, as various experts in Chile indicate, we often feel more insecure about a crime because of the sensationalized information reported in the press. I think that the media should be involved. Undoubtedly, all the efforts of political institutions must be supported by the media, given their role of social responsibility, since they have a strong influence on people's feelings and many times it's these feelings that make the ruling party adopt decisions that aren't necessarily the right ones, but which are praised or expected by the population.

LD: And in this framework, how would you describe the role of the Chilean police?

FHB: The police are called upon to establish certain behavioral standards. In some ways, I'm referring to social conduct and safeguarding national security and public order to maintain the peace and tranquility that allow citizens to go about their daily business. Equally, to prevent and control crime, they must work effectively and in collaboration with the population. It's in this process that the police need to be prepared and have knowledge of the social reality. Specialized knowledge is fundamental in these matters, for example, regarding the territory, since in this way they can respond to the population's daily needs. Second, since the police are the only organization with its own legal system and constitution, it has the opportunity to use force to control the population. This role must be exercised with extreme caution and with respect for basic human rights. Honest people have the right to guarantees and the right to express their opinions within a democracy.

LD: While recognizing its central role in the democratization process, there are still many challenges for the police force. However, what do you think is the main one concerning its organization?

FHB: I believe that the evolution of the police force has been remarkable in many ways, but there are other matters in which there are still issues pending in a process that is evolving, although I'm sure they'll eventually be carried out. In this sense, I think that in the not-too-distant future, a career development system will have to be established, recognizing both time in the force and merit.

LD: Is this because the current process of professional rank is based only on time in the force?

FHB: Definitely. By developing a mixed system that includes time in the force and merit, any police officer who has participated outstandingly in an operation and who risks his life will see benefits to his or her career development. Furthermore, incentives should be incorporated to encourage officers to be more proactive.

LD: Finally, what are your observations on the challenges for civilian democratic leadership in these matters?

FHB: First, I think that the challenges are definitely connected to national security as a state policy, removing public security from electoral use and, in time, stabilizing public policies, independent of the government in power. The second challenge is to have a greater capacity for and knowledge of the realities for police so that the police are considered when making decisions about planning and strategy and in the development of practices and better security conditions. Third, international relations should be improved, not on the basis of academic cooperation but concerning the practical relationship between governments and police. Therefore, police forces worldwide and government authorities, in particular, should exercise control of national security and have greater levels of information exchange, with the aim of preventing and controlling organized crime.

LD: Finally, what are the challenges that need to be met to achieve effective control of police organizations, especially the police force?

FHB: First, we need to surmount our fear, because, in this country, politicians on the whole don't understand that civilian control is far superior to police power. This situation shouldn't, under any circumstances, mean that organizations become political. This situation is also difficult to envisage considering the high levels of training and the professionalization of police control. Therefore, there is no risk of police organizations being used as political tools in elections. If the country understands this process, the necessary modifications, which effectively permit public security strategies or the plans and programs that the government develops as state security policies, can be established without fear.

LD: Perhaps the change of police dependence reflects the increased trust between the government and police organizations?[3]

FHB: I think that the change of police dependence and the standardization of the police force, which has always been under the control of the Ministry of the Interior, was undoubtedly a fundamental step. Nevertheless, I think that more advances are needed, so that the civilian authorities in charge—from the government's point of view—have the capacity for greater participation in decisions about budgets, innovation, and management control issues.

LD: Thank you for taking the time to talk to us.

Endnotes

1. In Chile, the traffic accident mortality rate is close to 1,500 people per year, a figure that is much higher than the homicide rate.
2. For more information see www.cejaamericas.org.
3. It should be pointed out that in 2006, Chile approved a change in the dependence of both police forces, removing the police from control by the Ministry of Defense to the Ministry of the Interior.

Interview with Police Director Heinz-Ludwig Leding (Ret.), Former Police Chief of the Supreme Police School of the Federal State of North-Rhine-Westphalia in Münster, Germany

6

INTERVIEWED BY ROBERT F. J. HARNISCHMACHER

The Interview

The interview was conducted on December 19, 2007 in the house of Mr. Leding in Münster-Hiltrup, Westphalia. The interviewer and Mr. Leding have been friends for more than 20 years. In many prior discussions on the topic of policing, they have exchanged their points of view on actual police problems as these influence the education and training of the police, civil society, and the state.

Introduction

The Federal Republic of Germany is a democratic and socially responsible country divided politically and administratively into 16 *Länder* (states). The nationwide constitutional order, embodied in the "Basic Law," is expressed in the country's constitutional bodies, in the country's federalism, in the legal order, and in the electoral system. These institutions determine not only everyday political routines but also the everyday lives of the people of Germany.

After the end of World War II, Germany was divided into four administrative/occupation zones by the victors—the French, the British, the American, and the Soviet Zones. The American, British, and French Zones were abolished with the enactment of the Basic Law (the "Constitution" of Germany) in 1949, which returned political power to German institutions in what was then West Germany; the Russian Zone, which had become East Germany, was combined with West Germany in 1990 after the fall of the Soviet Union to create the current Federal Republic of Germany.

The law of the Federal Republic of Germany applies to virtually all aspects of life. Most legislation passed today consists of adjustments and amendments to existing laws to take social developments into account and to cope with social problems. Germany's legal system has been shaped by constitutional law but is also influenced by the law of the European Union and by international law. The body of federal laws now encompasses approximately 1900 acts and 3000 statutory instruments. Laws are passed by the *Bundestag* (the lower house of the bicameral federal legislature), and administrative decrees, based on federal legislation, are enacted by the federal government. State *(Land)* law is concerned mainly with such matters as schools and universities, the press, radio and television, as well as the police and local government.

Historically speaking, German law in part goes back to Roman law and in part also is derived from numerous other legal sources in the German regions. A uniform system of private law was created for the entire German Reich for the first time in the nineteenth century. To this day, the Civil Code and the Commercial Code have preserved the liberal spirit of those times. Their underlying principle is the freedom of contract.

As its name suggests, the Federal Republic of Germany is a federation consisting of several individual states, the *Länder*. The federal nature of the system of government is reflected in the fact that the 16 *Länder* are not mere provinces but states endowed with their own powers. They have their own state constitutions, which must be consistent with the principles of a republican, democratic, and socially responsible constitutional state as laid out in the Basic Law, to ensure that all Germans enjoy uniform rights and duties and the same living conditions. Within this framework, the *Länder* largely have a free hand as to what they particularly wish to stress or specify in their individual constitutions.

This form of federalism is one of the sacrosanct principles of the German constitution. But this does not mean that the boundaries of the constituent states may not be changed—as long as the citizens affected by any such changes or amalgamations are in agreement. Provisions have been made in the Basic Law for boundary adjustments within the Federal Republic.

Maintaining public security and order is one of the most important tasks of government. In Germany, this task is shared by the states and federal government. For the most part, the police come under the jurisdiction of the states, but in certain areas the Basic Law assigns responsibility to the federal government, such as border police and the Bundeskriminalamt (BKA, the Federal Criminal Investigation Office) responsible for collecting and compiling statistical information and assisting Länder police in investigations and research.

The jurisdiction of the states over the police encompasses all organizational and personnel matters pertaining to their state police forces. The branches of the police forces include the general police forces, the criminal police (CID), the alert forces, and the waterway police. The general police forces are essentially responsible for ensuring public safety and order. Their duties range from warding off dangers to prosecuting crime.

The criminal police are also responsible for the prevention and detection of crime. Whereas the general police forces are mainly concerned with cases of petty crime, the CID deals with dangerous crimes and criminal offenses. These especially include culpable homicide, serious property offenses, and, increasingly, organized crime. In the prosecution of crime, the police assist the public prosecutor's office in charge of the given proceedings. The criminal police have special police units—in some cases jointly with the general forces—to combat terrorism and hostage taking as well as for protective measures at special events, and for observation and searches.

The alert forces of the states, which are deployed as whole units, were instituted pursuant to administrative agreements between the federation and the states in order to be available in case of internal emergencies, natural disasters, and major accidents, in a state of tension or in a state of defense. In some states, the alert forces are responsible for the training of new police recruits. They also provide support for individual police forces during demonstrations, sporting events, and other major events, traffic surveillance, police raids, and large-scale search operations, and can be deployed to combat organized crime.

The Interview

RFJH: Can you tell me a little about your childhood and adolescence ? What influenced and convinced you to join the police?

HLL: I was born December 3rd in the year 1934 in Münster. My father had been a sworn officer, and a postmaster. At home, at times after World War II, there had been difficult relations. We were often hungry, because of a lack of money. We had to take care, moreover, of our sister who had been very ill, a disease with a lot of consequences for the family. My brother and I had to promise to do our very best for our sister when our parents should die. Because of all these severe personal problems, I left the grammar school (Kardinal von Galen) in Hiltrup and entered the newly established police of the federal state of North-Rhine-Westphalia. It was really a flight, not only an escape, but the decision was the right one. The future would be evidence of that. I have never in my life repented or regretted this step. In the police, I did not have all the economic and severe problems I experienced at home. I was immediately a fan of this new world. A new start in my life with an unknown career had begun.

My biosketch is a typical one for Germans after World War II. Remember the situation at that time. The writer and poet Wolfgang Borchert has compared it to a man who is returning home to Germany. He had been away, perhaps too long. And he returns changed, being other than when he left. It had been a time of chaos. The Allied Forces wanted to establish a new police organization, with decentralization guaranteeing the inner peace of the new democratic state of the Federal Republic of Germany. That was the real incentive for me joining the police of North-Rhine-Westphalia.

RFJH: Can you tell me something about your training and education in this new police institution ?

HLL: Well, October 12, 1953 was a red-letter day. As a rookie I began to learn the basics during training. Besides the instruction, I also had the wonderful chance to pass my final exam, the *Abitur,* and attain a high school education. That meant that now I would be able to study at a German university.

After this basic training, and time as a probationer, and a final check and test I became a police constable. I had the great luck that despite of two or three thousand candidates I had been selected to be one of five hundred police officers.

I always have loved sports activities, such as Judo, boxing, all kinds of athletic activity. But I have to note that this so-called police training really was a military one. My instructors were persons with much war and martial arts experiences. For instance, I had to learn using hand grenades and firing a machine gun. These examples are evidence of the military style of training at that time in the German police institutions. Today our police is a civil service organization serving our citizens. Nowadays, the rookies don't learn such disciplines as handling military weapons and equipment. Today they all begin their careers in the police as students of the police.

RFJH: When did you get your rank inspector of the uniformed police?

HLL: That was in 1961 after attending a course at the Police Institute of Hiltrup.

RFJH: Did you now change your tasks in the service of the police?

HLL: Yes, indeed. I got new tasks as squad commander, for example, in the riot/standby police. That was a wonderful time with very fond memories. Now I had to control fight riots, deal with catastrophies, and manage great meetings and important events.

RFJH: Would you please describe the tasks of such an emergency division (*Einsatzhundertschaft*)?

HLL: There is an emergency division (*Einsatzhundertschaft*). The deployment task force, for example of the Polizeipräsidium Münster (Police Presidency) in North-Rhine-Westphalia is an example of the work and duties of the *Einsatzhundertschaft*. The *Einsatzhundertschaft* works rather unobtrusively and quietly. Its goal is legally based policing, appropriate to the situation, in necessary proximity to the public. Efficient policing is always in the interest of public reason and not of public violence. We do not consider ourselves a special task force. With the whole range of our activities we want to keep the social peace, strengthen the sense of responsibility, achieve voluntary obedience to the law, the defense of the legal system and sustaining and strengthening of the trust in it, with a view to a general preventive effect on criminal activities. Our daily presence, either in uniform or plain clothes, should result in a conscious or unconscious [conditioned] reduction of criminal activities. Crime must not become part of everyday life and disturb society. The fellow man and woman with his or her legal rights, life, health, and property is the center of our attention.

In this field of tension between order and law, cooperation between citizen and police is a necessity for achieving the public interest!

RFJH: Is it necessary having such a special police unit in our state?

HLL: I would say yes. The events in many a German town paint a picture of conflict. Police actions against squatters, radical ecologists and environmentalists, members of the peace and antinuclear movement, political extremists, and terrorists cause us to take a look at the way the change of values in the society has taken place and how these events influence policing. Many policemen might remember a verse from Heinrich Heine's poem from 1843–44, "*Deutschland—ein Wintermärchen*" ("Germany—a Winter's Tale"). "You are the judge, I am the bailiff. And with the obedience of the servant I execute the verdict you rendered. And may it be an unjust one."

Young policemen experience more than ever that people—an instability factor—become a security risk, that discrepant interpersonal behavior consists of hurting one another, that citizens are permanently perpetrators and victims.

A non-political-minded mass population also feels the conditions of structural violence, though often indirectly, such as resistance against social reforms or as reign of bureaucracies a citizen often cannot succeed against. The seemingly forgotten fact that men share elementary legal goods and fears has become obvious again. But the desire of many is experiences that will assure one's identity and to receive recognition as individuals.

Nowadays, self-interest has become an actuality not to be underrated. Politics aim more than ever at a reanimation of existing conditions. The populace looks for signs of hope, for new horizons, new chances in life. But our era prefers to leave the field to eloquent inactivity. Livius wrote about the Roman times, "in our times we can neither bear our faults nor their remedies." Such pessimism must not find a basis nowadays. Given the choice to die upright or to live as a crook, man will always prefer the latter.

RFJH: Is our state in good condition and OK?

HLL: Where everything becomes a legal problem, law itself has lost its value. An illegitimate state can only be supported by a few but strong pillars which receive the repeated voluntary approval of its members, or it will lapse into severe elementary crises. One of the strong pillars is a popular police, serving the community.

One can suppose that political movements outside the range of established political parties are an expression of a gap between the populace and their representatives, a gap difficult to bridge. This is a signal that the mature citizen wants to participate in the decisions on details of problems, but always knowing that he or she has to give up some individual freedoms for the sake of the common good.

Perhaps a coercive institution everybody agrees to is necessary. The results need not be perfect as the alternative is too terrible to consider. Injustice might be preferred to total ruin. The government is more and more under the pressure of lobbies, leading to the danger that it cannot fulfill its task anymore.

The policeman, a citizen himself or herself, exists and works in this field of tension. Whoever orders forceful police action to take place has to reckon with a violent reaction. There is a justified public suspicion that police hope for the deterring effect of aggressive force. The deployed policeman has to stick to orders, conscious that he represents the law and that his opponent is a factual or potential criminal. This poses an incalculable potential for aggression and will estrange in time even moderate citizens from the state. The populace's desire for order and safety needs to be met, but especially through trust that democratic and legitimate solutions will be fostered.

RFJH: Is our history in Germany a bad heritage for successful police work?

HLL: Political education, the creation of a historical consciousness, could be a remedy, as clarifying the present means becoming conscious of the past, to understand the causes, to see the meaning of the future, to look back in order to progress. History must not be understood as a stale mass of events but as a relevant inheritance. Anybody ignorant of the past cannot manage the future.

That the view into history is the corrective agent for future policing concerns the citizens and the police alike. Concern and care for one's fellow men must lead back to Protagoras' realization that "man is the measure of all things." The use of technical aids is only of a subsidiary nature. The unrest of people is not only characterized by fears of all kinds, but also by the change of structure in their daily life, their social existence.

The courage for action, for involvement, the motivation to participate, need more than ever the backup of a lived tolerance and demonstrated virtues in order to foster creative personal values that might provide solutions for certain situations.

Especially the police are in need of this creative unrest. It enables them, by their self-reflection, to come to a positive image of their profession, remembering their role as mediator between the pluralistic opinions of the social groups, and to achieve a more sensitive legal understanding of their work and high professional ethics.

The future needs ideas and principles in order to progress. It needs people with the courage to speak out their own thoughts. Maturity, especially in the police, is the guarantee for ways to solidify the legal peace. As Goethe said, "Whoever has a swaying mind in swaying times, increases the evil and spreads it further and further. But whoever remains steady, shapes the world." This is especially valid for the police.

RFJH: Would you tell us more about the roots and the importance of an "*Einsatzhundertschaft*"?

HLL: The *Einsatzhundertschaft* today? The term *Hundertschaft*, a hundredship, is the German version of the Roman *centuria*, the smallest unit of a legion with a strength of 100. After World War I, this term was replaced in some German police forces by the term Kompanie, deriving from the Latin *companium* (*cum*, with, *panis*, bread) meaning bread company or table company. Members of the company were people who ate their bread together. And the *Hundertschaft* is indeed a community concerned with the simplest preconditions of living—shelter, food, and economy. Today it really only means board and lodging in their own barracks.

In North-Rhine-Westphalia, there are several Hundertschaften, such as the Hundertschaften of the Bereitschaftspolizei, the Alarmhundertschaften, and the Einsatzhundertschaften. As a rule the Hundertschaften of the Bereitschaftspolizei are formed of police cadets. The duty in a Hundertschaft is part of their training. The cadets are confronted by special situations they have to respond to in closed formations, for example, riots, demonstrations, etc.

The *Alarmhundertschaften* are as a rule attached to a *Regierungspräsidium* (government agency), an administrative agency representing the government of the federal state in a certain district. The uniformed policemen of this district can be drafted and deployed to special situations in closed formation. The

Einsatzhundertschaften were formed with certain regional focuses. They are part of the local police department (*Polizeipräsident,* Police President). The *Einsatzhundertschaft* attached to the *Polizeipräsident* Münster differs from others insofar as its members have served for at least 8 years, are locals, and want to remain on duty in Münster for a longer period of time.

This meritorious concept was the idea of *Erster Polizeihauptkommissar* Udo Struebbe, the commanding officer, who wanted to avoid frequent change in the staff. The *Einsatzhundertschaft* was intended to integrate the members' professional and private lives in the spirit of comradeship, leading to the identification with one another, improving in the end the communication and interaction with the population by serving as an example of observing certain values.

RFJH: What especially are the tasks of the Einsatzhundertschaft? Can you give some examples for a better understanding?

HLL: Combating street crime. Street crimes include offenses, the pre-committing, committing, and post-committing phases of which happen or originate in a location open to the public. Most often these are spontaneous and uncomplicated offenses against people or inanimate objects. But *street* is not a static term; it is to be understood as a public interest issue. The most frequent crimes are robbery, burglary, theft, muggings, homicides, vandalism, and sex crimes. Frequent perpetrator groups include prostitutes, pimps, and criminal gangs. On foot, by bicycle, motorbike, or car the men and women of the *Einsatzhundertschaft* patrol their assigned beats, concentrating on meeting points of potential criminals, such as certain pubs, discotheques, and similar places; conduct reconnaissance beats at locations with a certain attraction for youths or social outcasts, such as public merry makings, fun fairs, pubs, motorcyclists' meetings; and do protection beats if there is information on riotous mobs or intended attacks on property or between gangs. Further they can perform raids, traffic controls, and checks in order to combat illegal immigration.

Combating the main causes of road accidents. In order to improve road safety the *Einsatzhundertschaft* performs speed checks (radar), alcohol and drug checks, checks on truck vehicle drivers in reference to their driving and rest times; checks on traffic lights; and does normal traffic duty. They suggest measures to slow down the traffic by barricades (chicanes), flower pots, depressions or humps, or the creation of 30 km/h zones, give hints on traffic lighting improvements, the securing of school ways, the erecting or taking down of traffic signs, etc.

The protection of the environment. The protection of the environment requires conscientious handling by people. They have to learn that they are the environment's custodian and not its exploiter, which means its destroyer. Chief Seattle from the tribe of the Dunwamish Indians said in 1855 in a speech in the presence of Franklin Pierce, the 14th president of the United States of America: "What is a man without the animals? If all animals go, man would die from great loneliness of the mind. Whatever happens to the animals, soon happens to the people. Can you buy the buffalo back, once the last one is killed? Teach your children what we taught our children: the earth is our mother. Whatever befalls the earth, also befalls the sons of the earth. When the people spit on the earth, they spit at themselves. Because we know: the earth does not belong to the people, man belongs to the earth. Everything is connected with each other, as blood unites a family. To injure the earth means to despise her creator. When all buffalos are slaughtered, the wild horses tamed, the secret corners of the forest heavy from the scent of many people and the view of lush hills disgraced by talking wires—where is the thicket? Gone! Where the eagles? And what does it mean to say farewell to the fast pony and to hunting? The end of life—and the beginning of survival."

Eighty percent of environmental crime is water pollution, 15% waste, and the remainder emission offenses. Patrols in the rural areas and suburbs of Münster have brought many hints on the disposal of oil, petrol, liquid manure, silo leakage juice, wild rubbish dumps, etc.

Detachments to special groups of the CID. It has become common practice to detach members of the *Einsatzhundertschaft* to special groups of the CID. The officers learn new insights and creative ideas and take part in an important exchange of information.

Detachments to the Politically Motivated Crime Unit. In 1948, HM (His Majesty's) Military Governor of the British Zone of West Germany ordered the formation of an information squad on antidemocratic, neo-Nazi activities and a unit to fight politically motivated crime. The information squad is now integrated in the Ministry of the Interior, the unit formerly known as "14. K", and now part of the local Police Presidency and is directly controlled by the *Polizeipräsident*.

Detachments to the Organized Crime Unit. The Organized Crime Unit of the *Polizeipräsident* deals with offenses by professional criminal gangs that work largely clandestinely and aim at material gain or seek influence in public life. Some examples: counterfeit money, drugs and illegal weapon trade, and abduction and sale of children and women, theft of luxury cars and lorry freights, prostitution, computer crime, terrorism, illegal gambling, check fraud, investment fraud, copyright violations, etc.

Cooperation with the Drug Enforcement Unit. The *Einsatzhundertschaft* supports the Drug Enforcement Unit in its departments—Information and Evaluation, Organized Trade and Smuggling, Street Trade and Acquisition, Hard Drugs, Surveillance.

RFJH: What's the structure or organization of this emergency police unit?

HLL: The structure of the *Einsatzhundertschaft*. The *Einsatzhundertschaft* has a strength of 120 in three platoons (*Züge*). The experienced platoon commanders are of inspector rank. Each platoon has three groups of 11 men each. The group commanders are inspectors and members of the *Einsatzhundertschaft* for many years; members now are frequently inspectors as well. One officer serves as the platoon commander's driver and radio operator.

The Evidence Attribution Detail. This detail connects or attributes any evidence to a particular perpetrator in a way that is usable and acknowledged by the jurisdiction. This end is achieved mainly by video demonstrations. The EAD is deployed in squatter situations, football matches, demonstrations, state visits, etc. The members undergo special training in the *Landeskriminalamt* (State Agency for Criminal Investigation) and are equipped with up-to-date electronic devices.

Then there are the *Einsatzhundertschaft's* stars, their dogs. The *Einsatzhundertschaft* is supported by eight lovely German Shepherd dogs and other breeds with the courage of a gladiator if need be. They are used as guard, search, or sniff dogs and have passed the test in many drug raids and state visits.

RFJH: How do the police officers keep fit doing their job successfully?

HLL: Sport is an aid for integration and achievement. Sport is a definite must in the *Einsatzhundertschaft*. Team sports are particularly popular, as well as running, swimming, skiing, boxing, jiu jitsu, karate, judo, wing tschun and kendo and, last but not least, shooting. Especially, officers are trained in shooting/nonshooting simulated situations. North-Rhine-Westphalia's best marksmen are in the *Einsatzhundertschaft*. Their commander is a good example. The trophies of many competitions in various disciplines vouch for a high personal involvement and intensive contacts with the German, British, and American armed forces and other institutions which turn out to be very useful in pursuing their policing aim.

RFJH: What is the secret of the success of the Einsatzhundertschaft?

HLL: Working relationships and human capital—interdependence of both is required for success: I am just saying this philosophical sentence: One doesn't just radio one another, one also speaks with one another. The internal relations of the *Einsatzhundertschaft* are characterized by a positive social competence, which shows in talking and listening ability, reliability, empathy, adequate and appropriate interaction with others, admission of emotions, being able to praise and give compliments, encouraging others, holding one's own.

Police forces anywhere, wherever in the world, live by their personalities. The *Einsatzhundertschaft* serves standards of justice; it serves as a model. Its members encounter their community not merely as a job, but as a vocation that needs positive, creative people, a vocation that asks everything of them and yet gives them back plenty. The men and women of the *Einsatzhundertschaft* are always eager for any further training. They have understood that if they want to be successful in understanding their potential opponent they have to learn from anything and anybody. So it is no wonder that they invite speakers from all walks of life in the expectation of controversial opinions (e.g., contacts with universities) and keep seeking contacts with foreign colleagues (e.g., EUROPOL in The Hague), or that many of them are members of the International Police Association (IPA), the varied seminars of which they enjoy.

The esprit de corps is greatly enhanced and consolidated by joint social activities such as summer, children, or Christmas parties, bicycle tours, etc. Everybody feels like part of a great family. The *Einsatzhundertschaft* lives by the maxim: "We live with one another, not against one another. We honor freedom. We work for the peace. We obey the law. We serve our internal standards of justice."

RFJH: Having learned so much about the standby police I am now eager to learn more about your further personal development during your times in the uniformed police service?

HLL: Excuse my emotions, but these times in my life were very important for my later career in the police. By 1962 I had to teach, based on my practical work experiences, at the police school of the land in Münster about traffic problems, constitution law, penal law, etc. And furthermore I had to arrange championships in skiing and other athletic disciplines, because I had been always active in various sports. It was a logical decision to become an organizer and supervisor of the "German Police Sport Committee" *(Deutsches Polizeisportkuratorium)*.

RFJH: When did you achieve the rank of *"Polizeirat"*?

HLL: In 1971 I started my course at the Police Academy in Hiltrup. On February 10, 1972 I was promoted to the rank of *Polizeirat* (in the military system comparable to the rank of major). Then I learned to administer some police institutions in North-Rhine-Westphalia where I had to do my job now as a leading police officer. My assignments have been in Oberhausen, Recklinghausen, Datteln, and Münster, where I had been ordered to serve as teacher of public law at the "Higher (Supreme) Police School of the Land" (*Höhere Landespolizeischule "Carl Severing"*). There I served as teacher and evaluator of judicial drafts for the Ministry of the Interior in Düsseldorf, the capital of the state North-Rhine-Westphalia. I later instructed police inspectors, and have trained personnel for the course at the Police Academy in Hiltrup. In the Ministry of the Interior, I worked for some years as expert advisor.

On March 19, 1975 I received the rank of "*Polizeioberrat*" (comparable in the military to a lieutenant colonel). I then became deputy chief of the school in Münster. On October 17, 1978 I was promoted to the rank of a police director. But then I had to go to the Police Presidency of Gelsenkirchen, where I had to organize security for the European Championship in soccer, as well as the visit of the Pope, and the huge event for the pop star Michael Jackson. I worked in Gelsenkirchen for two and a half years. On April 1, 1987 I was promoted to the rank of leading police director (*Leitender Polizeidirektor*). But I returned to Münster, becoming chief of my school in 1989. I was the first chief born in Münster to become head of this important police institution in our land.

RFJH: What were your goals in this important position?

HLL: I always wanted to realize in my life, as a sportsman, being a very good coach with personal principles and being supportive of all my staff and personnel. All problems should be solved with fair play and by communicating face to face, because with the new political situation in Europe at this time, all was changing. There was now a lot to do besides daily work. My school had to train police officers, for example, from Russia and other countries of the former "East Bloc."

We had to support after the reunion of the two states of Germany (FRG/GDR) into one Germany, and support the Police School in Bernau of the new German Federal State Brandenburg. Some of our police officers left the school, going to Bernau or other police institutions in the former GDR (German Democratic Republic), where they started a new career. As many sudden, brand new problems had to be solved by me and my staff members, I often had to travel by car to Bernau, a long-distance trip, to assist them in solving problems for establishing a functional and effective school organization which followed the spirit of the law of the Federal Republic of Germany. In this way I have spent a lot of my private leisure time, but I really wanted to do my very best for them, because my state expected me to do my duty with high respect, total police knowledge, and busy engagement.

And finally I am very proud that all this stress and business has been the basis for a real success in getting an institution committed to education, training, and learning by solving problems in all fields of police tasks and activities. There has not been a mentality in the sense of "the winner takes it all." Active and engaged cooperation was the secret of this success. Now this school is a welcomed and important partner in the German police organization.

RFJH: When considering your life as active and engaged police officer what, in your opinion, are the basic results?

HLL: In the FRG, since World War II, there has been a stress on training that teaches how democracy works, the separation of powers, and so on. Police reform after World War II has tried to include demilitarization, communalization, democratization, and improved community relations and public accountability. The latest reforms involve having a community-oriented strategy, communication, conflict resolution, and modern management skills and techniques.

In police training, students learn a great deal about police laws, which one cannot learn in the university because courses for law degrees contain more information and knowledge of general laws. The police laws also tend to be taught with a greater focus on the importance of the principle that the state must be built on the rule of law (*Rechtsstaat*) and that the democratic state (*Demokratischer Staat*) must coexist with it. Law is the primary focus in all forms of training, especially in the training of lower ranks, with less emphasis on social sciences. Senior superintendents have criminal courses. There used to be a strong emphasis on militaristic discipline. Now, particularly with women coming in, there is more stress on practical police training and less on militarism. There are even a lot of programs geared toward training police officers as social workers. But, in summary, you may recognize that the "re-education" by the Americans and the other Allies has been successfully done after World War II. The Germany of today is a peaceful country, far away from military thinking and acting.

The basic police training is imparted at the Police Technical College (*Polizeifachhochschule*). There exist different models of police training. One model is the former common police school, more of a theoretical school. Another model is the training provided by the Emergency Police as it is done in the Länder where the academic aspects are separate from the operational police. But the trainees see the work of the other part, the operational part. Another model is that officers apply to the police station, take leave from police work, then come to the police school training. This model is very much practice oriented.

The Police Technical College (*Fachhochschule*) is for regular training, which lasts 4 years. If officers do not have university entrance qualifications, they must have a certificate from the Police Technical College. They have to study in the Technical College for 4 years (because one year is taken up by studies to get the certificate from the Technical Police College). After finishing the Technical Police College, the pupils must go to work with the Emergency Police. However, they are sent to the police stations to work when there is no emergency. They also may be sent to other states. According to the German constitution, one state is required to help another. And moreover they are also deployed for special projects like drug operations and to control demonstrations.

Finally I can say this. The profession of policeman has always been in the center of my heart and thinking and feeling, the most important part of my thinking besides my family. It's a hugely attractive profession for young people. It is a multifunctional profession for human beings because of the many possibilities in the organization for fulfilling their dreams. One can do a lot of things, learn a lot of things, teach and organize a lot of things, search a lot of things, always keeping in mind that the most important duty is serving as partner of the public and rescuing the lives of people, fighting all forms of crime, and helping in special situations, such as extreme catastrophes. And until your retirement you'll be engaged in a process of forever learning more and more for the better understanding of current life. As the motto of the San Diego County Sheriff's Department says, "The honest motive is the public good!" That is our police mission worldwide. I have always been a man engaged in the practice of daily police life. The special gift to me has been that a lot of experts accompanied my professional work with scientific advice and consulted in solving severe problems and dangerous situations. It has often been even brain storming, very important for the success of police activities. Police equals *POLITEIA* [the Greek local self-governing community or city state]; that is the multifunctional discipline of the police—to serve citizens, society, the state, and, being a borderless profession, acting as the civil advocate and attorney for the living community to help in building the state that serves all.

The police have been really dominant in my life. Now in my retired phase of my life I am studying a lot of literature of writers, authors, poets. But I thank you cordially for giving me the chance to tell something about my experiences and career in the German police.

RFJH: Thank you. It was a pleasure.

Interview with Commissioner of Police George Asiamah, Ghana National Police Service

7

INTERVIEWED BY GORDON A. CREWS AND ANGELA D. CREWS

Background

In January 2007, Drs. Gordon and Angela Crews traveled with their graduate assistant, Kofi Annor Boye-Doe, and Ghanaian Fulbright Scholar, Ken Aikins, to Ghana, West Africa, in order to conduct a research project. The original research plan was to conduct a three part examination of: (1) the blend of indigenous government (rooted in religious practices and strongly associated with spirituality and mysticism) and state government in the Ghanaian justice system; (2) the treatment of women and children within these systems; and (3) the alternative dispute resolution, restorative justice, and conflict resolution strategies within the two systems.

During this trip, the researchers met with Commissioner of Police George Asiamah (who has become the driving force for the current community policing initiative in Ghana), other officials from the Ghana Police Service (GPS), and faculty of the University of Ghana Legon and the University of Cape Coast. In the course of these meetings, the Crewses became better informed about the practice of justice in the country and some immediate law enforcement needs related to the development of the nation, specifically the dire need for training in "community" and "intelligence-led" policing.

Citizens in Ghanaian society (as well as citizens in most sub-Saharan African countries) do not trust the police, preferring to rely instead on "magico-religious" forces and traditional authority figures to settle disputes (Abotchie, 2002). When circumstances do reach severity levels such that citizens are forced to contact law enforcement, the police role is best described as reactive. Unfortunately, this tends to reinforce the perception of citizens that police only exist to take away the "bad guys." Ghana's police force has a tradition of being used as a militaristic tool of oppression and this history, unfortunately, remains entrenched in the collective social conscience.

The current project has been developed to meet the needs of a more modern Ghanaian law enforcement agency. A recent name change from "Ghana Police Force" to "Ghana Police Service" reflects the desire of a more progressive administration to provide service to the community, rather than act strictly as an agent of governmental force. Of primary concern to the Ghanaian government and to the GPS is the development and implementation of an effective "community policing" program.

Since early 2007, the Crewses, working closely with Commissioner Asiamah, have developed a team of researchers and practitioners who currently are developing training programs to be delivered onsite in 2008 to Ghana National Police Service administrators dealing with "community" and "intelligence-led" policing. This team includes practitioners, experts, and academics, from the University of Ghana Legon (Ghana), the University of Cape Coast (Ghana), Washburn University (United States), and the National Organization of Black Law Enforcement Executives (United States). This team is also currently working with the U.S. Embassy in Ghana to ensure the implementation of programs and training that will be most beneficial to Ghana.

The Interview

This interview was conducted through a series of conference telephone calls between December 1 and 17, 2007, due to Commissioner Asiamah's duty schedule. The interview began in early December while Commissioner Asiamah was stationed in Tbilisi, Georgia serving on the United Nations Observer Mission in Georgia (UNOMIG). UNOMIG was established in August 1993 to verify compliance with the ceasefire agreement between the Government of Georgia and the Abkhaz authorities in Georgia. UNOMIG's mandate was expanded following the signing by the parties of the 1994 Agreement on Ceasefire and Separation of Forces. The interview concluded in Istanbul, Turkey as the commissioner was traveling back to Ghana for a brief holiday break.

Views on Career

GAC: Let us begin by discussing your policing career. Tell us a little bit about your career, educational background, and training.

GA: I am currently the commissioner of police for the Ghana Police Service, having held this position since 2006. In this capacity I serve as the director general for legal and special duties. Prior to this position I served over 27 years with the Ghana Police Service in various positions, such as assistant staff officer to the Inspector General of Police (IGP), district police commander, divisional police commander, deputy regional police commander, and director general for human resources.

I hold a postgraduate Professional Law Certificate (Barrister at Law) from the University of Ghana School of Law, Master of Arts in Police and Criminal Justice Studies from Exeter University of the United Kingdom, and Bachelor of Arts (with Honors) in English Linguistics and Russian from the University of Ghana Legon. Early in life, I had trained as a teacher at Nkoranza Training College. Later, I was very fortunate to have received extensive management training from the Ghana Institute for Management and Public Administration. In addition, I worked as a police trainer and human rights trainer in a workshop in Abuja, Nigeria and helped to develop a human rights training manual for West African police training schools.

I have always tried to maintain a very high level of service to the international law enforcement community. I have served as the Ghana Contingent commander to Bosnia (UN Mission), police trainer in human rights at Tito Barracks in Sarajevo, and many other peacekeeping missions around the world. I am currently serving another tour of duty with the United Nations Observer Mission in Georgia (UNOMIG).

ADC: I am not sure how many people know of this security effort. Could you please tell us more about this group?

GA: I am currently on special assignment as a police advisor of the police component to the United Nations Observer Mission in Georgia (UNOMIG). The UNOMIG was originally established in August 1993 by Security Council Resolution 858. Its mandate was revised following the signing, on May 14, 1994, of the Moscow Agreement, which established a cease-fire and separation of forces plan.

In accordance with this agreement, a Security Zone (SZ) of roughly 12 kilometers was created on either side of the cease-fire line. In this zone, military units are forbidden; only personal weapons, including RPGs (rocket propelled grenade launchers), may be carried. On either side of the Security Zone is the broader Restricted Weapons Zone (RWZ), in which tanks, armored transport vehicles, and artillery and mortars equal to or greater than 81 millimeters are prohibited.

The mandate tasks UNOMIG to monitor and verify compliance with the Moscow Agreement, and to observe the operations of a CIS peacekeeping force (PKF), as was stipulated in the Moscow Agreement. The CIS PKF is currently composed of some 1700 officers and soldiers from one single contributing country, the Russian Federation. The CIS PKF maintains stationary checkpoints along both sides of the cease-fire line. UNOMIG operates independently from the CIS PKF, but keeps in close contact with them.

UNOMIG maintains a political head office in Tbilisi, mission headquarters in Sukhumi, and sector headquarters in Zugdidi and Gali, on the Georgian and Abkhaz sides of the cease-fire line, respectively. Its primary tools for ensuring compliance with the Moscow Agreement are observation and patrolling, reporting and investigation, and close and continuous contact with both sides at all levels. To facilitate its operational patrolling tasks, UNOMIG has two helicopters and 38 mine-protected vehicles. UNOMIG patrolling teams not only observe and conduct liaison; they also promote dialogue among CIS PKF, heads of local administration, security personnel, and local residents. Each sector usually conducts one helicopter patrol per week. Currently, UNOMIG consists of 120 military observers from 25 countries, approximately 99 international staff, and 183 local staff. Its mandate is reviewed every 6 months by the UN Security Council.

UNOMIG personnel patrol unarmed in the face of armed threats such as mines left over from the war, attacks by insurgents and bandits, and kidnappings. UNOMIG patrols have been ambushed and come under direct fire on several occasions. The most common threat is hostage-taking. Seven hostage-taking incidents have occurred in UNOMIG's history. The last four took place in the Kodori Valley, most recently in June 2003.

ADC: Have you been surprised by anything related to your career development?

GA: I joined the police as a direct entrant from the university. In those days there were few college graduates in the police service. Many graduates believed that the police service was "anti-graduate," and rightly so. A few graduates who entered were regarded as people who had entered a profession that had very little to do with book knowledge. The old crop of police inspectors and chief inspectors who had served for more than 20 years and had to take a highly competitive entrance exam to police college, believed that direct entrants had come in without taking exams thereby making worse the competitive nature of entrance exams to police college. Consequently, the few graduates in the service in those days were looked down upon with disdain.

In terms of practical police duties, direct entrants had to undergo on-the-job training to acquire practical knowledge. It was therefore the case that direct entrants had to be submissive and friendly in order to learn from the old station officers. Graduate officers who appeared to be snobbish had much difficulty in learning on the job. And, the old and experienced station officers who had passed through the ranks often boasted or bragged whenever some graduate made little mistakes and tried to vindicate themselves saying graduates had come to pollute the service.

These things have changed now that the service has got more graduates in the system. The tide began changing when the old crop phased out due to retirement and the top brass eventually became filled with college graduates. When I look back 27 or more years ago, I do smile in my head that at long last I have made it to the rank of commissioner of police. Since there were no policy guidelines for promotion, it was sometimes a matter of luck or depended on the connection that you had at the top. I had no connection or godfather and so I always got a raw deal. While some graduates came straight away as senior officers, I came in as a chief inspector and had to serve as a trainer at the police academy for almost 3 years. This all occurred before I entered the police college to be commissioned as an officer. Anyway, I do not regret it because the solid foundation I got in policing can be traced to those days when I wrongly thought that I was being delayed in climbing the professional ladder.

ADC: Did your work prove as interesting or rewarding as you thought it would?

GA: Yes, I could not imagine doing anything else with my life. At one time I thought about dedicating my life to the practice of law, but I did not think that would be fulfilling enough. I found law enforcement and the service to my country a career that has given me enormous pleasure in seeing the results of my work. Actually seeing how my efforts help others is the greatest gift a police officer can experience.

Changes Experienced

GAC: Let's talk a little bit about the changes you have experienced during this time. What do you see as the most important changes that have happened in policing over the course of your career?

GA: Many changes have happened in Ghana police. Philosophically, there has been a great shift from postcolonial policing philosophy to democratic policing. From the time of political independence in 1957 to early 1992, the Ghana Police Service operated in the shadow of a colonial hangover. The new African elite also stepped in the shoes of the colonial masters (i.e., the British). The top hierarchy indeed suffered in the hands of the new breed of politicians who dislodged police independence and wanted very much to dictate to the police.

Police officers who tried to assert their independence were victimized. Whereas the colonial masters through their white officer corps used the police to maintain the status quos, and to protect trade and commerce of the colonial powers, the postcolonial political elites very much interfered with police operations and in many cases politicized the police.

In terms of organizational arrangement, very little has changed. The hierarchical structure with IGP at the top, followed by schedule offices down to regional commanders, divisional commanders, district commanders to station officers remains the same. Police powers are centered at the HQ and the IGP seems to be too powerful. It is a pity that now that we have two deputy IGPs, the IGP's overall powers have not dwindled. The deputy IGPs continue to function like schedule officers. The so-called decentralization of political power to the regions and districts did not affect the police. To date regional commanders down to the district command and the stations do not control their own finance. Even though they are nominally consulted during budgeting season their contributions are mere formalities.

In terms of specialization, it is true to say that little emphasis is placed on police specializations. Even at the senior officers level there appears to be no distinction between detectives and uniformed police officers when it comes to postings. It is therefore not uncommon to find that the officer of say the Narcotics Unit at the CID HQ has been transferred to head a police district, and vice versa. The same goes for the junior ranks to some extent. At that level, IGP has given the power to transfer detectives to the director of CID, but in many cases these are punitive transfers and IGP reserves the right to revert the detectives and post them to general duties irrespective of level of specialization of the affected officer.

The most contentious policy has been that of Police Policy Guidelines for promotions. Until that policy came into force the service had no formal policy in terms of promotions in the service based on academic qualifications. Generally promotion had been on merit, seniority, and through examinations. Even though meritocracy seems to be holding sway its application has not been all that equitable. The present administration has taken the bull by the horns to streamline the policy guidelines on promotions [however] very many gaps remain in place.

In terms of equipment, very modest gains have been made. But the police still remain under-resourced and ill-equipped. The 2001 May stadium disaster in which several lives were lost when police fired tear gas to dispel football hooligans, little did the public know that the police were indeed ill-equipped and that public order equipment needed to be modernized to reflect international standards. Public outcry and resentment went into how the police were trained to handle public order situations and the need to give them better equipment to do their work efficiently and effectively.

ADC: What changes in external conditions (i.e., support from communities, legal powers, judicial relations, relations with minority communities, resource provision, political influence, etc.) have had a significant impact on policing?

GA: Police powers in Ghana are unambiguous. They are found in the Statute books (e.g., The Police Service Act 320 and the accompanying Letters of Interpretation). The Public Order Act also guides the police in the exercise of their powers in times of public demonstrations.

The police enjoy the support and cooperation of the judiciary and the Justice Ministry. Being a common law country, the police prosecute minor offenses on behalf of the Attorney General Department, and leave the indictable offenses for the AG lawyers to prosecute. Since the police are not part of the Justice Ministry (but of the Interior Ministry) many gaps remain to be filled in terms of police prosecution. Many judges and even the media as well as the general public seem to have very little confidence in police prosecutors and accuse them of inefficiency and corruption; police prosecutors will have to be countenanced for many years to come. This is because the AG lacks professional lawyers who are prepared to prosecute criminal cases. In recent days many serious attempts are being made by the Police Service in collaboration with the Justice Ministry to enhance the capacity of the police prosecutors through training courses.

The Ghana Police has no minority problems to deal with as may exist in many countries. Nevertheless, many critics seem to opine that the police are more inclined to protect the rights of the rich and powerful in society than the poor who are vulnerable. A social commentator once observed that the police indeed spend more time in protecting people with political power than the ordinary people who are left at the mercy of criminals in their neighborhood. Community policing, if well implemented, can make the neighborhoods safe for all. If the public continues to think that sporadic police swoops in the deprived communities can solve the crime problem, they are far from right.

GAC: Overall, has the quality of policing improved or declined (street work, specialized units, managerial capacity, self-evaluation, interagency cooperation, etc.)?

GA: The present Ghana Police Service appears to be very undermanned. The police are encumbered because most of the men who should be on the street to fight crime are invariably posted for guard duties (e.g., financial houses and the houses of dignitaries). There is a need to encourage the more private police to do guard duties so that the police can concentrate effectively on their core duties of fighting crime.

The police in recent times have sought assistance from the French government in terms of public order policing, from the U.S. government in terms of criminal investigations and basic officer skills, and the British in terms of organized crime and money laundering. The police also do cooperate with Interpol in the fight of transnational crimes (e.g., child trafficking, drug trafficking, and terrorism).

For many years the police have paid lip service to community policing as an organizational philosophy and strategy. There is a need for political will and serious commitment from both the police managers and the people in government to concretize community policing and make it work. The recent community police officers drafted from the unemployed youth to assist the police cannot be a substitute for proper community policing. The newly community formed community police appears to be an avenue to find jobs for the jobless in society, but its efficacy as a crime prevention tool suffers from so many gaps.

ADC: In general, is it more or less difficult to be a police officer now than in the past?

GA: The present day vigilant press, which is always very critical of the police, has put policing into sharp focus. Police misconduct and malfeasance can no longer be swept under the carpet. The general public is wide awake and sensitized about their rights. Gone are the days when police brutality on campuses went unreported [because] people in power thought that it was not in the national interest to do so. Now we have a free press and the government no longer has the monopoly on the media front.

Policing in such an atmosphere is not only challenging but interesting. The present day police must be accountable not only to the law, but to the people. The new police managers must rethink their strategies and adopt operational measures that are in conformity with the tenets of democratic policing.

In the good old days when we were young officers, information and communication technology (ICT) had not reached such an advanced stage. The security services including the police had monopoly over wireless messages which were deemed to be faster and convenient but with globalization, even a street corner FM station can easily outdo the police in terms of reporting incidents. The reality is that if as a police manager or commander if you don't get on your feet you will be overtaken by events and will find yourself in a tight corner where you can't explain away your inefficiency.

Personal Policing Philosophy

GAC: I am very interested in your own personal policing philosophy; what do you think should be the role of the police in society? What should be their job, functions, and roles? What should be left to others?

GA: I think policing should be a mixture of combating crime, law enforcement, public order maintenance, and a social service. In a sense policing strategy must be crafted to suit the society in which it operates. It must be dynamic in order to cope with new crimes and public safety issues. In the area of public order maintenance and crime prevention and public safety issues, the police must forge a close partnership with the larger society.

The job of the police must be not only performed according to the mandate prescribed by statute, which may be restrictive, but should perform in the overall context to ensure that there is peace and order in society. And, by extension, I mean to say that policing functions should not be put into water-tight compartments, so that the police would be selective in their operations and say no to public safety issues that are crucial to the survival of society. What needs to be done is to ensure that policing roles are performed in the larger interest of society and within the law.

I think that as much as possible certain roles of the police can be civilianized. For example, guard duties can be performed by ordinary civilians. Much more so certain secretarial and administrative work in the offices can be civilianized. Police property management must be left for civilian professionals. Certain aspects of traffic management, apart from investigation of accident cases, must be given to civilian agencies to operate.

ADC: What policies on relations with the community, with political groups, with other criminal justice organizations work well?

GA: I think that, for the police to be efficient and effective they must win the trust and confidence of the people they police. If there is widespread perception of corruption in the police organization and policing strategies also tend to alienate the general public, police legitimacy will be undermined.

Police neutrality must be sacrosanct. There must not be attempts to politicize the police. The police must be law abiding, because if law enforcers become law breakers then the society is doomed. Police as an organization should work in harmony with the criminal justice society, including those in academia. Policing research must not be shelved, must be given the chance to be tested just as the scientific community and industry collaborate to bring technological advancement in society.

GAC: How should policing be performed? What should be the preferred priorities and strategies; hard edged crime control, prevention, services, order work, what mix for which types of problems; proactive-reactive; community policing-law enforcement, etc.?

GA: I think proactive interventions should be more prominent, and that as far as possible police work must be intelligence led. The police must avoid labeling of certain social groups, especially the poor communities, as the cause of crime. Stereotyping in policing operation can be counterproductive so there must always be covert intelligence reports before the police embark on swoops in deprived communities.

Problems and Successes Experienced

ADC: Let's move on to discussing problems and successes you have experienced. In your experience what policies or programs have worked well and which have not? And can you speculate for what reasons?

GA: At a certain point in my career as a commander I found out that police swoops in deprived communities always tend to rope in innocent passersby, thereby making the whole operation a failure. It is also my contention that, much as regional security committees have a role to ensure police operational efficiency in the overall context of national security, they must give the police the chance to do their professional work for which they have been trained. The fact that one has been given a political appointment does not mean that he should carry himself as a security guru. He should depend on the police and other security agencies for informed security advice.

GAC: What would you consider to be the greatest problem facing the police at this time?

GA: To me the greatest problem facing the police is not so much about logistics and resources, but the crisis of legitimacy. The police must earn the respect and trust of the community so that the community can support the police in its work. If there is apathy among the general public and the police are singled out as the main organization to fight crime, the police will woefully fail.

The modern media also appears to be one of the main agents more often prone to exaggerate police misconduct and malfeasance thereby massing public resentment against the police. In the effort of the police to boost its public image they need the media to deliver the goods. But, invariably, the same media that builds up police image is the same organization that nibbles police image to extinction. In the bid of the police organization to boost its image, when police take 20 steps forward, the media comes in with damaging reports to send police 100 times backward.

I think that, as much as the media has the right to criticize the police, it must not be done in such a way as to kill the very spirit of the police organization. Policing as a service organization must be owned by the community. It should not be seen as an external occupation force in society. The police and the public must always be involved in a healthy partnership for the good and survival of society and for the sustenance and safeguarding of individual rights and liberties. Policing issues must be put on the public agenda for a healthy debate and a few press houses should not be given the monopoly to determine what is good policing and what is bad policing.

ADC: What problems in policing do you find are the most difficult to deal with?

GA: In my opinion, it is the enormous responsibility of trying to build the capacity of the police service to serve the needs of its people and government. This capacity building involves so many things internally and externally. Internally, we need to increase the resources given to police officers to fight crime. Externally, we need to find ways to increase public confidence and trust in police. These things are obviously connected.

Theory and Practice

GAC: In our courses and training we are always discussing the connections between theory and practice. In your opinion, what should be the relationship between theory and practice?

GA: Yes, of course there is a strong connection between theory and practice. I should probably say, theory is driving practice. In Ghana we have tried to do just that, we have tried to learn from our own academic pursuits and those of others from which we can seek assistance. We have a large number of police administrators who are college educated. They have the background in education to see how what they have learned can be implemented in their daily practice.

ADC: What is the relationship right now? Does it exist? Does it work? What holds collaboration or interactions back?

GA: A good example right now is the work that you [the interviewers] and I are doing with the GPS and with NOBLE (National Organization of Black Law Enforcement Executives) from the United States. We currently have a wonderful team working together to implement community policing in Ghana. We have you as current research-ers/academics and former practitioners, and others who are current practitioners and currently involved in community policing training in many parts of the world. This is currently one of the biggest initiatives we have in Ghana working towards proper implementation of community policing from a theoretical and practical foundation.

GAC: What kind of research, in what form, on what questions would you find most useful for practice?

GA: Again, the current Police Officer and Household Surveys that you are administering in Ghana in support of our mutual research/training efforts are the kinds of information we desperately need. The findings that you have offered to us so far on police officer perceptions of the citizens and the citizens' perceptions of police are incredible. And, it confirms what we know; there is a very strong lack of trust between these two groups. But, it is nice to have the research to back up these beliefs.

ADC: Where do you find theory-based information? Where do you look? What journals, books, publications, reports?

GA: Those of our service who are educated read and study any and all information they can find. We are all avid readers and sponges for any information that can help us do our jobs more effectively.

GAC: Does the organization do research on its own? On what types of issues or questions?

GA: No, actually, we have very little internal research being conducted. It just has not been an organizational priority.

Transnational Relations

ADC: I want to ask you a few questions about transnational relations and Ghana. Have you been affected by, and how, in the work of your organization by developments outside the country (human rights demands, universal codes of ethics, practical interactions with police from other countries, personal experiences outside the country, new crime threats, etc.)?

GA: When I was a postgraduate student at Exeter University in the UK in the early 1990s I had a rare opportunity to travel to most European countries, including Germany, Holland, Denmark, and Belgium on a study tour. I visited police organizations and police academies and shared professional experience with my colleagues. I was also in Bosnia to serve under the IPTF (International Police Task Force) where police from 42 countries worked harmoniously together to monitor the local police and also to entrench internationally recognized police standards which had at its base the protection of human rights and democratic policing. I see that these exposures have positively impacted my work as a police officer and I see policing as a service-oriented profession designed to promote world peace through protection of the rights and human rights of all, irrespective of color, sex, religion, station of life.

I am also convinced that through international police cooperation we can fight transnational crimes and all crimes (e.g., genocide). I am convinced that crime and criminals do not know state boundaries. Criminal operations are stateless; therefore, we need concerted and deep police internal cooperation to confront all crimes that defy boundaries.

ADC: Have those interactions been beneficial or harmful? What kind of external international influences are beneficial and which ones less so?

GA: Ghana is very receptive to outside assistance. We have been very fortunate to have received help from a number of countries. In recent years, we have been fortunate to receive training and assistance from the French Police, the British Police, and from the FBI and International Criminal Investigative Training Assistance Program (ICITAP) in the United States. Given our training needs and problems, these types of assistance are greatly appreciated.

ADC: How have developments post September 11 affected your work?

GA: The developments in the aftermath of September 11, 2001, brought to the fore that international terrorism, organized crime, and international drug trafficking issues must be tackled with intense policing cooperation globally. Police forces must share intelligence information. Developed countries should assist in building the capacity of police organizations in poor countries. Global terrorism is not only a problem for the United States and her allies but a problem confronting the whole world. The whole world must appreciate more than ever before that global conflicts must be resolved peacefully. The UN and the regional groups including the United States must agree that there must be peaceful resolution of conflicts worldwide and that in all attempts to solve conflicts, the UN must take a leading role.

General Assessments

GAC: In that same vein, I wanted to discuss with you briefly your general assessments of policing. Are you basically satisfied or dissatisfied with developments in policing?

GA: Generally, I am satisfied with the developments in policing. Especially with Interpol, as well as UN police peacekeeping, capacity building, mentoring and monitoring, supervision of elections, and confidence building in post-conflict environments thereby encouraging safe return of IDPs [internally displaced persons] and refugees to their original homes. In the old days the police were concerned only with the internal security of their countries, but now the wings of police operation are stretching far and wide and police men and women are cooperating to fight crime in this global village of ours. This means that policing has responded positively to globalization.

The "police" is an institution that had very little regard for book knowledge but has now opened its door wide to intellectuals and professionals of all shades. Policing research has doubled in most universities.

Community policing as an organizational and operational philosophy has gained currency in most police departments and organizations worldwide. The future of policing as an organization better placed to safeguard human rights and guarantee fundamental freedoms is deeply entrenched. Democratic policing is gaining roots in areas that were once noted for repression and abuse of human rights.

Policing has embraced gender issues in its planning and women police are now coming to the forefront to champion the cause of peace. Many more women have joined the police and policing has lost its poor image as a profession reserved for men only.

But what is more worrying to me is the incipient perception of corruption that is working like a virus in a computer. Another worrying factor is the politicization of police work such that in some societies policemen with political connections but little experience are being promoted over and above their hard-working professional colleagues. Generally most police forces are underpaid and are working with poor conditions of service (e.g., in third-world countries).

I think that there should be an international movement to fight for better conditions of service for the police. The so-called corruption eating up most police organizations can be traced to the fact that the police are not well catered for by the society. The larger society should not simply take it for granted that the police can thrive and survive on corruption. An incorruptible police service should not be an ideal, but a requirement.

I watch with trepidation a new crop of police who are trigger happy and very sadistic. I condemn people with ulterior motives who join the service for selfish gain. I abhor the wicked practice whereby criminal organizations sponsor people to join the police in order to protect their interest. I dislike officers who are not prepared to learn the job of policing but only prefer accelerated promotion to fill round holes with their square pegs. The service should not be a place for people who reveal the identity of police informants.

GAC: What are the most likely developments you see happening and which would you like to see happening?

GA: I had been yearning for an organization attracting the best cream of society to address crime problems and public safety. I see this happening. I had a vision of a police service that regarded the service role as supreme; a service that saw itself as a calling, like the priesthood. I am optimistic that the light is at the end of the tunnel. More police officers are becoming more professional and highly committed. I will be happy for the day the title of corruption will be wiped away from our professional garb.

GAC: What is most needed now to improve policing?

GA: I think what is most needed to improve policing is to take a critical look at the human resource base of the police and ensure that the police are well trained. The police service needs a customer-oriented approach in order to work to satisfy the aspirations and the security needs of the public.

There must be an aggressive capacity drive in all police forces so that the police will update their professional competence and thereby provide efficient and effective service to themselves, citizens, government, most importantly, their government.

Conclusion

The central themes of this interview are obvious. First, this represents the views of a man who loves his profession, organization, and mostly his country. Second, his dedication to police professionalism and credibility cannot be overstated. Third, he demonstrates a keen understanding of the connections between police resources, practices, and eventual police perception. Finally, as is being adopted by more and more international police leaders, he points out the crucial connection and understanding that law enforcement must have with those they serve. Without such connection and understanding, all is potentially lost.

Ghana Background

Ghana is occupied by approximately 22 million citizens over roughly 92,000 square miles (about the size of Illinois and Indiana combined). It is now in its fourth republic, having endured military rule and political upheavals since gaining independence from British rule in 1957. The president, H.E. J.A. Kufuor, represents the New Patriotic Party, and was elected to his second 3-year term in 2005.

There are 10 governmental administrative regions, similar to U.S. states, each with corresponding capital cities except for the Greater Accra region, which is the Ghanaian capital. Those regions, with capital cities in parentheses are: (1) Greater Accra; (2) Ashanti (Kumasi); (3) Brong Ahafo (Sunyani); (4) Central (Cape Coast); (5) Eastern (Korofidua); (6) Northern (Tamale); (7) Upper East (Bolgatanga); (8) Upper West (Wa); (9) Volta (Ho); and (10) Western (Sekondi/Takoradi).

In addition to the formally elected government, the country's political, social, cultural, and economic landscape is significantly affected by the National House of Chiefs and the 10 regional houses of chiefs. These entities represent more than 32,000 traditional rulers, designated by lineage, who are the trustees of communal lands and resources and who are believed to be the living representatives of the ancestors (Gyekye, 1996). The Ghana Constitution recognizes and protects the chieftaincies as an integral part of Ghanaian governance.

Although there are 10 governmental regions, the country is divided into 13 police administrative regions, with additional regional offices for the National Headquarters, one in Tema, and one to deal with railways, ports, and harbors. Within these 13 regions are 51 police divisions with divisional commanders, 179 police districts with district commanders, and 651 police stations and posts, headed by station officers.

The GPS is headed by the inspector general of police (IGP), Patrick Acheampong, who is aided by two deputy IGPs, one in charge of operations and one in charge of administration. The GPS has nine main divisions, each headed by a deputy general. Five of these divisions are the responsibility of the deputy IGP of operations, and four are the responsibility of the deputy IGP of administration. A chief staff officer operates directly under the IGP and serves each deputy general. Seven other individuals/units have administrative relationships with the IGP (e.g., executive secretary), or are in a lateral relationship with the IGP (e.g., Audit Unit). The GPS currently numbers approximately 17,000, with a police/civilian ratio of about 1/1200.

Ghana has six police training schools: (1) National Police Training School at Accra; (2) Kumasi in the Ashanti Region; (3) Pwalugu in the Upper East Region; (4) Koforidua in the Eastern Region; (5) Ho in the Volta Region; and (6) Winneba in the Central Region. All recruits must be Ghanaian by birth, between 18 and 25, of good character with no criminal record, and of minimum height and medical fitness. There also are minimum education requirements. Police recruits attend a 6-month training academy, consisting of instruction in physical training and drill, firearms use, unarmed combat, and first aid. Recruits also attend classes such as ethics, criminal law and procedures, methods of investigation, human rights, and domestic violence.

A 10-member National Police Council, established by Article 203(1) of the 1992 Constitution, is charged with advising the president on "matters of policy relating to internal security, including the role of the Police Service, budgeting and finance, administration and the promotion of officers above the rank of Assistant Commissioner of Police." Until March 2006, however, there was confusion in Ghana as to whether this Council actually existed (Foley, 2006). This uncertainty adds to the evidence that the GPS is plagued by questions of administrative and legislative oversight.

More information on the Ghana National Police Service can be located at:
    http://www.ghanapolice.org/

More information on the UNOMIG can be located at:
    http://www.un.org/Depts/dpko/missions/unomig/ and
    http://unomig.org

References

Abotchie, C. (2002). *Social control in traditional southern Eweland of Ghana: Relevance for modern crime prevention*. Accra, Ghana: Ghana Universities Press.

Foley, E. (June 2006). *Roundtable on police accountability: The police, the people, the politics: Police accountability in East Africa*. Arusha, Tanzania: East Africa Law Society.

Gyekye, K. (1996). *African cultural values: An introduction*. Accra, Ghana: Sankofa Publishing Co.

Interview with Police Lieutenant General Dr. József Bencze, High Commissioner, Hungarian National Police

8

INTERVIEWED BY POLICE COLONEL DR. JÓZSEF BODA

Background

On June 1, 2007, Dr. József Bencze was appointed high commissioner of the Hungarian National Police (HNP), a force of some 45,000 personnel, including 37,000 sworn officers, in a country with a population of 10 million. Dr. Bencze joined the HNP in 1985 as chief of police station. During the major political changes in Hungary between 1989 and 1990, he worked in the Ministry of Interior (MoI). For 2 years—in 1990 and 1991—he was mayor of a small village called Farmos. Between 1991 and 1995 he was asked by the then high commissioner of the HNP to take over command of one of the most difficult police districts of Budapest (District Five). After 5 years in the district, he was transferred to the MoI again. From 1997 until his appointment as a HNP high commissioner, he was director general for law enforcement (second-in-command) of the Hungarian Customs and Financial Guards (HCFG). When returning to the HNP, the prospects were that he would face resistance and opposition at every turn as an outsider. But he quickly gained extraordinary popularity within the HNP.

The Interview

This interview was conducted on January 8, 2008, in the office of High Commissioner Dr. Bencze, which is on the top floor in the Hungarian National Police Headquarters building and overlooks the River Danube and the many construction projects in the booming inner city of Budapest and the large suburbs of this big city. In Hungary, policing is entirely a state function, with a central police structure overseeing 20 county police headquarters, covering extremely diverse urban and rural environments. Therefore, police executives manage highly complex organizations, with many stakeholder groups, and numerous challenges associated with geographical distances and the diversity of population.

JBO: Could you please tell me a little about your childhood and adolescence? How did you become an active duty police officer?

JBE: I was born into a family of army service members. My father and mother were active duty service members of the army, and my future career, as it were, could be foreseen. That is, I was expected to choose some military career field. I started my higher educational studies at a military college, but after 2 years I changed my mind and decided that I would prefer a civilian profession to a military one, and for some time I lived the life of a civilian. In the mid-1980s, when a law degree was a prerequisite in most of the senior positions within the police, I was asked if I would take on policing work, namely the command of a central police station in a town. At this point I already had a law degree. In those days I worked as mayor of a large village, as the term is now called; then the position was called president of the village council. I agreed to accept the offer on condition that this position be not of a political nature, and that I would be given sufficient time to prepare for policing work. My conditions were met, and I was given one year in which to prepare for the job. I completed the retraining course at the Police College, and I implemented a personal preparation plan, during which I spent periods of varying length in all specialty areas of the police, before assuming the office of chief of station.

JBO: How and when did you join the HNP?

JBE: This happened in 1985. That was the year when I became a sworn police officer.

JBO: Were you then a young man full of self-confidence?

JBE: Positions, as it were, found me, because at the age of barely 20 some years, I became the elected leader of a village with a population of 4,000. I was hardly 30 years old when I was selected for the post of chief of police station. I think events just came my way. Of course, you had to have self-confidence for these things to happen. By the way, I think no one should shoulder a single leadership task without being self-confident.

JBO: What did you do during the major political changes in Hungary? How did you feel about those changes?[1]

JBE: I was already a chief of police station during the regime change, and among other things, reforms were on my mind. I was keen on communicating and indicating the need for serious reforms within the police, not only with a view to the impending regime change, but because reforms were necessary anyway. In those days I was even nicknamed the "Reform Chief of Station." This, however, resulted in me being appointed head of the Law Enforcement Department of the Ministry of Interior, to supervise the professional operations of the police and the Border Guard. This was in 1989–90, that is, during the regime change.

I had had great hopes and expectations, because I did believe that the police would start on a road to modernization. At that time, I pinned my faith to some extent upon the establishment of the local government type police, but which failed right at the very start. As a matter of fact, only one sentence on the local government police was inserted into the provisions of the Act on Local Governments, the essence of which, to this day, is that the local government, as an optional function, "ensures the execution of the local tasks of public security." The extent to which the local government undertakes to perform such functions is, of course, a matter of financial resources. At the same time, it is clearly visible that the centrally structured police can cope with a number of tasks only with difficulty. So at the local government level policing, private security services assumed an ever-greater role. I think that the great challenges of tomorrow for policing are precisely how to find their respective place and role; how can we identify the obligations of the police as state functions; and how to identify other areas of security where external service providers can be hired?

JBO: What were the main stages of your professional career before being appointed high commissioner of the HNP?

JBE: As regards policing, I worked as chief at a police station in the countryside, in Nagykáta town, Pest County. Following that, I was head of the Law Enforcement Department at the Ministry of Interior for a short period. A bit of civilian work followed. For one year I was a mayor of a small village called Farmos. Thanks to that I could rock the cradle of the Hungarian local government system. Next, during the period of the job-application system following the regime change, I was appointed chief of District 5 Police Station in Budapest, as the chief police officer in a central district of the capital city. From that position I—already a senior police officer—was seconded to the Prime Minister's Office, to coordinate the actions against the black [underground] economy. Here I performed the functions of a government commissioner as a member of the prime minister's staff. From this position, I was transferred to the National Headquarters of the Customs and Financial Guard, where I held the position of director general for law enforcement for 10 years. From that agency I was invited back to the police to fill the position of high commissioner.

JBO: What is your philosophy of policing? (Trust, Safety, Honor)

JBE: I think it is included in the program that I made known to my senior fellow executives at the police on the day of my induction. If you allow me, it can be described in three words: safety, trust, honor. It is extremely important that the police are able to guarantee safety to all and equally so, both in the area of preventing and detecting crime and of eliminating traffic offenses. The police can guarantee this safety in such a way that the legal aid professionals, and not only average citizens, and legal aid NGOs should rightly have confidence in this safety. This safety should be underpinned with appropriate legal guarantees, and the police should also be able to deliver safety to its own personnel, so that those members of the police who work hard and honestly could also rely on a certain kind of safety. Safety should be provided in such a way that the legal rights of both the public and the police are safeguarded.

Trust is extremely important, because this profession will not work without self-confidence, and in the absence of public trust, the police will only muddle on. So it is important to have self-confidence and public trust. To have the confidence of the citizens, and to have, of course, on a higher level, the confidence of legal aid and advocacy groups. With respect to the key term of confidence, it is also important to emphasize that the top-level leadership of the police should have justified reasons to trust the personnel of the police, including the conviction that the Hungarian National Police are able to meet the modern policing challenges of the twenty-first century.

As for honor, I think it is self-evident that the police must be an honorable agency, an exemplary agency. In certain issues, the commanders' expectation based on zero tolerance for violations with respect to their own staff must be made clear. And it is all the more important, because if any single member of the police violates a law, the public at large—and, by the way, the law itself— will consider this act to be a much more serious offense than the same offense perpetrated by an ordinary citizen, and, to boot, the offense perpetrated by a member of the agency will in no time be projected onto the whole of the force, it will appear on the level of generalization. So I always say, on this point, that even one corrupt police officer is one too many.

JBO: What do you think about the principle of zero tolerance policing employed by the NYPD?

JBE: I know it because earlier I also studied what Commissioner William Bratton and later Commissioner Safir introduced and employed. I know myself that the partner criminal justice authorities, the prosecution service and the courts, were scared and were critical before the introduction. I think that zero tolerance can be made to work if there is appropriate political support for it. There is no favoritism; citizens can expect the police to do their job in firm actions, no matter what kind of offenses have been perpetrated. And of course, one can also expect the police not to be so heavy-handed everywhere and with everybody. Once again, I say that it is a matter of political support. If you have political consensus, then the police can do just one thing: take action against all forms of offenses, within the law—this is zero tolerance for me.

JBO: In your view, what have been the main changes in policing in Hungary since the regime change? What is your assessment of these changes?

JBE: During the change of regime, the police were politically committed, because the regulations and expectations in the one-party system made it clear that the police were under the direct control of the single political party that supported the prevailing government and the prevailing head of government. Even today, the government directs the police, but today the Constitution makes the situation of the police quite clear in the sense that, quite obviously, the police must primarily act within the laws. The police must act professionally and constitutionally and, of course, the police must be loyal to the elected government, no matter under what ideologies that government controls the police. During the regime change, there was a legislative deficiency, and consequently a deficiency in legitimacy. Those cardinal laws and legal regulations governing issues protecting the rights of the citizens at a high level that we have today did not exist then. Nothing regulated the operations of the police, or their covert intelligence gathering activities. I could continue by stating that there existed no high-level legal regulation governing the service relations, so there was a deficiency or gap in legislation. I believe there were more deficiencies, because political affiliation also generated a sort of deficiency of trust in those who, let's say, did not like the previous political system.

The top-level leadership of the police correctly perceived the circumstances and got out of this predicament by boldly moving forward after the regime change. They tried to build up a citizen-friendly police model in the early 1990s. I remember it well, because, thank God, I took an active part in it. I was chief of station in District 5 in Budapest, and we tried hard to establish good relations with the local community. This was done, in addition to finding, voicing, and implementing the slogan "To Serve and Protect," for the purpose of manifesting a truly community-friendly approach, but also to make certain that the police took action with the necessary firmness and steadfastness. I think this was a relatively good period for the police, and in 1994 the legislature managed to lay the legal foundations by enacting the Act on the Police, and a number of subsequent legal regulations provided guarantees for the operations of the police.

The real problem was rather the fact that, in the absence of a long-term strategy, the political elections, the various election cycles always rewrote the expectations for the police. This, by the way, obviously resulted in changes in the police leadership on several occasions and frequent turns in the course of reforms, which led to all manners of uncertainty. In addition, serious problems existed in the financing of the police, because a kind of waste, and a kind of deficiency at the same time, was continuously present in the budget, in the management of financial resources. To wit, the systems in personnel management and financing had already evolved and the budget was the basis of the system that had evolved by then. Possible budget increases were added to the existing budget, and whoever had earlier been in a better position, could more strongly bring to bear their interests and enjoyed better conditions. And, police stations that had been struggling with understaffing for years were stuck with the same problem for years to come. Likewise, in the areas of development and operations, achievements could be made, to a certain extent, on the basis of lobbying for one's interests. In addition to this, the police were continually given extra tasks, without the extra financial resources.

It was clearly visible that, at the end of the day, we had to come to terms with clarifying what is a policing responsibility that the state intends to devolve on the police as a state function, and what it is that is not a state function. And it should have been made clear that these core tasks will require this much money and for that, in turn, a zero base budget should have been prepared. Unfortunately, this has not been done since then. Instead, a number of tasks that could in the meantime be partly civilianized were turned over to the public administration, and these positions were taken out of the remit of the police. Here I have in mind the customs aspects of security administration. On the other hand, the private security initiatives and services developed, which partly have taken the burden off the shoulders of the police today.

Earlier, the protection of collective property was given priority. Today, the police must not discriminate between collective and private property. The Constitution also prohibits such discrimination; therefore, whoever has the means and strength to protect their own property will ensure such protection on the basis of ownership. They may not use their own resources, but they will pay for the protection as a service. These arrangements are all very helpful for the police.

Likewise, the law enforcement systems at the local government level include the inspectorate of public wardens or any other type of organization established to perform law enforcement tasks at the local level, such as the rangers, gamekeepers, river-keepers, etc. I believe that slowly, slowly areas of specialization are taking shape that must permanently stay within the remit of the police. The fact that in the period of integrating the Border Guard into the police we cannot engage in a deep restructuring of the police is a different cup of tea, because the amendment of the Constitution and of the Act on the Police took place on the basis of political consensus. And the price for that was that it was impossible to change the centuries-old county system in Hungary's public administration, not even within the structure of the police. There were concepts supporting movement toward regionalization, but regionalization could not take place. I think that, in the future, the question remains to be answered whether Hungary needs 150 major police stations and even more field offices and police substations. The law enforcement strategy must decide, and decide very quickly, in which direction legislation on law enforcement, the law enforcement mentality, financing, training, human resource management, the system of awards and bonuses, and the settlement of interests, etc., should go.

JBO: Where were you and what did you do during Hungary's EU pre-accession period?

JBE: I was director general for law enforcement at the National HQ of the Customs and Financial Guard, second-in-command to the national commander, and we were preparing for European Union membership there. I can safely say that European Union membership, as of May 1, 2004, affected, first and perhaps foremost, the Customs and Financial Guard, because the moment Hungary acceded to the EU customs control ceased along a 1,100 km-long section of national borders. Accession did not have an impact on the police then but only has now that we joined the Schengen area[2] as of January 1, 2008.

As a matter of fact, the European Community started off as a customs union, and strange as it may sound, the EU could address every specialty area of agriculture, industry, and the common matters of everything else by translating them into the language of customs. If it was about any object, about any commodity, then the commodity was identified on the basis of the accepted EU customs tariff numbers, so that it would be acceptable and understandable for everyone. So I believe that the time I spent with the Customs Service and the preparation for EU membership was indeed a great challenge, because we had to see these tasks clearly. From the very first moment, we had to review some 801,000 pages of EU customs regulations, and become familiar with them before preparing for EU membership. Later on, we had to apply these regulations.

JBO: You were the director general of law enforcement at the HCFG for 10 years. What were your main achievements during that time?

JBE: It was important to build up an effective team in the areas of criminal investigation, border customs administration, and border policing. We were given ever-wider scopes of authority, since there were four distinct crime categories in which the Customs and Financial Guard have exclusive investigative powers. When I started work at the General Directorate of Law Enforcement, we did not have the opportunity to use court-authorized surveillance techniques. Ten years on, the HCFG could—and still does—investigate 28 different crimes, while the investigative authority related to financial crimes and drug abuse were also devolved to the HCFG. The Investigative Service of the Customs and Financial Guard has also unfolded and become stronger, and has received all authorization to use every single court-authorized surveillance technique and to conduct covert investigations. So the Investigative Service of the Hungarian Customs and Financial Guard has all the means and assets that the Hungarian police have. This was one of the achievements. The other one was the completion of the required border development projects. In the meantime, I—as the commissioner appointed by the minister of finance—chaired the intragovernmental committee that was responsible for preparing all sections of the national borders for the accession. We were responsible for the development and enlargement of the land border crossing points, for the construction of new BCPs. Earlier, the development projects were financed from PHARE[3] funds, later these investments were supported from the Schengen funds. Quite clearly, the architectural aspects of these projects were not my responsibility; I was mainly in charge of the professional preparation, the conduct of international negotiations, preparation of these international agreements, ratification and preparation of these draft agreements for signing.

JBO: What difficulties did the HNP have to face during and after the accession to the EU?

JBE: Accession to the EU did not bring about stunningly big changes in the life of the police, because the Border Guard was left behind and still operates at the so-called "internal borders" where they exercise some sort of control. The most the police saw was that EU citizens started to arrive in Hungary in greater numbers and possibly Hungarian citizens also started to travel to countries of the EU in greater numbers. This process started and grew right after the introduction of the new passport valid for all countries in the world. So I believe that accession to the EU was not as great a challenge as joining the Schengen area quite recently, on December 21, when borders and all forms of border control ceased on a 1,100 km section of the state borders.

Undoubtedly a security gap emerged here. To counter that, a number of actions had to be taken, partly in cooperation with the neighboring countries, with Slovenia, Austria, and Slovakia. We had to organize cross-border criminal prosecution and the joint patrolling of the border area. The establishment of the Common Contact Points on the borders was one of such actions, as well as the establishment of an integrated in-depth control system within the borders of Hungary. Because, along the Schengen "external borders" [the Hungarian borders with countries that do not belong to the EU] we now must ensure, along 1,100 km of the border, a strict control in line with the Schengen criteria to ensure the security of the total population of 600 million of the whole EU. We must also provide guarantees that if someone should slip through this screen, or if they should evade control, then it may be expected that the illegal immigrant is possibly apprehended in the middle of the country, and that is why we built up the in-depth control system. These challenges resulting from our membership in the Schengen space, I think, are more significant.

JBO: What is your relationship with the major political stakeholders?

JBE: I formulated the expectation for myself and my fellow chief constables that we must keep an appropriate distance from all political parties and party politicians. If possible, keep an appropriate distance. That is my tenet and the expectation of the community as well. I do not think that the current minister or prime minister expects me to do otherwise, either. So it is my expectation that the players of the political arena, and here I mainly have the governing parties in mind, but also the players of local politics, should be at an appropriate but equal distance from the police, and the senior executive officers of the police should do everything they can to make it happen. If this is not the case, any police executive and the whole of the police will quickly be stigmatized.

JBO: How do you handle police corruption and misuse of police powers?

JBE: We do not cover up cases of corruption. Soon after I took office I issued a Code of Ethics and a High Commissioner's Instruction on rolling back corruption and on the improvement of the morale and discipline. I reestablished the Internal Affairs unit which was regrettably disestablished earlier. I think that a police officer's corrupt act cannot be tolerated, not even in a single instance. It would be like a preacher committing blasphemy before the high altar. If a police officer is corrupt or commits a theft, I think he or she has no place in the force. As for misuse of police powers, I also think that it can fall into this category. The police are the depository of legitimate state coercion, therefore all actions taken by the police must, more than anything else, comply with principles of lawfulness, professionalism, and proportionality.

JBO: Leadership is a key issue in policing. You changed most of the country's chief constables and senior police executives recently. What is the reason for these changes?

JBE: The main reason for that is the fact that the Hungarian National Police were given a number of new tasks when, as of January 1, 2008, the police took over all the responsibilities of the former Border Guard. These new tasks require new skills, new senior executives with leadership and management skills, who, for example are able to operate those 29 border police field offices along the external Schengen borders that are responsible for performing the primary Schengen search, screening, and checking activities. Furthermore, they have to be able to perform all the border policing tasks related to migration that emerge along our eastern and southern borders. So, when taking account of these new skills, I thought that in several places, in several positions, the former Border Guard directors who, based on their personal and professional qualities are otherwise able to fill executive positions and carry out executive tasks, would be suitable for the position of county chief constable.

In other positions, changes took place for other reasons, basically because I think that the program I announced is a 5- to 6-year program. If that is the case, I need to join forces with and I need to find, people to fill executive positions to implement the program on whom I can rely in the next 5 to 6 years. That is the reason why I reassigned several of the hard-working, respected chief constables among my fellow executives who were drawing near retirement age, or had been working on an extension of their active duty service. I offered those different positions, different tasks. That was another one of my considerations.

I also considered that a senior executive at this level should not spend more than 7 to 8 years in his or her position, and this is now a widely accepted basic principle of organizational management. In other parts of Europe, in France and in Germany, by and large it is predictable that senior executives are rotated, that is, reassigned to a different duty position, every 4 to 5 years. They know, 5 years in advance, where their next duty position or career station will be. In Hungary, the majority of people live in a system that is tied to the ground. Everyone builds a detached home for themselves, that is their lifework, and by settling down in an owned landed property, they limit themselves. In a number of countries in Europe, people live in rented houses or flats, so it is much easier, more flexible for them to change jobs. I think that we need to make a significant move in this direction in the future, we must implement the appropriate rotation of the police staff, but the conditions for that must also be created.

JBO: What were the main difficulties in integrating the Hungarian Border Guards into the HNP?

JBE: Here we had a case of two distinct organizations with different traditions and partly different sets of responsibilities that had their unique traditions. Because the Hungarian National Police, if I take the date of the establishment of the first state police, was founded in Budapest in 1873. The Hungarian Border Guard was created 100 years ago, and clearly, changes were made after World War II.

The most difficult part of the integration was not the heaps of amended legal regulations, not the organization building, nor the drafting of the new organization chart, but the stage of the personal interviews. Many already looked forward to this period with relief, waiting for us to offer them a new position. The emotional aspect of the disestablishment of the stand-alone Border Guard was perhaps the most difficult part. An organization with traditions over 100 years old ceased to exist as of January 1. The Border Guard as an organization, as a term or concept, ceased to exist. It was perhaps the most difficult task to handle it with appropriate circumspection, and that is not so easy after all. We offered work for everyone, we offered a position for everyone and as a matter of fact, 90% of the BG personnel did accept the position offered.

JBO: What is your preferred model for the nexus between recruitment, education, and training?

JBE: Recruitment and training should be separated. Since only young people having a secondary education certificate can apply to the police, I see a problem here, namely the fact that mainly secondary schoolleavers who cannot make it to college or university apply to the Police NCO-Training Vocational Schools. So this circumstance by and large limits the selection pool.

With respect to selection, there is no problem, because some of the young people perceive it as a kind of challenge to try out this career field. There is interest and pre-admission screening is very rigorous. I think that the personnel should be further screened; not only in the traditional way but, in a given instance, a great number of personality traits should be screened during the admission process, from the propensity for corruption to the ability to endure stress. Modern medicine and psychology today are inventing appropriate methodologies to test these. I think that the system of admission needs to be changed, by all means. Within the training area, we have achieved the ability to impart knowledge to the students within a 2-year law enforcement vocational training system, and upon completion of the training the students are promoted to NCO ranks. This must be rethought, because the reform of the law enforcement vocational schools and police training is under way. It is not absolutely certain that everyone needs to be given 2 years of training. By the way, the law enforcement qualification provides the students with professional skills that can be utilized in civilian life as well. The police may have functions and tasks that can be performed with "semi-skilled" staff. I know of a best practice even in the United States, where people, following extremely hard basic training of 10 weeks duration, are assigned policing tasks.

So we must stop to think whether the current practice is efficient enough, and I believe thought must be given to whether the same kind of training should be provided to the traffic police officer as to the would-be district police officer, whether a criminal investigator should be given the same training as someone working in another service branch of the police. In my opinion, our system of training needs to be made more differentiated.

And the designing of a predictable career system would be necessary so that after the elapse of a certain time in service and after proving eligibility we might say, that the police officer can now apply again for a higher position, stepping on the next rung of the "career ladder," as it were, following the acquisition of the next higher level of training. I would build in stages in the police training system, which would mean a sort of career offer—for the best officers, of course. And the other thing, I do miss management training and follow-up training, mainly among senior police staff. Hopefully, we will be able to change that, by all means in the very near future.

JBO: The HNP seem unable to establish an effective system of management training. What is your view on that?

JBE: As chief of station of Inner City Budapest I attended one such management training course, which I keep referring to ever since. I can say that it was to my benefit in many respects. I would like to implement it, and a very important aspect of that will be one week this coming spring when the new chief constables will be trained by a specialist from the FBI, based on an agreement we concluded with the director of the FBI. But I will go one step further. I think that senior police executives not only include chief constables of county police forces, but commanders at lower levels as well. For them, master's degree education is provided for the time being. About 800 police officers participated in this two-stage training recently. This must be carried through consistently. But even more important than that, I think, is to reach a point where the executives are not selected and appointed on the basis of fluctuation or under duress, or on the basis of ad hoc decisions. We should reach a point where somebody, if selected for a leadership role, is given systematic and methodological training to prepare that person for carrying out the executive tasks. I think the police will truly move forward towards modernization, also from a human resource management point of view, if we have succeeded in starting these processes.

JBO: How do you see cross border crime trends after Hungary joined the Schengen Area?

JBE: By the fact that the internal Schengen borders were pulled down, the criminals were obviously given greater opportunities, because persons involved in criminal activities have to cross fewer checkpoints. The EU Member States and the countries of the Schengen Area and the so-called third pillar[4] is a rather sensitive area, and therefore everything was done to improve cooperation. The introduction and operation of the Schengen Information System is a major step forward in this direction. The so-called Prum Treaty,[5] which Hungary is also a party to, offers an opportunity at the level of an international convention to share DNA and fingerprint samples and data, stolen vehicle and travel documents data, and to include these data in our system of security checks. Only international organized criminal prosecution can provide an effective response to international organized crime.

JBO: How would you describe relations between the police and criminologists in Hungary?

JBE: Hungarian criminologists, who are recognized and accepted also at the European level, all know the Hungarian police very well, because they were related to it in some way or other; partly, either by serving in the ranks of the police when they were young, before choosing an academic career, or because they took part in one way or another, in the development of the police. Yet I think, we must achieve a situation where there is greater interest in criminology and law enforcement sciences also within the ranks of the police, and where the law enforcement scientists, and criminologists for that matter, do not write their otherwise brilliant studies exclusively for the desk drawer, but as far as possible try to find answers to the current practical issues of the police, with the help of science and theory. The Hungarian police have renewed their scientific and innovation activities. A major step was taken last year by establishing the Scientific and Innovation Council of the Police.

JBO: Are there areas of police practice that are currently under-researched?

JBE: There are a number of such areas, but even more important, I think, is that we fail to properly utilize the findings of those international research projects that exist today. For that to happen we need intensive foreign language training and progress in the language skills. An international law enforcement study might not be exciting for an academic expert, but it would be very important for everyday practitioners to have access to such information.

JBO: The average age in the HNP is 32 years. How does this affect the efficiency of policing?

JBE: Indeed, one generation is missing. In addition, it is the generation that possesses theoretical and practical knowledge and expertise. Legal regulations today allow an active duty service member to retire on a service pension after 25 years of service, or during restructuring, as has been the case quite frequently over the past few years, they can choose to retire on a normal pension because there are differences in the amount of money they will receive in service and normal pensions after 25 years of service. Quite clearly, it is an achievement by the police unions or employees, and I believe the unions. It is, however, an undisputable fact that the police are continually losing a significant amount of gray matter. Most likely, this trend must be reversed in two directions. On the one hand, the junior officers need to be given more self-confidence, in policing, or in the executive positions of the police. I tried to do just that, by the way, when I replaced the county chief constables, because the average age of the top level leadership of the police has gone down by almost 5 years. The other direction, respectively, is to make that part of the police personnel motivated who have completed their 25 years of service, so that they will not seek a way to retire at all costs, but they should find it worthwhile to go on serving in the force until they are 60 or 62.

JBO: What is your position on civilian control over law enforcement agencies?

JBE: The so-called civilian control is not from the devil. It is something that is working today, because the local governments, for example, have the right to debrief the chief constable and the police force staff once a year. In the appointment procedure of the high commissioner, a required step is the nominee's appearance before and hearing by the Defence and Law Enforcement Committee of the National Assembly. Hearings by the committee can happen later as well, at any time, and similarly, the local governments can request such a report on top of the mandatory annual report. So civilian control does exist. The ombudsman, the Parliamentary Commissioner also carries out a sort of civilian control over criminal cases, although the Public Prosecution Service is the owner of the case, and, if you will, it is also a civilian part of the justice system; the ombudsman is not part of the active duty personnel. Recently the National Assembly decided to establish an Independent Civilian Complaints board. All that is left to do for the National Assembly is to agree on the five members of the board. I think that this is all right, because the citizen has the right to know and see that the police perform their duties in a professional and lawful way, and that they deal with the complaints made by the citizens, the members of the public.

JBO: How do you explain your appointment as commissioner of HNP?

JBE: I do not think I need to explain that, because my past expertise, my activities for several decades in law enforcement and successfully demonstrated achievements in my work are, I believe, sufficient in the way of explanation. Anyway, it is not me who should explain my appointment, but the person who nominated me for this position, and the person who did appoint me, respectively, the minister and the prime minister when this appointment took place. In my understanding, my position is a service, an extremely great challenge, in an historic moment that rarely occurs in the life of a police officer or a police executive. To me, it was given.

JBO: There was a series of scandals over police brutality, heavy-handed tactics in public order policing, and raids, abuse of power, police misconduct. Do you feel you have walked into a trap?

JBE: Let me specify something. During the events of the autumn of 2006, charges were brought against the police of exceeding their powers on occasion, charges of acting unlawfully in these cases. The competent investigative unit of the PPS (Public Prosecution Service) launched investigations into these charges. Criminal procedures against colleagues subjected to the procedure are still under way. I have knowledge of 45 such cases, against 45 officers. It is quite another matter that, in many cases, the judgment of the police public security operations in the autumn of 2006 by legal aid bureaus and by other players is still on the agenda today. And here again, it is primarily the negative experience that occasionally comes to the foreground in the press again. It is extremely important to note here that the police cooperated with the competent Public

Prosecution Service units in order to clarify the procedures and possible offenses or legal violations perpetrated by police officers. The fact is that the procedures are slow or the fact that the specific perpetrator could not in every case be identified or their guilt proved, or that the perpetration of an offense cannot be proved at all, is a question of penal procedure.

May 2007 held a couple of cases in store that shocked the public. There was a case in which police officers were charged with a criminal offense, like raping a young women during duty hours in the service car, and in the present stage of the procedure it turned out that no crime was perpetrated by the police officers, and the police officers will be held responsible for minor violations of the service regulations only. In the other case, a large amount of cash disappeared from a crime scene. It turned out that one of the police officers taking part in the crime scene investigation purloined it. One such case would have been one too many.

At that time, under that popular feeling, several things occurred at the same time, and there were cases when the police and the PSLEA [Protective Service of Law Enforcement Agencies—the Hungarian equivalent of the Anti Corruption Command of the British Police Service], following joint preparation and a covert operation, established a case related to the Motorway Police Unit in which the criminal offenses perpetrated by about a dozen police officers were detected. Quite obviously, this case of police corruption was held against the police, although it was the police commanders who detected this case and instigated the arrest of the corrupt police officers. I think that these cases further worsened the index of public confidence on the one hand, and the self-confidence of the police on the other. As I mentioned before, in each case when a police officer is found guilty or even just suspected of perpetrating a criminal violation, the whole agency is stigmatized and people will form their unflattering opinion of the whole of the police. That is why it is utterly important that not a single such case is covered up, and that investigations of these cases are completed as quickly as possible.

I arrived at the police in a hot atmosphere. It was no mistake that my very first actions were directed towards consolidating discipline and the situation, strengthening the morale, and towards the consistent introduction of actions against corruption. Later on I found a very good team and then excellent partners in the police commanders for this task. I think that the new corps of police executives that emerged after the personnel changes at the top levels entirely identifies with these executive expectations.

JBO: Did you experience hostility to you personally, particularly as an outsider, in the early days of your appointment?

JBE: I am quite sure that there were self-proclaimed nominees for the position
of high commissioner, and there were some who were encouraged
by certain individuals and by certain circles, and I think it is also
natural, in a way, that the question may emerge in the minds of several people that their names are possibly being considered during a
personnel change at the top level, which may even bring a promotion to them. To my understanding, this is quite natural. When
the answer to a question of appointment is given quickly, order is
restored in a law enforcement agency. It is important that there be
no uncertainty in issues like this, that the necessary actions are
taken quickly, in order that everyone understands clearly who the
leader is and what expectations are formulated for him or her. With
respect to myself, I did not perceive reservations or negative voices
coming from my fellow executive officers or senior commanders,
not at all. This is a large organization, which was unusual for me,
because actions cascade down several levels, the organization as a
whole is slow in making a turn, slow in implementing the actions. I
intend to change and improve this, by all means. And there followed
an account taking. I tried to indicate, among the first actions I took,
that I not only make the decisions, but will hold those in charge
accountable for the implementation of my actions. This had some
unexpected effects. Perhaps the corps of general officers was unac-
customed to being asked questions, to being held accountable.

JBO: What is your relationship with the police unions?

JBE: I have good relations with the representative police unions. In the most
difficult period, when the public esteem of the police was at its low-
est in May and June 2007, the unions organized a demonstration,
obviously not in the streets, but on the premises of a police facility,
in a sports hall, and I also attended that demonstration, I delivered a speech, and put on the T-shirt with "Serving with Clean
Hands" printed on it. I did all this to show that the police deals,
in a responsible way, with the ideas and concerns coming to light
that ruffled tempers in that period, and that unequivocal answers
are given to these so that they are appropriately dealt with by public opinion. So that due to the guilt of a couple of police officers
perpetrating offenses, the whole personnel of the police should
not wear the blue uniform of collective guilt. So our relationship
with the unions started off well. Obviously we stand together for
a common cause, which welded the personnel together even more
tightly. We involved the heads of the unions in the entire process of
integration. Upon our invitation they attend every major executive

meeting and conference. We can work together to the maximum extent. My view is that the line commander must be the fiercest protector of the interests of the staff. But, where the means and ways of the line commander end, the opportunities of the union are still not exhausted. It is obvious that the powers of the unions are somewhat more limited in law enforcement agencies than in civilian trade unions. Our cooperation with the unions is good.

JBO: What about your relation with the minister of Justice and Law Enforcement and the prime minister and the main opposition party police experts?

JBE: In one word fair. I mean good.

JBO: What are your priority areas for change in the HNP?

JBE: The Hungarian National Police today, with its 150 central police stations, 29 border police field offices, the Budapest Metropolitan Police HQ, and the 19 county police service headquarters, which is a large organization, and here I add the 126 police substations, which I think is uneconomical, less manageable, because the police have to respond to events in a 24/7 system. In this day and age of information science and telecommunications, distances do not necessarily mean that the 24/7 duty detail and the 24/7 response capability must be present in all settlements, or at least in all towns. Obviously, it is a kind of political success for a politician, if he or she could successfully lobby in the past decades in order to set up a substation somewhere or perhaps for a mayor to have a new police station opened in her or his town. The organizational structure of the police must be adapted to the trends in crime, to the workload crime represents, and if we take a look at the map of this workload, then the present staffing levels probably do not reflect a distribution of personnel in proportion to workload. A change needs to be made in these areas, by all means.

I add here that all this, on the other hand, requires full political consensus, because the Hungarian police will not be able to cope with yet again changing the course of the organization every 2 to 4 years. So it takes long-term decisions to identify the tasks that must be decentralized and the tasks that must be centralized, to identify the level of decentralization, and the most effective structural model that can meet the challenges presented by criminality. Local answers are of primary importance, that is, answers must be given where crime is perpetrated, naturally with the proviso that in the case of crime crossing various town and county boundaries the answer must be given not at the local level in the first place but by a unit with national jurisdiction.

And sooner or later we will have to operate, design, and make efforts at a structure crossing the national borders. This is one of the substantial components of the changes, namely how we will be able to stand our own ground and become integrated in international cooperation, or even, in a particular case, design a joint investigating team structure or arrangement for that purpose. Or even to assume an appropriate role in large-scale international cooperative efforts, and here of course I have in mind the Europol in the first place, or, in a given case, the Interpol or Southern European Criminal Initiative (SECI), but, on account of the challenges in border policing, also our contribution to the FRONTEX.[6]

JBO: Thank you very much.

Endnotes

1. Political changes: in 1989 Hungary had a peaceful political changeover from a socialist system to democracy. We had a free and fair election and an opposition party called the Hungarian Democratic Forum won the election. Two years later the Soviet troops left our country. A new democratic public administration, including the law enforcement system, was built.
2. Schengen Agreement: an agreement concluded in Schengen, Luxembourg in 1985, the purpose of which is to abolish border controls along the internal borders of the EU.
3. PHARE: the European Union's grant aid program for restructuring the economies of the East European countries.
4. The European Union (EU) was established by the Maastricht Treaty in 1992 and based on three pillars. The first pillar deals with EU Community, the second is the EU Common Foreign and Security Policy, and the third is Police and Judiciary Cooperation in Criminal Matters.
5. Prum Treaty: concluded in 2005 by Austria, Belgium, France, Holland, Luxembourg, Germany, and Spain. Its purpose is, with a view to the terrorist threat, to intensify international cooperation, particularly in the area of information sharing.
6. FRONTEX: the EU integrated border management office in Warsaw, Poland.

Interview with Kiran Bedi, Director General, Bureau of Police Research and Development, Indian Police Service, New Delhi

9

INTERVIEWED BY ARVIND VERMA

Introduction

Kiran Bedi is an icon in India. As the first woman to join the prestigious and powerful cadre of the Indian Police Service (IPS)[1] she has attained fame and recognition as a no-nonsense, dedicated, and professional officer. IPS had been the domain of men for 112 years and she had to get an order from the court to force the government to allow her to join this service. By strictly enforcing traffic laws in the chaos of Delhi, irrespective of rank and position in the hierarchical Indian society, she attained early fame and came to be known as "Crane Bedi" for towing and impounding illegally parked vehicles. By confronting a sword-wielding Sikh agitator with her bamboo cane she set a high standard in leading her subordinates from the battle front. Unfortunately, her outspokenness, uncompromising attitude, and refusal to follow the dictates of power mongers deprived her of important positions in the police organization that she richly deserved. Recently, she was again overlooked for the post of commissioner of police of Delhi even though she was the most senior officer. Further, she was shunted to posts outside the police as a way of punishment but in every position she set a new standard of excellence. Her 4 years as the head of Asia's largest prison, Tihar Jail in Delhi, were supposed to be a period of punishment but she turned around the prison, introduced Vipassna meditation, and brought order to the chaos reigning there. For her work at Tihar and with several voluntary nongovernmental organizations she received the prestigious Magasasay Award— known as Asia's Nobel Prize. She has served with distinction as the head of UN CIVPOL and at present, she heads the Bureau of Police Research and Development and is working to reform the Indian police through research.

She is a regular speaker at panel discussions across the country and abroad and is completing her fifth book.

She resigned from the IPS in 2007. The interview took place in her office and home, on various days in December 2006.

Career

AV: Tell us a little bit about your career: length of service, organizations worked in, postings, specializations, etc.

KB: I joined the Indian Police Service [IPS] in 1972 through a national examination selection process conducted by the Union Public Service Commission—a statutory national body that conducts examinations and selects candidates for various senior posts in the government. As destiny would have it, I became the first woman in India to join the officer ranks of the Indian Police Service.

I have served in many field assignments such as policing cities, for crime, law and order, traffic management, administration of large police organization; narcotics control bureau, police training, prison management, policy making with the lieutenant governor of Delhi. Besides this, I did a 2-year assignment at the United Nations as civilian police advisor to the secretary general in New York. This involved operational planning and implementation in 16 international peacekeeping operations or missions in Europe, Asia, and Africa. Currently I am a director general in the Bureau of Police Research and Development in New Delhi, Government of India.

AV: Did the way your career developed surprise you?

KB: No, it did not. For the reason that I never let go the reins of any responsibility I was assigned, whatever these may have been. I came into the service for the potential it held which to me was the "power" to prevent deviance and criminality in society. Right from my childhood I wanted to function to the maximum of my capacity. From my school days, I excelled in studies and sports and became the first Indian woman to win the Asian Tennis championship. I brought this zeal to my work in the police where I did not lose time in contemplation and became a sensitive observer. I also learned from my seniors, particularly what was good and what was not right for the service. I never accepted the practice of working as a remote control and carried my supervision directly into the field, working alongside the subordinates who looked up to me as their leader. This was unusual in the police subculture where senior officers operated from the air conditioned confines of their offices and demanded subservience as the rule of administration. There are of course exceptions in any situation and in Indian police too there are and will be good and bad officers. However, I was determined to work according to my ethical principles even though the success from my work came at a tremendous personal cost. But I have the satisfaction of getting results in great abundance and in particular, the immense goodwill of ordinary citizens.

AV: Did your work prove as interesting or rewarding as you thought it would?

KB: Yes it did. I achieved a substantial sense of achievement, albeit with the maximum effort and persistent risk (not physical but of annoying my insecure seniors) in forcing changes and altering the status quo. But it was absolutely needed to meet my own expectations of the responsibility based on ground needs. I remained focused on the inherent power of prevention and participative, accountable, and transparent policing, and continued to optimally maximize and empower all possible resources, instilling in them a sense of ownership and self-worth. Due to these operating principles my work continued to evolve and took the shape of firm, effective, and yet welfare policing.

I believe the inherent power of correction is there for anyone to achieve provided certain personal and professional systems are adhered to. If I had not kept the focus this career for me would have been one of control, subservience, injustice, self-centered living, and monotony. I would have been an invisible entity who would have been marginalized with gender being another possible reason. The ruling establishment made large efforts to break my will and force me to compromise but I think I thwarted them again and again.

Changes Experienced

AV: What do you see as the most important changes that have happened in policing over the course of your career (philosophies, organizational arrangements, specializations, policies and programs, equipments, personnel, diversity, etc.)?

KB: Just as everything else has changed in our society for the good or the bad so has it been with the police. The transformations seen over the last three decades have been phenomenal.

The police have expanded their potential to serve the community and provide a variety of services. The police are now contributing in a big way to the governance of a large, diverse, and democratic country. Police are no more, strictly speaking, a firefighter of crime detection and prosecution. Policing is now about larger prevention. It has moved over from keeping security to creating security.

The expectations from the police too have changed considerably. People reach out to them as first responders for any emergency that is life threatening. The police too realize this and are constantly under pressure to live up to these expectations.

The police face considerable criticism, many with little justification. For example, the media and the resultant 24-7 exposure, presents every single incident of deviance by any single police person in India (almost the size of a continent) as an issue of national police failure. However, when every state has its own police service and each one of them operates with its own resources and adequacies, the criticism of national failure seems unwarranted.

Newer challenges demand more and modern training. However, this cannot be done unless there is an adequate supply of additional resources and funding. Unfortunately, there is always a lag between demand and supply, which impacts the police services adversely.

Police leadership in India is under great stress. The challenging issues are growing rapidly and the number of incidents now is large. Yet, the political insulation is wafer thin and in the end it's all about living on the edge. It was not so in the early seventies when I joined the police department.

AV: What changes in external conditions (support from communities, legal powers, judicial relations, relations with minority communities, resource provision, political influence, etc.) have had a significant impact on policing?

KB: During the British occupation period the police were designed and operated to support the raj and maintain the foreign colonial rule in the country. The immediate post-independence period was marked by a high degree of idealism and a dedicated political leadership deeply concerned about development of the country. However, this idealism has declined and the political class has degenerated into selfish ventures that are deeply affecting the governance today. The rich and the well-connected blatantly influence the system and get away with their criminal behavior. The courts too are seriously slow in the delivery of legal services and losing credibility among the people. The criminal justice system is overcrowded and moving extremely slowly. This impacts police performance too. No wonder people are losing patience and are angry at the police who work among them. Another particular impact of this delay in providing justice is the resort to vigilantism that is occurring with frightening regularity, especially in remote areas. Mobs have lynched suspects of crimes and want to carry out street justice, having lost faith in the legal system.

It must be kept in mind that the Indian police were designed to maintain the hegemony of the British rulers and deliberately restricted from mixing with the people. There has never been a system of local accountability and the police have always been an authoritarian centralized organization controlled from the top by few people. The system has not changed after independence and therefore there is still little cooperation from the citizens since they do not trust the police and remain in awe of their extensive powers.

The Supreme Court, being independent of the political establishment, has been able to carve a new dimension for itself by keeping in check excessive executive powers. This is a change from the British period when the judicial powers were exercised by the executive magistrates and who worked closely with the police. At present, the judiciary does not believe in the police and imposes severe constraints over its functions.

The police have also been shackled in the exercise of its powers and many legal powers needed to combat terrorist activities have been denied due to politics. Indeed, the political influence over the police has increased to an unprecedented extent and is badly affecting their performance. Politicization of the police is now an established sad fact and proving extremely harmful to their performance. Despite the increasing number of challenges being faced by the police, the resources are slow in coming. Modernization of the police is still in its infancy in many parts and wings of police in the country.

Politicization, historical legacy, poor resources, and outdated organizational dynamics are proving serious constraints. Notwithstanding constitutional safeguards the police are unable to protect the minorities and victims of crime. Consequently, relations not only with the minorities but also with the citizens remain strained and hostile.

AV: Overall, has the quality of policing improved or declined (street work, specialized units, managerial capacity, self-evaluation, interagency cooperation, etc.)?

KB: The question is improper as it makes a presumption about the way "quality of policing" should be construed. Providing more resources and managerial capacity is not the index of measuring the quality of policing. There is no doubt that the government has spent money on procuring more vehicles, wireless communications, and even computers but the warmth of human concern is missing. I measure the performance of police in terms of its ability to mitigate the suffering of victims of crime and in building a just, equitable, caring society. It is the role of police leadership to set an example and focus upon enabling police personnel to be humane in their actions.

Unfortunately, the Indian police have not evolved as a service-oriented organization for the people but as an instrument of control working on clear partisan directions. The system of policing is still very hierarchical, almost nondemocratic, traditional, conservative, focusing on order maintenance. The police leadership is extremely insecure and there is no attempt to develop long-term policies. This is lamentable, since honest and humane response to the problems of the people does not cost money but goes a long way in alleviating their sufferings. I would say that overall the quality of policing measured in terms of addressing the concerns of the citizens has declined despite induction of more resources, specialized units, managerial capacity, and technological inputs.

AV: In general, is it more or less difficult to be a police officer (street, manager) now than in the past?

KB: Yes, it is like that today. The policing is much more demanding than ever before.

Personal Policing Philosophy

AV: What do you think should be the role of the police in society? What should be their job, functions and roles? What should be left to others?

KB: The role of the police should be to ensure rule of law and this role should be exemplified by personal examples. Police officers should not be afraid of investigating and prosecuting the high and the mighty of the society. They should also ensure that justice is done to all without discrimination based on class, gender, race, ethnicity, or any other consideration.

The job of the police is to provide safety, security, and services that are demanded by the citizens. The police truly have to act as philosopher, guide, and friend to the citizens, especially in India where a vast multitude are impoverished, exploited, and lack the capacity to defend themselves. The functions and roles therefore need to be determined in view of the peculiar circumstances of the Indian state where a rapidly expanding economy is nevertheless leaving a large number of people behind and the callous establishment is not responsive to their problems. Clearly, functions catering to the economic development, education, health, shelter, and general well-being of the citizens have to be left for other agencies but ensuring a life of dignity, empowered citizenship, and democratic participation are areas where police need to play a role. The police need to be the upholder of probity in enforcing and upholding the law.

AV: What organizational arrangements work and which do not? What policies on relations with the community, with political groups, with other criminal justice organizations work well?

KB: I am not sure about the question. Organizations that learn from their environment and constantly endeavor to improve their performance will work better. Complacency or indifference to the role will affect its performance and ultimately reduce its importance in the society. Nothing but the best cordial and respectful relations will work with the community. The police need to work with the people and be accountable to them for their actions. The political groups have their own arena to function in and need to operate through democratic principles. The problem comes when the politicians begin to exercise constitutional power directly, violating the safeguards and institutional arrangements. So long as all the different institutions, criminal justice agencies, interest groups, and community-based organizations operate in accordance with the constitutional principles and in keeping the development of society as their ultimate lofty objectives, arrangements will work smoothly. However, problems emerge when power is sought for narrow, sectarian, and personal enrichment and exercised in violation of constitutional principles. In such a situation institutional arrangements do not and will not work.

AV: How should policing be performed? What should be the preferred priorities and strategies; hard edged crime control, prevention, services, order work, what mix for which types of problems; proactive-reactive; community policing-law enforcement, etc.?

KB: Policing should be performed in accordance with the rules and regulation evolved by careful deliberation by the people and their trusted representatives. It must take into account the wider questions of human rights, due process, and checks and balances. There must always be a system where the police agents are held accountable by external evaluation and beholden to the people they serve. Clearly, police must work to prevent crimes, take a proactive approach, and adopt a style that promotes community participation and cooperation. Professional criminals by definition are difficult to deal with and need expert handling. But this must not translate into "hard edged crime control" policies that operate at the edge of law and human rights. Police need to be smart and not hard in order to deal with professional offenders. At all times they must keep in mind the larger issues of citizen rights, rule of law, minority apprehensions, and long-term rehabilitation of law breakers rather than punishment and incarceration that cause suffering. The Buddhist principles of compassion, detachment, and seeking ways to end suffering provide a better path than hard-nosed punitive measures.

Problems and Successes Experienced

AV: In your experience what policies or programs have worked well and which have not? And can you speculate for what reasons?

KB: Policing is easy when it is straightforward and principled; it is very complex and draining when it is selective. I followed the easy path all the time. This path won great support from my juniors but not from my peers and seniors. Consequently, this made my work personally demanding. I was never sure how long I would be at any place. I was kept out of postings where it was known that I could deliver and the department would progress. Yet, those who could deliver were problems for the establishment and I was one of the "difficult" officers in the organization. The appreciation of my work by the citizens has been a cause of envy to many of my peers and many of them left no opportunity to undercut my achievements and contributions. They have succeeded in denying me positions where I could deliver, evolve policing to new heights, and bring fundamental transformation of the organization. In the end all were losers and when all lose it is no one's loss in particular.

AV: What would you consider to be the greatest problem facing the police at this time?

KB: Very controlled and dependent leadership; one that is heavily dependent not on its professional capability and support of the personnel but suitability to the political bosses and manageability of issues dictated to them. The present police leadership in command of the organization seeks political connections and ways to serve narrow partisan interests of rulers. The leadership is unwilling to stand up to the politicians and develop professional competency in the organization.

AV: What problems in policing do you find are the most difficult to deal with? What would be easy to change? Internal problems (culture of the organization, managerial deficiencies, allegations of corruption, or gender-related problems, etc.) or externally generated problems (resources, community support, etc.)? Is anything easy?

KB: As the first woman officer in the Indian Police Service I was prepared to face problems from my male peers, but the most difficult problem I faced was that the policing is still in the hands of people who have patriarchal mindsets. Unless there is a change in their thinking, women in leadership will be dormant.

I do not think there is anything easy to change in the Indian police today. There are also vested interests keen to maintain the status quo. Therefore, any police reform that leads to a shift in power is difficult to implement. Wherever this is happening in the country it is being forced by the judiciary rather than by the executive. Management and resource mobilization cannot solve fundamental problems as police administration does not occur in isolation. The problems of policing in the country are interwoven with the politics and democratic functioning of the society. Today, the pursuit of power is blatant and sought by any means even if these are illegal or downright criminal. Unfortunately, the police leadership has succumbed to political dictates and has become completely malleable. There is little that an individual can do except step aside and not sully his or her hands.

Theory and Practice

AV: What should be the relationship between theory and practice? What can practitioners learn from theory, and what can theory builders learn from practitioners? What is the relationship right now? Does it exist? Does it work? What holds collaboration or interactions back?

KB: Clearly, theory must guide practice and practice must inform and teach theory. The two are inseparable and should not be conceived to be different entities. Practitioners can learn the consequences of their action from theory. They can also learn to apply the implications of theory to shape their work and improve upon their performance. Theory builders too must learn from the practitioners to understand what they do, how they do it, and why. Theory is empirical in nature and this empirical base can only be provided by the practitioner who is dealing with facts and realities on the ground.

Unfortunately, there is no relationship between the two and if it exists it does so in isolation among individuals. Despite vocal support for research and theory building, the government, police leadership, and policy makers have never supported those who want to do or are doing research. The rulers have always been reluctant to face the truth and would not support those who present it through their empirical approach.

AV: What kind of research, in what form, on what questions would you find most useful for practice? If not very useful, what could or should theory builders do to make their products more useful to you?

KB: Research [searching for something again], so long as it is concerned about seeking the truth and understanding what is going on and for what reasons should not be limited to particular issues only. Research should be concerned about every aspect of policing and should endeavor to go beyond the existing framework to seek alternate ways of improving the situation and performance. The colonial model is clearly unsuited for policing a democratic society. However, India is an ancient civilization, a diverse society of people living together for thousands of years with their own culture, beliefs, and skills. The existing model of police, designed by the British, cannot be simply cut and reshaped for a new dynamic country. A new system, designed by its own genius and wisdom, has to be developed that can serve the people and build a healthier, stable and harmonious society. At present, there is really very little research on policing in India. In such a situation, almost every topic of research has to be undertaken and encouraged. India needs a new police system and this can only come from extensive research that is developed by its own efforts.

Theory builders need to communicate in ways that are understandable and that help solve immediate problems.

AV: Where do you find theory-based information? Where do you look? What journals, books, publications, reports?

KB: I find theory-based information from books, journals, and articles published in a variety of formats ranging from newspaper and magazine articles to media reports in the form of audio and video as well as through the Internet. I look everywhere and am always ready to go to anyone to seek the information. There are far too many outlets to list but the *Indian Police Journal* that is administered by my organization is one that I utilize frequently. I have also restructured and redesigned the web page of my organization where I bring in all the available sources providing information to the police officers working in the country. I also meet a large number of citizens, academics, serving and retired police and criminal justice personnel who provide valuable information to me.

AV: Does your organization conduct research on its own? On what types of issues?

KB: I head the Bureau of Police Research and Development organization that has the mandate to conduct research on its own. Unfortunately, it has no support from the government and lacks even a skeleton staff to conduct meaningful research. I have initiated many projects, notwithstanding government's apathy, looking into improving police performance, working with the people and gaining their cooperation, focusing upon the training of subordinates, and encouraging educational institutions in India to conduct research on policing issues.

Transnational Relations

AV: Have you been affected, and how, in the work of your organization by developments outside the country (human rights demands, universal codes of ethics, practical interactions with police from other countries, personal experiences outside the country, new crime threats, etc.)?

KB: I have served as head of the United Nations Civilian Police Force and certainly in that capacity I have been affected by developments around the world. I have also served in the Narcotics Control Bureau of the Government of India and issues of drug trafficking have influenced me to develop new mechanisms to control trafficking, prosecute perpetrators, and rehabilitate users. I was also posted as the inspector general of Tihar prison, the largest in Asia, where many foreigners were incarcerated. Administration of this prison involved major issues of human rights, universal code of ethics, and personal interactions with a variety of Indian and foreign prisoners. I introduced a system of compassionate healing of these unfortunate people through the mechanism of Vipassna meditation that brought many encouraging results and outcomes. All these experiences of dealing with human suffering led me to develop a volunteer organization called Vision India that takes care of children whose parents are incarcerated and who have nobody else to take care of them. I am also involved with a large number of nongovernmental organizations that are working for issues of human rights, ethical conduct in public service, gender issues, exploitation of children, and democratic functioning of the Indian society, to name a few.

AV: Have those interactions been beneficial or harmful? What kind of external international influences are beneficial and which ones less so?

KB: I have always been open to new ideas and have sought to learn from others, whatever little they can teach me. Accordingly, I believe all my interactions, whether domestic or international, have been beneficial to me. I also believe that if a person has a genuine desire to learn from others, has no selfish motives, and is not afraid to admit mistakes then all influences are seen to be beneficial. Even if an interaction is antagonistic, it could be educative and a lesson for the future.

AV: How have developments post September 11 affected your work?

KB: Although there is no direct impact upon my work, reverberations of incidents anywhere in the world find echo in India. Post September 11 is a changed world and has affected everyone on the globe, directly or indirectly. The impact on India has been direct—the United States has at last been forced to accept the complicity of Pakistan in exporting terrorism and letting its base be used for terrorist activities. The United States has also moved closer to India and is now seeking a strategic partnership with the country. This has resulted in greater cooperation and economic partnership between the two governments. It is likely that there will be greater cooperation between the police forces of the two countries.

General Assessments

AV: Are you basically satisfied or dissatisfied with developments in policing? What are the most likely developments you see happening and which would you like to see happening? What is most needed now to improve policing?

KB: As described above, nobody can be satisfied with the existing situation in the country. India is transforming rapidly right now. There is rapid growth in the economy, which is increasing the wealth and well-being of the people. A new, young, and vibrant generation is emerging that is ambitious, confident, and determined to match the best in the world. However, in its rapid stride this economic development is also leaving a large number of people behind and causing greater disparities. The consequences of rapid industrialization and urbanization are also harmful to the environment and rapid changes are beginning to affect social relations and affect the cultural heritage of this ancient country. The country and its people have to resolve this dilemma. Nevertheless, this generation X is also bringing a promising development in policing where it is witnessing the induction of a large number of technologists and management-oriented young people who are preparing to take over the police leadership. They appear to be the best hope for the future.

There is no dearth of ideas. But you need people who can implement wisely. Where are they? Today, the police organization is suffocating and ready to kill new initiatives. It is all 24 hours policing which is controlled and subservient to partisan interests. It is a very hierarchical nonparticipative policing. In fact it is truly a monopoly organization with all its strengths and its weaknesses. It is afraid of opening up and deeply apprehensive of change. It does not research for it is afraid to know the outcomes. In fact it is the least researched organization. There are thousands of students in universities who would love to access information but it is hidden, just not given and no one can question the reason for this secrecy. It is going to take a long time for the mindsets to change. But since change is the law I remain optimistic.

AV: Thank you.

Endnotes

1. The IPS provides the leadership to Indian police and all ranks from superintendent upwards are reserved for members of this service. Recruitment to the IPS is done by the Union Public Service Commission annually when around 50 or so applicants are selected from a national competitive examination, which is taken by at least 300,000 university graduates. The service is attractive to university graduates for the opportunities of public service, status, and power it provides to young people. IPS officers are trained at the prestigious National Police Academy and are allotted a state "cadre" position where they serve for most of their years in service. IPS officers also command all the central police forces including units engaged in intelligence and covert operations.

Interview with Odd Berner Malme, Police Counsellor, Permanent Mission of Norway to the United Nations

10

INTERVIEWED BY JOHN A. ETERNO

Background

Odd Berner Malme is currently assigned as police counsellor/police advisor at the Permanent Mission of Norway to the United Nations. His career is very distinguished as he rose through the ranks to become the deputy national commissioner in Norway, the position of second in command of all of Norway's police. In this capacity, among other duties, he developed strategies to prevent and combat both organized and transnational crime. The interview with Counsellor Malme focuses on his views regarding both domestic and international policing. In order to place these views in context, some background information about the Norwegian police service and the UN is required.

Norway has approximately 4.7 million people. Its largest city is Oslo, with over half million inhabitants. Norway borders Sweden, Finland, and Russia (in the north). Norway is not part of the European Union but does work closely with its neighbors. To become a police officer in Norway, one must study for 3 years at the police university.[1] There is one national police service, with one police commissioner for the entire country.

The current national police commissioner in Norway is Ingelin Killengreen. She is in charge of the Norwegian Police Service, which has approximately 12,000 employees. According to her, the goal of Norway's police service is "to prevent and combat crime" (*The Police in Norway*, 2005). The police fall under the auspices of the Ministry of Justice and Police. They are a national force unlike the system that, for example, is used in the United States, namely, numerous police departments with overlapping jurisdictions at the federal, state, and local levels. Recently, the Norwegian police have undergone reorganization. The existing 54 police districts were reduced to 27 districts. The reduction was an effort by the government to streamline the bureaucracy.

In 2001, the National Police Directorate was formed. Its functions are "strategic co-ordination, agency management, personnel and organizational development, support and supervisory duties, administrative duties, contingency planning and handling complaints" (*The Police in Norway*, 2005). One reason for the establishment of the directorate includes the challenges emerging from current trends in crime and the need to adjust the organization of police to a new reality. There is an increased awareness of the importance of organized crime and the mobility and internationalization of criminal networks. Fighting these challenges requires concerted efforts both nationally and internationally. The National Police Directorate has overall responsibility for the coordination of efforts against organized crime. This includes participation in international police cooperation (*The Police in Norway*, 2005).

In general, Norway enjoys a low crime rate. The vast majority of crimes are property crimes, which average around 175,000 to 225,000 per year. However, organized crime and transnational crime are concerns to Norway. Counsellor Malme is an expert in this area and I did have the pleasure of seeing him speak on these issues a few weeks after my interview at the International Police Executive Symposium in Cincinnati, Ohio on May 15, 2008. Before I discuss my interview with him, I will go over the highlights of his presentation, which provides us with helpful insights for the interview: it is an excellent summary of his background, it is an informative discussion of transnational crime as it relates to Norway, it gives us some background information useful for interpreting the interview, and it helps us to understand Counsellor Malme. His presentation, therefore, provides an excellent foundation for the interview.

International Police Executive Symposium, Highlights of Presentation by Counsellor Malme

The title of Counsellor Malme's presentation was "Transnational and Organized Crime: A Perspective from the Northern Hemisphere." He pointed out that the discovery of petroleum products, in particular, oil and gas, in the 1960s gave Norway an economic windfall. While this is good, unfortunately, it has also led to more concern about organized crime as it is attracted to the growing economy. Criminal organizations readily adapt to changes and quickly learn how to take advantage of any weaknesses.

Norway, because it is not part of the European Union, needs to make special agreements to combat organized and transnational crime. Norway is part of the Schengen Agreement, which includes 24 countries. This involves removal of checks at common borders but also strengthening external

European Union border controls. There is also simplified cooperation between the police and the judiciary within member states. This means easier rules and faster routines for police among cooperating nations. Norway also uses the Schengen Information System (SIS) which has helped Norwegian police to obtain information about criminal suspects and the like.

Since organized criminal networks are cooperating across national boundaries, it is necessary for nations to use similar definitions. Norway is using the European Union's definition of organized crime. Based on this common definition, the greatest problem, as it is in many nations, is illegal drugs. Cannabis, amphetamines, and heroin are major challenges to Norway. The Balkan route with illegal drugs coming from Afghanistan is particularly troublesome. In addition, money laundering, human trafficking, and asylum-related problems are on the increase.

Other trends in transnational crime are also evident. Vehicle crime, arms trafficking, false passports, piracy of technical products (e.g., CDs), corruption, and terrorist groups financing themselves through criminal activities are all on the rise. Typical organized crime groups such as the "mafia," however, are not common in Northern Europe. The only exceptions to this are motorcycle gangs such as Hells Angels and Baditos.

To combat these problems, Counsellor Malme first recommended national coordination. At a minimum, this includes: a National Criminal Intelligence Sharing Plan, a national focal point of international connections, a National Criminal Intelligence Register, and incorporating innovative methods of combating serious crime. These recommendations for coordination transcend nations. That is, every nation should be doing something in these areas. In Norway, The Advisory Council for Combating Organized Crime (ROK) is the focal point for coordination for fighting organized crime (see Figure 10.1).

With respect to international cooperation between Norway and other countries, the National Criminal Investigations Service (KRIPOS), which has a 24-hour desk to allow global communications at any time of day or night, is critical. Many authorities are linked through this focal point, such as Schengen cooperation countries, the Baltic Sea Task Force on Organized Crime, Interpol, Nordic Police, and customs cooperation, regional cooperation, etc.

Counsellor Malme pointed out from his experience that of particular note is that the Nordic countries have a special agreement on police and customs cooperation. First, there are working groups such as witness protection and disaster victim identification. Second, the Nordic Police and Customs Co-operation Office (NPCCO) has about 36 officers stationed around the world as liaison officers. They assist the host country and, in turn, help the Nordic countries to fight international crime. These liaison officers provide a bridge to cultural differences. For example, differences in legislation between

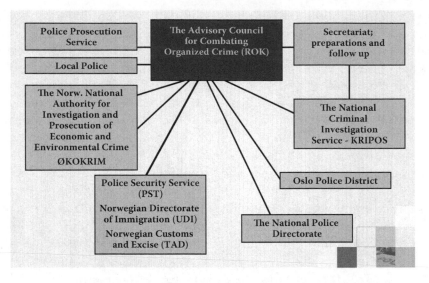

Figure 10.1 Combating organized crime and structural linkages.

the countries can be discussed and understood. These officers also provide a linguistic bridge. These officers also understand the language of police officers—search warrants, wire tapping, and the like. These officers can be useful for many transnational criminal investigations, especially cross-border surveillance.

Norway has also been a part of Interpol since 1931 and has had a cooperative agreement with Europol since 2001. Europol can assist with crime analysis and investigation of international crimes. There are two Norwegian liaison officers in the Hague.

Additionally, Counsellor Malme discussed improvements that could be made to the current system. Liaison officers, he recommended, should be used more extensively as the global threat from crime continues to expand. These officers should be allowed to exchange data, coordinate and provide analysis, develop operation and strategic planning and intelligence, and work together on research and development.

Overall, Counsellor Malme saw a need to work closely with other nations. He pointed out that mission statements and policies need to be developed at all levels, from local to international, particularly with respect to sharing intelligence. Then officers need to be provided with proper training on intelligence processes and sharing plans. Further, web sites and using the Internet in general need to be expanded as information resources. He also felt that intelligence-led policing needs to be expanded. He concluded that we need to develop our knowledge about conventions on privacy and civil rights.

Although the presentation focused on one aspect of Counsellor Malme's vast experience and knowledge, organized and transnational crime, in the interview he discussed the dual roles that he has played: as police officer in Norway and now as police counsellor/advisor at the Permanent Mission of Norway to the United Nations. He discusses the complexities involved in both roles. Clearly, his vast experience in Norway, including his presentation on transnational crime, is a tremendous asset to his work at the United Nations.

The Interview

This interview was conducted on March 17, 2008 at Norway's Mission to the United Nations. I had to pass through three security doors to get to Mr. Malme's office. This is not unusual but is certainly a sign of the times. The first door brought me to a secure holding area where a secretary greeted me and had me wait a few minutes until Mr. Malme came to get me. We cordially greeted each other as we were meeting in person for the first time. His hand-shake was firm, yet polite. We walked up one flight of stairs to his office—rather typical, with a desk, several chairs, and a small table in the corner. I noticed a map of Europe on the wall above his desk with the Scandinavian countries, including Norway, clearly visible. Evidently, this is helpful in his work especially with visitors like me. He had to move a few things around to make room for me to sit—obviously a busy man. The warmth of his greeting, offering tea or coffee, immediately set the stage for an excellent interview. Mr. Malme was clearly confident and highly professional, the consummate diplomat. Norway has chosen well.

JE: Can you give me some background information about yourself? What you did in Norway? What do you do now?

OM: My last position in Norway was as the deputy national police commis-sioner. To explain it to you, I was the second in command for the entire police in Norway. This is because in Norway we have only one police service unlike America. In America, you have many, many police services. In Norway, we have one police throughout the country divided into 27 police districts and central special units. Here in New York I am employed by the Ministry of Foreign Affairs to be a police counsellor at the Norwegian Mission to the United Nations.

We are here in New York to work with the United Nations and to be a contact point to our country. We are providing the UN assistance for peacekeeping operations around the world. Years ago these were purely military but in 1989 or so, the UN organized integrated peacekeeping operations. That number is growing. For the UN today there are something like 11,000 police officers in peacekeeping operations. Compared to the military, it is growing because they need police competence for these missions in order to build the rule of law. However, it is very hard to get police from member states because we are taking them away from the streets and communities where they are also needed. If we want to have an influence on UN policy and strategy, we have to be here in New York. I also do try to keep up with the FBI and New York City police by making contacts with them.

JE: Does Norway provide police officers to these operations?

OM: Yes. We are providing up to 1% of the operational police service to international operations. We provide officers to the UN and for other international operations as well, such as in Afghanistan, Liberia, and Sudan. We have approximately 70 police officers on these operations. There are 8,500 sworn officers in Norway, which means we have up to 85 officers on these operations at one time [i.e., 1%].

JE: Your job then is very political?

OM: Yes, very political but my competence in my craft is essential to this. I am appointed to the International Police Advisory Council (IPAC) for the UN. This council is made up of both academics and practitioners and provides advice to the UN on policing in post-conflict countries.

JE: With respect to your role, how might you use an academic person in anything that you do?

OM: Academics can give me very good insights for my use in operational matters. They can be especially helpful if I need to support my views. Academics tend to know issues in far more detail and I may be just passing through. If I disagree with academics, I might bring my practical background to explain why. The best academics have some practical experience as well. The academic world needs to produce work that has more value to the practitioner. Here in America, there are a lot of "think tanks"—a wide range of academics—you can see the diversity of views. This is far more interesting and valuable. I do try to keep abreast of what is going on academically.

JE: What is the proper role of police in a free society?

OM: The role of the police in a free society is to serve the public in the frame of law and regulations taken by the legislators. The police must also be a barometer of trends and incidents that can threat democratic development and security.

The role of the UN police in post-conflict countries is to build local police capacity and reform existing police such that they have the ability to conduct basic policing and respect human rights. In the past, especially during conflicts, police have been misused by leaders. Therefore, the UN police often have to start from scratch to build the local police and rule of law. When this happens it is then necessary to reform the entire security sector. The police and justice sector institutions are critical to a country's sovereignty and this is always a sensitive issue. National involvement is absolutely necessary.

As we build police capacity in post-conflict countries, at the same time we also need to be aware of the need to collaborate on a global scale to fight crime. This includes ordinary policing in well-developed countries as well. One of the major challenges in the world is overcoming barriers to cooperate as crime globalizes.

JE: Would Interpol be an example?

OM: Not really in all aspects. Information sharing is the greatest challenge to police on a global scale. And here Interpol can play an important role, but it must also be done bilaterally—nation to nation. Regional agreements are more likely to be successful compared to global agreements. Close collaboration between nations is needed where information is shared. We all have a lot of information but we are not always sharing it in a way that is useful. Human trafficking, drugs, terrorism, and other transnational crimes will best be fought with further information sharing among countries. It is not a lack of information but a lack of sharing information. Maybe half the cases we investigate in my country have some connection outside the borders.

JE: What about Norway? Do the borders of Norway influence its crime?

OM: Cross-border crime is a challenge for all countries and for my and the other Nordic countries as well. In the north we border Russia, Finland, and Sweden. There is crime coming across land borders as well as the sea. This can come from various places: the Baltic states, Russia, Germany, Poland, Ukraine, etc. Norway is not the center of the world. We are small and at the outskirts of Europe and need to build strong links internationally. We have a long tradition of cooperating with the other Nordic countries, Sweden, Denmark, Finland, and Iceland. In 1984 we did an agreement within the Nordic countries to deploy common liaison officers in production and transit countries of narcotics. Information with respect to crime is widely shared among the Nordic countries.

JE: Is this a good model for other countries?

OM: Yes, this is a good model for other countries. However, sovereignty gets in the way of other nations sharing such information. History and politics of nations are clearly very important to understand. Such understandings will help pave the way for agreements such as those in the Nordic model I have just told you about to be more widespread. This will allow information about criminal activity and terrorism to be more widely disseminated. This information sharing starts at the regional level.

JE: Norway did not join the EU. Is this an issue with respect to cooperation?

OM: Norway did not join the EU. However, Sweden, Finland, and Denmark did. Nevertheless, the cooperation agreements are still in place and working well. Norway does have some minor differences in foreign policies but the borders are so porous between our nations and we have so much in common with the other Nordic countries.

JE: With respect to international policing, what is the foremost problem that must be overcome by police?

OM: This is clearly organized crime and terrorism. These organized criminals are going from country to country and they know no borders. They have the cover, the money, they are violent, and are working in a very large area—larger than police work. International cooperation on this is extremely necessary. There is a need to develop contacts in various countries. For example, your FBI is involved with other countries on these matters. There is a need for Legats [FBI liaison officers] to be around the world because criminals are going back and forth all the time. You need to have an immediate contact to fight this. Of course, information sharing is also part of fighting this as well. This would include the concept of modus operandi [methods that criminals use to do their crimes]. Second, competence building is very important. This would include training and best practices and lessons learned. Training should also be done in partnership among cooperating countries.

JE: Who do you picture as a good police officer to be recruited—first, domestically, then for international missions?

OM: Recruit young, well-educated people who understand the society in which they are living. They must have a good understanding of the police role and how to serve the public. They must understand how the police fit into a democracy. Police are the police for the community and the people living there—that is simply a fact. Police officers should be nationally trained and informed about international policing. Knowledge of conventions and international rules is needed to understand the frame of international cooperation.

In peacekeeping operations we need experienced police officers who can represent their home country in a good way. Peacekeeping is getting more and more complex. In the past, you only needed a good general police officer. Today, there is a need for more specialists for international missions. These officers are going to be mentors and trainers in very specific areas. They, therefore, need specialist skills as well as experience using those skills. We train and we mentor. In Norway, these skills reflect the level of education with our police. The Police Academy in Norway is part of the official university system and requires 3 years of studies to be a police officer. The first year is training in the basic theory of police and the society they are living in. The second year the police students are out in the police districts practicing. The third year the police students are back in the academy for advanced studies. Norway is encouraging higher academic studies. The expectations of police coming out of the university system, however, are very high. They expect to become specialists almost immediately. That is, new officers have such high expectations that they are likely to be let down a bit when they realize they cannot become specialists immediately but must do their time in regular duties.

JE: Is there anything that you would do differently in your current role?

MB: I enjoy my work here. I can use my background and experience. Being in command in Norway for too long can be challenging. Here in New York there is an international community of which I am part. There are other police, military advisors, and diplomats that I cooperate with every day. I visit and cooperate with colleagues at the police division at the UN several times every week. There are academics there as well. The Department of Peacekeeping Operations (DPKO) is the biggest department at the UN, with over 170,000 personnel assigned in operations worldwide. There are three pillars of that department. Essentially they are Military Affairs, Operations, and the Office of Rule of Law. I deal at length with the people in these areas. My experience clearly assists me in these matters.

In Norway I was in uniformed Special Operations Corps after graduating the Police Academy. I then went to the Security Service as a senior police officer. There, I dealt with surveillance and undercover for 5 years and had several years of work with espionage cases and investigations. After that period, I went to the Ministry of Justice and Police where I was the head of the international branch for some years. I was later head of the Criminal Intelligence and Organized Crime Branch in the Oslo Police District. In the autumn of 2000 I was appointed deputy national police commissioner for a period of 6 years. I feel that I have a very extensive background which gives me an advantage in understanding the intricacies of international diplomacy and peacekeeping post conflict. At our Mission I also deal with the UN antiterrorism aspects and small arms as well. These are also areas of great concern for the police globally.

JE: If you could change one thing in policing today, what would it be?

OB: I would make police organizations more transparent. The more transparent organizations gain more trust from the public. We have a tendency to take the public trust for granted. Police officers in America, as in Norway, sometimes forget that they are serving the public. Of course, with the gangsters and other criminals, we need to be tough, but most of the time police are dealing with people who are in a time of high stress and are vulnerable. Often when police come upon a situation, it is not ordinary, not calm. Sometimes police think that people do not understand what they are saying, but it is such a high stress time, that police need to deal with people as the situation calls for. We still have some way to go before we are able to police people in the way they need to be policed.

JE: Do political considerations make it difficult for a police chief to speak his or her mind?

OB: It varies. In Norway the government appoints the chief of police and they cannot fire you without raising a case against you. Additionally, you are a political person [as an individual] independent of your professional duty. But professionalism is essential to a police chief. They need to be able to receive critics in an open way. Of course, if you are making a superior uncomfortable with what you are saying, you may get a phone call advising you on the issue. However, as long as the police chief is acting in a professional manner, this would not likely happen. You are generally free to discuss issues with the media and others. Police chiefs should take an active part in the public debate.

Final Thoughts

Counsellor Malme's experience and intellect make him the ideal person for the challenging job as police counsellor/police advisor at the Permanent Mission of Norway to the United Nations. I found him to be polite and professional (in every sense of the word). His ideas on transparency and understanding cultures are some of the most enlightening and interesting ideas that I have heard. They are based on many years of experience and education.

A few thoughts come to mind as I conclude our talk. Before we can even attempt to influence other countries, we need to be sure that the political will is there to make the change (Bayley, 2001). A change to democratic policing must not be taken lightly by any country. It is a difficult process that requires enormous effort and a paradigm shift among the rank and file. Assuming this prerequisite is met, then, as Counsellor Malme points out, sending officers as trainers to neophyte democracies requires, at a minimum, transparency (on the part of the new democratic police force as well as by UN police) as well as a deep understanding of other cultures.

Transparency, however, does not come easily. Even in many so-called free societies, transparency, especially among police agencies, is difficult to achieve at best. In the United States and Great Britain, policing has often been described as a profession that is filled with secrecy. This may be due to the nature of the police culture and the lack of clear guidelines (see, for example, Manning & Van Maanen, 1978; Manning, 1977). As far as the police culture is concerned, I have experienced an international fraternity among police officers. When I go to other nations, if they know I am (or was) a police officer in New York City, the entire tone of the conversation changes; it becomes more friendly and an unspoken understanding of what one has gone through occurs. This can be a good quality but also something that could hinder international missions. Many officers, for example, develop a sense of pride in fighting crime. Indeed, I think most officers genuinely want to work together to fight crime. However, the mission of police in free countries must always be one of respecting human rights first and then fighting crime. This is the dilemma for police, to fight crime while at the same time respecting rights (see Eterno, 2001). Counsellor Malme has touched on a key issue with respect to this dilemma. Being transparent helps to limit the power of police such that they do not abuse their authority. Furthermore, training on other cultures is important, as he rightly points out.

The need for clear guidelines is also an essential aspect to policing (Eterno, 2003, 2006) especially with respect to international missions. We cannot send officers into harm's way without giving them clear direction as to what we expect and what they can and cannot do. For example, a directive such as "do not torture" is meaningless. Officers need to be told, at a minimum, what torture is and be given explicit direction as to what they can do. In the United States, for example, we need to read a suspect his or her rights under the Constitution before interrogating that person. The United States Supreme Court created a bright-line rule for officers to follow.

In sum, Counsellor Malme is the consummate professional. His experience and knowledge of both local and international policing is exceptional. His presentation at the International Police Executive Symposium shed light on Norway's fight against organized and international crime. The interview captured both his national and international experiences. Counsellor Malme's ideas on transparency for police are particularly important especially given the nature of the police culture.

Glossary

Advisory Council for Combating Organized Crime (ROK): Norway's council to help combat organized crime. It is the focal point for national and international cooperation.

International Police Advisory Council: A recently created council, which is part of the United Nations. It is in the UN Police Division.

National Police Directorate: Established in Norway. Its main functions are "strategic co-ordination, agency management, personnel and organizational development, support and supervisory duties, administrative duties, contingency planning and handling complaints" (*The Police in Norway*, 2005).

Nordic Police and Customs Co-operation Office (NPCCO): The NPCCO has about 36 officers stationed around the world as liaison officers. They assist the host country and, in turn, help the Nordic countries to fight international crime. These liaison officers provide a bridge to cultural differences.

References

Bayley, D.H. (2001). *Democratizing the Police Abroad: What to Do and How to Do It.* Washington, DC: U.S. Department of Justice.

Eterno, J.A. (2001). Zero Tolerance Policing in Democracies: The Dilemma of Controlling Crime without Increasing Police Abuse of Power. *Police Practice,* 2(3), 189–217.

Eterno, J.A. (2003). *Policing within the Law: A Case Study of the New York City Police Department.* Greenport, CT: Praeger.

Eterno, J.A. (2006). Understanding the Law on the Frontlines: The Need for Bright-Line Rules. *Criminal Law Bulletin,* 43(5): 706–725.

Manning, P. (1977). *Police Work: The Social Organization of Policing.* Cambridge, MA: MIT Press.

Manning, P.K. and Van Maanen, J. (1978). *Policing: A View from the Street.* Santa Monica, CA: Goodyear Publishing.

The Police in Norway (2005). Publication of the Government of Norway.

Endnotes

1. If you would like more information about the Police University College for Norway, see http://www.phs.no/Om-PHS/Internasjonale-relasjonar-/About-the-Norwegian-Police-University-College/

Interview with Aleksander Jevšek, Senior Criminal Police Superintendent, Director of Criminal Police Directorate, General Police Directorate of the Republic of Slovenia[1]

11

INTERVIEWED AND TRANSLATED BY
DARKO MAVER AND GORAZD MEŠKO

The interview was held from 8:30 to 11:30 a.m. on October 19, 2007 at the Ministry of the Interior, Republic of Slovenia, and on the morning of November 10, 2007.

The Interview

DM & GM: Can you tell us, please, about your career in the police?

AJ: When I completed primary school in 1976 I enrolled in the Tacen Secondary Police School, thus fulfilling my longtime wish to become a police officer and somewhere along the line a criminal investigator. My interest in the vocation was reflected in my performance at school as I finished the education with distinction. My criminalistics teacher recommended me to the chief of the criminal police service at the Ljubljana Police Directorate, who took me on and assigned me to the homicide and sex crime squad. As a young and keen criminal investigator I was quick to grasp the first steps of criminalistics. By 1987 I completed my degree at the College of Law in Maribor.

   In 1987 my wife and I moved to her family's home in Murska Sobota, where I started working as a criminal investigator in the General Crime Department, mostly dealing with homicides and property crime. I stayed in Murska Sobota until 1992, when the director of the Maribor Criminal Investigation Service invited me to take over the management of the General Crime Department in the second largest police directorate in Slovenia, which I did from 1992 to 1995. In 1994 the police sponsored my further studies at the Faculty of Law in Maribor, which I completed two years later and returned to work to the Maribor Police Directorate as assistant director of the criminal police.

In 1997 the director of the criminal police appointed me director of the criminal police at the Celje Police Directorate, which is the third largest police directorate in Slovenia, and I stayed there until 1999. In November 1999 I returned to the Murska Sobota Police Directorate to become its director, which I remained for 7 years. In November 2006 I was transferred to a demanding position of director of the largest police directorate in Slovenia, Ljubljana. After only two months I was appointed director of the Criminal Police Directorate in the General Police Directorate, the position I still hold today.

Since 1990 I have been teaching criminalistics courses to new criminal investigators, lecturing on criminalistics at the Police College and taking part in the education process of the Faculty of Criminal Justice and Faculty of Law in Maribor. I am a founding member, the first president and currently vice president of the Criminal Investigators Association of Slovenia. In December I am planning to defend my master's thesis in the postgraduate study of criminology at the Ljubljana Faculty of Law.

My career has enabled me to be creative and to learn to adapt to new challenges, which is very positive. It has to be pointed out that my career was not systematically led and directed but rather a combination of hard work and study as well as some lucky coincidences. I have every reason to be pleased with my professional career and I can say it has exceeded my youthful expectations. Its progress was such that my efforts and hard work were awarded by promotion.

DM & GM: What changes in policing have you experienced during your career?

AJ: Without any doubt one of the key changes in the work of the police had to do with the independence process and the building up of a democratic political system in the country. This brought key changes not only in the content of police work, legal bases for the work, organizational structure but also in work philosophy. Building up work philosophy is a process that is still ongoing. It needs to be mentioned that in the period before, during, and after independence the police had the honor as well as the burden of achieving independence and defending the country. The state did not have its own army yet and a large portion of defense duties were on the shoulders of the police, who were the only organization with the equipment, weaponry, and knowledge of combative tactics. The police performed their historic role with excellence and as a police officer I am proud to have actively participated in the process of gaining independence and defending the country.

After independence the police did not have time to celebrate as they immediately had to assume their duties in the field of protecting lives and property of citizens, fight against crime, protecting state borders ... It has to be emphasized that the police enjoyed the exceptional support of the community as people regarded us very highly because of our instrumental role in the independence process. Unfortunately this support quickly dropped, which causes considerable grief to some segments of the police community.

The introduction of democratic principles in police work was not without its problems. Demands for greater security and a reduction of police powers compared to the previous political system on account of fundamental rights and freedoms of individuals caused certain problems. House searches with the obligatory presence of a lawyer and based on a court order, shortened duration of police detention, higher standards of proof, etc., are the milestones that caused considerable difficulties in the practice of policing.

A further milestone in policing was the beginning of preparations for Slovenia's membership in the European Union. The adoption of legal standards of the EU, their transposition into the national law, changes in the field of international cooperation towards strengthened contacts with other police forces, and preparations for the Schengen arrangement had an important effect on the organization and philosophy of police work.

I can say with certainty that to be a police officer today is harder than it used to be. Police officers have to be well informed and educated as formal and informal control over their work is reinforced. They often feel trapped in a situation in which the public on one hand demands greater safety and on the other hand criticizes every small mistake in their work and tries to limit their powers. Despite all this, the Slovenian police have also gained a lot and are still gaining. The education structure has completely changed. If in the old times we used to have problems with uneducated staff and had a distinct deficit in this field, today the situation is radically different. The level of education within the police force exceeds the needs, and as a consequence police officers with college or university degrees do work for which only secondary-level education is necessary. This brings additional difficulties.

Moreover, equipment has improved dramatically in the 27 years of my career within the police, not only as regards new computer technologies and possibilities for accessing and using them but also as regards working conditions. Police officers work in modern buildings, where they have good working conditions. Personal and protective equipment is state-of-the-art and the same is true of vehicles.

With the transition to a new, democratic system the police acquired a huge number of additional tasks that they had not had before, which are a consequence of the poor functioning of other state authorities. Thus, the police do a lot of work on the basis of the new legislation, assist inspection services, deal with minor offense procedures and petty crime. As a result, police officers, despite their relatively high number, spend too much time doing other tasks and documenting them, which leaves them with too little time to do their basic activities, which are directly linked to the duty of protecting people and property. This is another reason being a police officer today is harder than it used to be. As a consequence there are fewer police out in the field than in the old times. This is a fact we have come to realize and we are doing all we can to ensure that a police officer spends as much time as possible among people in the field, not as a repressive figure, but as a point of contact with people.

High standards regarding the protection of human rights and freedoms have entered the philosophy of police work and are an integral part of police procedures. The attitude towards minorities and other nationalities has changed. There are of course some violations in this field within the police, to which we react with disciplinary action, including the termination of employment. The standards of protecting human rights and freedoms in the Slovenian police have changed considerably.

Specialized police units have made good progress, which is also a consequence of international exchanges of police officers and good policing practices. The equipment as well as tactics and methods of specialized units' work have changed and are being adapted to new security challenges.

A big change and shake-up was caused by a departure of 700 police officers from the force on the basis of a statutory amendment in 1998, which enabled them to retire at the age of 45. The loss of such a high number of police officers was a big shock, which is still felt today. A lot of young officers were left without mentors, the management structure got younger (which is not necessarily a negative thing), and I have a feeling that the police force is only just recovering its wind.

In the last 5 years the Slovenian police directed a lot of human resources and equipment into the adoption of Schengen standards and work forms. The orientation of priority goals (it is undoubtedly a priority of the country) into only one field of police work, that is, in this case protection of the state border, is felt in other fields. Personnel policy in general work fields has been made more difficult and the flow of funds is directed predominantly to the border. I am convinced that we managed to perform this task without negative impact on the safety of our citizens.

DM & GM: What is your personal philosophy of police work?

AJ: A police officer in a community must continuously be in contact with the environment and be physically present. To put it simply, people in a village, part of town, or a street must know who "their" police officer is. They basically perform both reactive and proactive activities and it is important that they are a contact point people can turn to for advice or solution to their problems.

The fundamental role of a police officer is providing assistance and safety and the feeling of safety to people. They must be a person of public and personal trust. Minor traffic violations, minor accidents, petty crime, and the work of other state authorities (inspection services, etc.) should not burden the police.

In the police field of work those organizational changes have been effective, which enable police officers to be present in the community, that is, dispersed organization and deployment of police forces in the field. A centralized organization and the creation of large police stations and the relocation of police officers from the rural areas to town centers has proved to be ineffective as it causes lower presence of police officers outside of city centers.

The police must maintain an apolitical position to political parties. It would be unacceptable to have politics decide who will be the commander of a police station or director of a police directorate, which was the case in the past. The police must be open to the community and solve security problems together with the local community. The police and the local community must be jointly responsible for maintaining safety in a community. Placing all security responsibility only on the shoulders of the police (drug problems, road traffic, etc.) makes police work and cooperation with other authorities and groups more difficult. Safety is not solely a responsibility of the police.

A primary priority of police work is protecting citizens and property. The police are primarily a reactive agency. With their know-how and experience they can also take part in preventive projects, where they should be one of the participants and not the sole holder of the project. For instance, drugs and drug addiction are a problem that needs to be dealt with by public health, schools, the ministry of labor and family and the police. The same is true of public safety. The police can act reactively, but is it not in their power to build pavements, safe roads, traffic islands, roundabouts, educate young people, etc. However, they can and should act as a partner. Partnership is the key.

Only by knowing security conditions in an environment down to their microelements can the police react—quickly and adequately— to a security problem and this is the kind of police people want.

DM & GM: What problems and successes have you witnessed?

AJ: A problem in our police organization is that good solutions often do not last. It tended to happen in the past that with the arrival of new people to the management structure of the police a reorganization was imminent, bringing new solutions to police work that were not well thought through or reflected poor knowledge of the system as a whole. A concrete example was the project of closing police departments and centralizing and concentrating police forces in larger centers. We should not impose too many guidelines and directions for work on the police as this reduces the possibility for creativity of police chiefs at the local and regional levels. It is especially wrong to burden the whole organization with directions for work based on a concrete negative security-related event. The reasons for many failed organizational changes can be found in a view held by those not familiar with the police organization (which is a complicated system) that everything is wrong in the police and everything needs to be changed. As police chiefs at the top level, due to the nature of policing, change frequently, this causes a lot of confusion and annoyance in the police for it often happens that an existing reorganization is not even finished in a particular area when a new one starts being devised. The police need a stable and solid system that police officers know well and which makes them more effective.

Currently a big problem in our organization is that in the last 5 years a lot of energy and resources, educational capacities and personnel have been devoted primarily to the establishment of the Schengen arrangement at the border with Croatia. This broke the flow of human resources both in police education and consequently at the general police stations at the local and regional levels. A lot of police officers retired and were not replaced by new personnel. Favorable security conditions had to be provided with fewer staff, less experience, and greater workload. We are already working on a solution to this problem.

I believe that the Slovenian police have relatively good material support for work and support in the community that affords it a high level of trust.

DM & GM: What are your views on the relationship between theory and practice?

AJ: It is my firm belief that theory and practice must complement each other. This need may have been less pronounced in the past but in the modern society it is a real necessity. Police work and ensuring safety in a contemporary society that has just undergone some changes of values are becoming increasingly demanding. And for this very reason police work cannot be done without good theoretical background, bases for work strategies and clearly set goals. On the other hand, theory needs findings from practice as its only source of materials. Otherwise theory would be based on assumptions only and not on real problems in the field of providing safety in everyday life.

The current relationship between theory and practice in our country is relatively good and cannot be assessed only on the basis of the relations between particular institutions or concrete individuals. Police officers, especially those who have had some further training in the last years, upgrade their practical knowledge with theoretical bases. They approach solving problems on the basis of the knowledge they acquired during theoretical training. Education and training in the Slovenia police are very well organized.

What the police expect from theory is to be able to trust it. Surveys that the police request and finance must not be abused for retaliation against a police chief. If results of a survey become a weapon of political retaliation, this of course has a negative influence on the relationship between police theory and practice. Every police organization in the world has problems it wants to identify and solve. If it enlists theory and has its trust abused, this can be a big obstacle for further cooperation.

In the Slovenian police we are doing our utmost to reduce administrative duties of police officers to the minimum, to reduce the time spent at their desks writing reports so that they can spend more time in the field among citizens. There are a number of projects devoted to this goal (reporting and informing, petty crime, modernization and rationalization of entering data into databases, etc.) in which theory could take part by conducting surveys and making international comparisons. Theoreticians are expected to prepare solutions to a particular problem with proposals for concrete measures.

The police obtain theoretical information through the network of training provided by the Police Academy. Training is organized in different fields of work and external experts and lecturers from faculties and different education institutions take an active part. The police have their own library, which collects practically all the most important publications on policing in the world. Every police officer has an opportunity to find the publication he or she is interested in on our intranet and obtain it. The police have a modern Internet network so every police officer has access to any literature (via the Co-operative Online Bibliographic System & Services—COBISS, press clipping, legal information system, IUS info, etc.).

The police do not carry out their own surveys, such as public opinion polls, victimology research; they are done by external institutions.

DM & GM: What international relations do the Slovenian police engage in?

AJ: Changes in our country and beyond (as mentioned in the introduction) affected the work of our organization. The raising of standards of the protection of human rights and fundamental freedoms and of standard of proof in case of new forms of criminal offenses demand constant adapting on the part of the police. In addition to acquiring new knowledge, organizational adaptation, technical support, etc., experience we obtain in international exchanges of police officers is very valuable. Slovenia has been taking part for many years in the international exchange of criminal investigators and police officers in the framework of CEPOL—European Police College, Central European Police Academy, other forms of training and international exchange of experience offered by Europol and Interpol. I also believe that other police forces find the experience of our police useful. These interactions are very useful for our organization.

Good practices of foreign police forces are useful as long as they bring about positive shifts in the field of the provision of security in a particular country. Blind copying of security measures used in other countries not taking into account the specifics of our country cannot be good. It is especially for this reason that we adapted the security measures after September 11 to the level of terrorist threat in Slovenia, which is currently low. In practice this means that in the field of the fight against terrorism the police carry out a number of activities both at home and in international exchange. However, citizens do not feel any restrictions.

DM & GM: What is your assessment of the general conditions and progress of the Slovenian police?

AJ: In general I am very pleased with the progress in our police organization. What the Slovenian police have achieved since the country's independence, membership in the EU and the entry into the Schengen area, was a huge step, which demanded a lot of effort. It is important that the security conditions in the country have not deteriorated. On the contrary, in the case of the clear-up rate of criminal offenses, this has even improved.

Changes in the future will take place in accordance with the national strategies in the field of crime prevention, road traffic safety, and others. It is my wish that everyone performing tasks linked to the strategy would do their job thoroughly. Strategies give the basic points of departure so that security problems can get tackled at their root causes. In the long run it means a better security situation and the fact that the police will have more time to be in contact with people and be present in the field.

In the future, further globalization of crime, especially organized crime, can be expected. This will require police forces to get even more closely connected and in a way globalize the fight against crime.

DM & GM: Thank you for your time.

AJ: You are welcome.

The Police in Slovenia

General

The Slovene Police had departed from the totally centralized management of the Yugoslav Federation to complete independence in 1991. A new Constitution and numerous new laws were passed, which extended to the field of state administration and especially the field of human rights protection. The organizational structure changed, as did its name. In 1992 the Militia became the Police. The Slovene Police wanted to become a modern institution, shaped by European criteria. The Police Act, enacted on July 18, 1998, provided the legal basis for the establishment of the police as an autonomous body within the Ministry of the Interior. Through this, the police acquired a high degree of autonomy, especially in the field of the performance of police tasks and police powers.

Three-Level Organization

The police perform tasks on three levels: the national, regional, and local levels. From an organizational point, the police are composed of the General

Police Directorate, 11 regional Police Directorates, 106 police stations and (50) police offices. The Slovenian Police headquarters is situated in Ljubljana. All together, Slovenian police consist of around 9,000 uniformed and 900 plainclothes police officers.

The General Police Directorate performs the regulative, coordinating, and supervisory functions needed for the functioning of the entire police; police directorates perform the same function at regional and local levels. Police stations take care of security on local levels and carry out more than 90% of all police tasks. Within the General Police Directorate are (among others) the Directorate of Uniformed Police, Directorate of Criminal Police, Center for Forensic Examinations, Special Unit, Police Academy, and others. Criminal police are responsible for major criminal investigations in the country (about 20% of all criminal offenses) and are also located at all regional police directorates. Most criminal offenses are therefore handled by the uniformed police.

The police are headed by the director general of the police, who is also the manager of the General Police Directorate. Besides this he or she also coordinates, directs, and supervises the work of organizational units of the police and internal organizational units of the General Police Directorate, ensures the legitimate performance of police tasks, issues regulations and other acts for which he or she is empowered, decrees measures and decides on compliance with law or regulations, issued on the basis of laws. The director general answers to the minister for his or her work and for the work of the police. Thus, the Government of the Republic of Slovenia may discharge the director general upon the minister's proposal. The director general has a deputy.

Endnotes

1. Mr. Jevšek defended, on November 30, 2007, his MA/LLM thesis on "Fear of Crime and Attitudes towards Punishment in the Context of Contemporary Dangers, Risks and Uncertainties." (The thesis was co-supervised by Dr. Kanduč and Dr. Meško.)

Interview with Director Jeremy Vearey of the South African Police Service, Mitchell's Plain, Cape Town, South Africa

12

INTERVIEWED BY ELRENA VAN DER SPUY

Background

In the early 1990s, as negotiations towards a political settlement in South Africa began, the issue of police reform crept onto the agenda. Across the border, the Namibian experience of security reform provided some useful pointers and a fair measure of optimism to the policy elites at home. In April 1994 the first multiparty democratic elections were held. Shortly thereafter a Government of National Unity was formed. The South African Police Services Act of 1995 consolidated the new legal parameters within which the public police agency of the new constitutional democracy was to operate. A retrospective assessment of the trials and tribulations of police reform in South Africa is bound to emphasize the complexities involved in a process that aimed at translating the broad principles of democracy into everyday police practice.

In 1995 Jeremy Vearey, an African National Congress (ANC) intelligence operative and former cadre of its military arm (*Umkhonto we Sizwe*—MK for short), became one of a small group of "lateral entrants" into the South African Police Service. Symbolically, the entry of these personnel into the police signified a variation on the theme of post-conflict experiments in amalgamation and integration of former adversaries into unitary structures.

Vearey's career within the police organization took off first in the crime intelligence and special investigations environment. Thereafter he became station commissioner at various police stations in the Western Cape, followed by a spell as area deputy commissioner. Currently he is director of the police station in Mitchell's Plain, a large dormitory suburb of Cape Town and formerly a segregated "colored" area. At Mitchell's Plain, Vearey has faced the challenge of policing a high-density urban area where the legacies of socioeconomic deprivation and political marginalization have bred large-scale destitution reflected in high crime rates and gang activity. Mitchell's

Plain has been selected as one of the nodes within the National Urban Renewal Strategy which aims at reducing historic inequalities and improving the quality of life of residents. Against the broader background of political change on the one hand and the continuities of socioeconomic inequalities on the other, Jeremy Vearey speaks to a number of thematic issues of concern to this volume: of far-reaching changes in policing philosophy and policy, in structure, management style, and operational practices as the police organization began to adapt to a new political era of constitutionality amid growing concern about public insecurity.

The Interview

The interview was conducted on April 14, 2008 in the multimedia seminar room of the Centre of Criminology at the University of Cape Town. The room has a wide-angled view of Table Mountain, that icon of international tourism. To the northeast of this location lie the sprawling townships of Cape Town, consisting of shack lands, council estates, and a mixture of lower- and middle-class suburbs. The interview lasted for three and a half hours. The discussion was wide ranging and touched on many details regarding a complex process of organizational change. Extensive editing was undertaken so as to structure the discussion under thematic headings. Two further conversations followed during which issues were clarified and the text finalized.

EVDS: Can you tell me about your past and how you came to be a police officer?

JV: I was born in 1963 in Elsies River, a working class area on the Cape Flats, which after the forced removals of the 1950s became "home" to large numbers of the so-called colored population. I became politically conscious through my mother who was at the time actively involved in the Garment Workers' Union. Through this exposure I was provided with a unionist type of understanding of politics that was socialist in orientation. At the age of 20 I was recruited into the military wing of the African National Congress, *Umkhonto we Sizwe*. I qualified as a teacher in 1984 at the University of the Western Cape [the designated university for coloreds at the time]. My involvement in the formation of the Western Cape Teachers' Union led to my suspension by the education department in 1985. In 1987, after I started teaching again I was arrested, went on trial with 15 other *Umkhonto we Sizwe* members, and was sentenced to imprisonment on Robben Island. In June 1990 I was part of a phased release process of political prisoners and became active in the intelligence wing of the ANC.

In the ANC's intelligence circles we were then primarily concerned with opposing state intelligence agencies involved in attempts to destabilize the ANC and engineer conflict in the townships. We also focused on recruitment of sources within state structures to extract information of benefit to the ANC, identified state informers within ANC structures, and were responsible for protection of the national leadership of the ANC. In 1992 we started focusing on the integration of ANC intelligence officers into the National Intelligence Service and the military of the apartheid state. We did not at the time prioritize integration into the South African Police. As political negotiations got underway I was first employed in the national intelligence environment. In the course of the early 1990s, however, we discovered that security police structures, in particular covert intelligence units, posed a real challenge. Those units continued to fight covert wars with the sole purpose to neutralize the ANC's influence in a particular area. As a consequence, these units within the police became our primary adversaries. In mid-1993 it was decided that key individuals should start engaging the covert side of the police, that is, the security police directly. Such an engagement had two purposes in mind: first, to try and stop this engineering of conflict situations, and second to start preparing the police for integration from the side of the liberation armies.

By then some of us were already in the National Intelligence Agency. We were asked to start preparing the cadres for engaging with the police agency. So in 1995 we went in as part of a strategic maneuver which was designed in political and police management circles. The Western Cape had the largest contingent of cadres—21 in total—who were integrated into the South African Police Service. Among the rank and file of the police, however, there was still a lot of hostility. At the time there was no clear program of demobilization or of integration. There was no acculturation process to speak of. It was a tense situation—understandably so. We're talking about people who were on the sharp edge of things with each other. Not all could cope with the situation. Some of us [i.e., the lateral entries] left. A lot of them too [the old guard] resigned from the intelligence environment. So the first phase of this amalgamation involved the deep end with the real adversaries who would have killed each other a few years earlier. Later, towards 1997, things started to change. The security police's influence declined ... As this happened some of us moved elsewhere in the organization. Some went into visible policing, others became detectives or got involved in intelligence structures.

EVDS: This process of integration must have been challenging?

JV: Yes, very. Training, however, provided a conducive context for building links. Most of us [lateral entries] received training both outside and while in service. But the actual police were in the same position in fact. Everybody, old and new, needed retraining. After 1994 you had a large number of "experienced detectives" who were used to unconstitutional ways of extracting information and evidence. Convictions in court often rested on confessions and point-outs [line-ups] which resulted in investigative tradecraft and professional evidence procurement methods being underdeveloped. They had to realign their approach. They too had to be retrained just like we had to be trained. So there was a lot of training at that point in time where we were jointly exposed to new ideas and new methods in the training environment. Back then in 1996 the course I did was for specialist detectives in the serious violent crimes environment. We came from very specialized units all across the country and it was something entirely new. We had to focus on the nitty-gritty of crime scene management and proper interrogation procedures. Things you never worried about before, you know, in the specialist tradition. For the first time investigators also received training in conducting organized crime investigations. Previously, detective training focused on crime scene-driven investigations methodology. Training in intelligence and process-driven methods of investigation required to investigate organized crime and commercial crime were underdeveloped. And so the specialist environment underwent a major change. One thing that was good about that change was that it was accompanied by retraining. Retraining did not focus only on one group such as newcomers for example, as opposed to other groups. It threw us all into the same pool for a period of a few months. Joint training cultivated a new investigative culture and created conditions conducive to integration.

EVDS: Looking back, what would you describe as the most critical changes in policing, in policing structure and methodology, that took place in South Africa after 1994?

JV: A number of changes really. What stands out in particular is the decentralization of command and control, particularly over resources. Formerly the South African Police had a culture of overcentralized decision making and bureaucratic control. The space now exists within the guidelines of policy, of course, to be much more creative in terms of our approaches to crime at the precinct level. The other critical change relates to certain major stations. We now have specialized units active at station level. We have our own vehicle theft investigation in Mitchell's Plain, we have child protection services, we have organized crime capacities. Previously these things were all centralized at a provincial level. Furthermore post-1994 these resources are now primarily servicing areas that they didn't service before. There's been a total reprioritization in terms of where specialist services are required and where 90% of the effort is going into capacitating them. We have greater control of our own budget at station level in respect of things like overtime and expenditure on resources. All of these things were done formerly at a stratospheric level, that is, at the area, provincial, or national level.

EVDS: That presupposes that you have good managers at stations?

JV: Yes. And that is also another part of the change. The result of bringing most of these specialized functions that come from specialized knowledge, including finances, from the provincial level, has meant that we needed to train more of our own station people at that particular level to have the specialized managerial skills. Furthermore, we had to restructure provincial offices and area offices so that the expertise that existed there is placed out to certain key stations. Key stations that would become what we call *accounting stations* around which other stations would be clustered. As managers we now have much more control over our resources and over processes that were far removed from us before. More control of course brings more responsibility. We basically run things as station commissioners now. Decentralized management and control has improved our capacity in the South African Police Service to micromanage according to local needs and ensure greater compliance with service delivery standards.

EVDS: What about the criticism that decentralization runs the risk of fragmenting and dissipating rather than building capacity?

JV: In terms of the answer to that question, I think the fragmentation argument assumes that you have a loss of information flow regarding threats that cross precinct borders. However, what this argument ignores is that we now have a centrally managed but station-level-accessible national electronic crime intelligence database. Information about trends that cut across our boundaries, our crime intelligence capacity, or the crime analysis capacity can be accessed from an integrated database. So there is not a loss of flow of information. We now do have access to extensive databases including those of other state departments such as Home Affairs. And there is a stronger culture currently of data capturing and of sharing information. At the area (or cluster) level we also integrate our intelligence efforts around specific crime problems such as hijacking, for example.

By the way, what is "specialized crime"? How do you distinguish that from normal crime? The other point is the type of crime. In a place like Mitchell's Plain 90% of the crime that makes people feel unsafe involves violence—violence perpetrated within the domestic environment. This requires that most of your resources need to be directed at solving that kind of crime. If most of your house break-ins have no organized element at all but primarily involve break-ins by sometimes parents, kids, or neighbors into their own homes to finance drug habits, then the resources need to be focused on that. Only 10% of crime at present involves specialized investigation because there are, of course, sophisticated drug dealers and car theft networks in Mitchell's Plain. When we do need a degree of specialization, it is task or project specific.

EVDS: What other changes in policing deserve mention?

JV: There is a further important change in policing that deserves mention, namely the shift to a crime prevention ethos in visible policing. Crime prevention in visible policing was not something we focused on in the early phase of police reform. In the past the emphasis in visible policing was restricted to attending to complaints, that is, it was entirely reactive. Within the Western Cape the shift to crime prevention within visible policing primarily came with the appointment of the existing provincial commissioner, Commissioner Petros. As part of a people-oriented strategy the emphasis became policing at a precinct level, which included building sustainable relationships with the community. This new ethos led to an emphasis on proactive visible policing and the implementation of sector policing. This approach was pursued particularly at "priority stations" that accounted for most violent crime, such as Khayelitsha, Elsies River, and so on. After 1995 many of us lateral entries found ourselves in the station environment. Some of these stations were still dumping grounds for "problematic people." Such stations were still poorly resourced.

Although community police forums existed, the engagement was superficial—not really qualitative. Community Police Forums (CPFs) became bureaucratized in the form of meetings and it didn't serve any productive purpose. People in these structures were not necessarily representative enough of the precinct area. Against this background we first focused on the role of the police inside the CPFs as a starting point for developing accountability towards the community. Police needed to play an active role in strengthening the CPFs in terms of its structure and representivity on the ground.

We focused on the development of more neighborhood watches and letting them become a sort of street sector based presence tied to the CPFs. Some of us took it a little bit further as in Mitchell's Plain with the establishment of a street committee system which also focuses on mobilization around the other underlying social crime issues and localized stakeholder representation more effectively.

Lastly, there have been very positive developments with regards to oversight. Now Community Police Forums are much more empowered. In Mitchell's Plain they attend our weekly meetings, where we brief them on crime. Also, even the relationship with the provincial government and local government has changed. We appear on their discussion forums in the form of community meetings called *imbizos*. These things never used to happen in the past. In the context of decentralization we cannot hide behind the central monster anymore. We are held much more accountable at the precinct level. The time of hiding behind the national commissioner is past. You do not have the past luxury of deferring every sensitive policing issue to a provincial or national communication department where airbrushed answers are provided in your defense. You deal with such issues yourself, directly with the community.

And the media ... let me talk a bit about the importance of engaging the media. Outside of the normal structural lines of accountability and oversight, there is a totally unpredictable wild card element that can come to your station, that can engage you, and can add a refreshing perspective to what you are doing. It is called the media. I believe that the media constitutes a territory that we must learn to engage with. It is a terrain where unpredictability makes it difficult to manufacture superficial responses.

Another challenge is for the South African Police Service to become more involved in the opinion-making processes, informal policy processes involving discussions about policing. I don't see oversight accountability only in terms of explaining what really went wrong, but also engagement around the policy issues of policing and research oriented thinking in policing. I mean we are doing ourselves a disservice. I say this because I know there are some very good strategic policy thinkers *inside* the police who just don't talk. They talk to each other yes, but I mean who could engage policy units and research institutes on the outside. The discourse on policing will be enriched if we stop talking only to ourselves and engage those who are talking about us from a policy-making or research perspective.

EVDS: Which raises a question about the role of research. Is there a need for greater synergy between research-based institutes and the police?

JV: Look, if our job only involved structured organized criminal threats requiring sensitive and covert investigations, then we would never have spoken to people in the research environment. But policing as it is now—particularly in an area such as Mitchell's Plain—involves social and economic factors in crime. The primary sources of insecurity in areas like Mitchell's Plain are social in nature. It is not robbery driven by organized criminals. It is robbery or house breaking driven by people who need money for *Tik* [local slang for methamphetamine]. So what I'm saying is the most prevalent forms of crime we confront in Mitchell's Plain are crimes influenced by socioeconomic factors. Such crimes require a type of analysis that can inform an integrated approach that goes way beyond the confines of what we as the South African Police Service can deliver. I'm always going to think as a cop when it comes to analyzing certain trends. As a cop I'm going to be dealing with the problem from a tactical perspective. But addressing the crime problems we confront requires much more than just a tactical approach. Dealing with such crimes requires research and knowledge that a wide variety of organizations working in the field can bring. We talk about the need for an integrated approach, but we do not really understand what it requires. Such an approach needs to be informed by further research that cuts beyond our sector-specific emphases or approaches. And that's where institutions like the Institute of Security Studies, NGOs, and even universities play a particular role because they can, through independent research findings, contribute an approach beyond our sectoral focus.

In engaging with drug addiction and domestic violence—both big issues for Mitchell's Plain—we need research to understand what is happening. Patterns have been changing. Rape and indecent assault used to happen in the context of public spaces, often with gangs involved. Now the rapes that you see are in the domestic environment and make up 70% to 90% of those crimes. The indecent assaults happen in the home. Our highest percentage of rape cases come from the domestic context. Fathers and boyfriends: that's the profile of rape perpetrators in Mitchell's Plain now. Cases of indecent assault still happen in schools. But most of it we pick up in the domestic environment. Now that requires research to identify predisposing factors at play. In the past we didn't see it for we were all too focused on gangs, gang violence, and organized crime. Crimes in the private spheres have become more visible. I believe that one of the challenges is developing an integrated approach suited to this. That requires a much greater emphasis on social crime prevention strategies undertaken in collaboration with other government departments. But not only at a level up "there" of planning, but at a level where we start looking at actual integrated delivery at the local level.

EVDS: What about the challenge of social crime prevention? Is this an area of concern to you as station commissioner in Mitchell's Plain?

JV: Very important. Let me use the Mitchell's Plain example. If we talk about the Safer Schools Strategy we are involved in, it's not a publicity driven event that we go and speak about at schools. It is no longer cosmetic stuff at the level of fancy displays and glossy leaflets. The Safer Schools Strategy involves working with youth at risk, and using our intelligence operatives to identify, at particular schools, those potential "trouble makers" or future gangsters. I then try to target those groups directly for involvement in social diversionary programs. We have one in soccer and another in pool. Both are very popular sports which are practiced on the streets or in *shebeens* [informal drinking places] which expose youth to gangs. We've started reviving certain legitimate pool clubs. Currently we have 12 active police officers trained as soccer coaches or trained pool champions who do nothing else but work on diversionary activities with youth at risk. Prior to 1994, it would have been taboo to ever think about a police officer wearing a uniform being involved in playing soccer or pool—something that others would not perceive to be classically associated with a police officer in uniform. But with these diversionary programs it became essential to allocate 12 police officers to do just that. This has been worth much more than trying to put another police vehicle on the street. We have 16 vans 24 hours in Mitchell's Plain. Compare this to the previous era where we had only four police vans. Another van on the street was not going to make a difference to youth-related crime in the area. Now if you're dealing with the kind of youth population we have in Mitchell's Plain—if you have five fights at 10 schools out of 77 schools in the area you have most of the crimes for the week. So you must prioritize the youth in schools. Apart from the fact that they become gangsters at a later stage, you must prioritize dealing with aggressive types of criminality at the schools in social diversion programs. So it justifies us allocating our police officers to that exclusively and they only work with youth.

EVDS: Is this approach home-grown or are you drawing on experiences elsewhere?

JV: When I arrived at Mitchell's Plain in April 2007, some police officers had been to the UK, the Metropolitan Police, and elsewhere. There they became involved in diversionary programs involving cadets and all those kinds of things. They came back here and tried to transplant the model in exactly the same way. It didn't quite get off the ground. While doing so they were still tied to other functional policing duties and didn't have the type of time required. When I arrived, I recognized the limitations. For example, there was little engagement on the part of the community. The police were trying to come in as an external force into the school. The time was not quite right for there was at the time still a lot of hostility in Mitchell's Plain towards police officers.

The police also didn't engage the Western Cape education department or the educators. I knew some people in education—people I taught with in Mitchell's Plain in 1987. By 2007 they were quite senior figures. We opened up a discussion forum in Mitchell's Plain. We started engaging these issues and I started talking to them every Monday morning, engaging teachers and just trying to get a feel for how teachers think about these issues. It took us a month or two to break the ice. Thereafter we started working at schools openly. Now we can go into the school and kids won't jump around thinking that we're coming to do a raid. In fact I stopped raids at schools. I told the principals that I was going to do that. The raids were quite common—drug raids and other kinds of raids.

EVDS: This sounds like a change in policing method?

JV: Yes. I explained to the principals that I was no longer going to conduct blanket raids. If they had information about a particular group of students they would have to put that in a statement. We would take that statement and apply for a search warrant targeting a specific classroom or venue involving a particular group of students. The big raids where everybody goes out onto the school field may scare some people but it really doesn't work. Instead I explained that 12 school officers have been appointed and 12 sector commanders. Our emphasis is going to be engagement with the community in a sustainable way. We are not going to be seen as *sticks* (i.e., enforcers). If a principal has a discipline problem with some kids it's of little use using the police as a threat because such an approach is not sustainable. School raids all too often come at the cost of our engagement with youth.

On the other hand we insisted that crimes on the school ground should not be handled informally—like in the case of sexual offenses. We told them that crime is crime in our jurisdiction everywhere, including schools. So we are going to make greater attempts to find out what type of criminality is prevalent in schools. We are not only interested in the break-ins. We are interested in other types of crimes affecting the youth especially, crimes of aggression and crimes against women in particular. For

school principals to resolve sexual offenses informally would constitute itself a criminal offense and defeats the ends of justice. We
have a much more open relationship now. Down to a fight in the
school yard, our school officers will know what is happening. This
strategy has brought about a decline in school-related crime. We
don't have that many incidents and where we are more organized
you can see that we actually do weekly analyses of school-based
incidences in Mitchell's Plain. I measure the officers' performance
by the absence of school-related crime and by the success of the
youth diversion programs. Mitchell's Plain crimes now, or in the
last 6 months at least, are domestic. The most violent people are
the people who live together in their houses. That's where most of
our sources come from. At present the violent crime threat doesn't
come from gangsters.

EVDS: Why is that? Is it a change from what used to be?

JV: Yes. I think gangsters realized that if you fight you attract too much sup-
pression from the state. Constant operational focus is bad for a
business like drug dealing. So people rather prefer to steer away
from those types of conflicts. In Mitchell's Plain, for example, I
know of some gang leaders who say that they are going to sort out
the problems *outside* of Mitchell's Plain. The other thing is drug
turf. Things are fairly structured and settled in Mitchell's Plain.
It's unlike an area like Delft, for example, which is relatively new.
In Delft drug dealers are still trying to establish control over territory. Then it becomes a very volatile situation. In Delft there are at
present too many crooks battling for control. In contrast Mitchell's
Plain is fairly settled, also because gangsters have expanded into
legal businesses outside Mitchell's Plain—as in the property market. So our policing of drugs follows two pathways: at the one point,
we try to strangle the business by executing three warrants in a
24-hour cycle at unpredictable times. In addition to that, through
the information we get from the street committees we are able to
identify clearly the customer clientele. So what we do is to target
those individuals. Sector commanders are involved in street-level
mobilization against the drug dealers.

People do very creative things in Mitchell's Plain. For example,
older people would be standing around a drum fire close to a drug
outlet. They would then intercept all "customers" of drug dealers.
This actually resulted in the closure of drug outlets combined with
strategically timed raids when the community (drum fire) squads
were not there. This achieved better results than any exclusive
police tactics.

EVDS: What are the key challenges confronting the South African Police Service in the near future?

JV: I think internally a critical challenge is to continue the decentralization process, bringing down to cluster and station levels all the specialized abilities. Every station should have its crime intelligence capacity. Every station should have its organized crime specialist capacity. Bringing those core skills, those disciplines of policing and actually start to locate them at every single station. Every station should have its crime intelligence capacity. So that's the challenge, to extend what we are doing now further.

At the community level the challenge is to ensure greater representation of CPFs, because at the moment in some areas it is uneven, in other areas it's fairly well developed, in other areas it's just intellectuals who think about community policing. You know it takes various forms but is nowhere near the levels of stakeholder representation that is required on the ground, especially on the Cape Flats. In general, dealing with youth at risk requires integrated police training involving other stakeholders and institutions as well as diversionary programs that are sustainable and regular, not event oriented.

EVDS: You have spoken a lot about the routine nature of crime in Mitchell's Plain. What about transnational crime in the context of globalization?

JV: Transnational crime—that's another one of those constructs that we use all the time without much clarity as to what we actually mean by it. Before globalization we spoke about multinational syndicates and we gave it a neat little structure with somebody at the top with some "Hollywood" understanding of cross-border criminal activity. Prior to 1994 we saw a Nigerian and thought he was tied to some syndicate links. But things have changed. First, Mitchell's Plain has a lot of immigrants—illegal and legal. There are Somalians and Nigerians and many others. Some of them are involved in the same type of criminal activities that the locals are involved in. For example, Chinese nationals who are involved in counterfeit Levis and Lacoste clothing that they sell openly from shops. It fits in with our prejudices, our assumptions about the so-called Chinese or Nigerians or Somalians, but it doesn't translate to them being part of some transnational syndicate or international network, you understand.

We are dealing with a type of criminality that is common even if it had been perpetrated by a local. Some people are a little bit more skillful at putting these things together out of experience, but not as an example of being part of some global syndicate. The Nigerians, they have been involved in selling cocaine in the town center like the others sell coke. But nothing makes them distinctively transnational. The Somalians are ingenious business people who basically undercut the competition because of their methods of selling. They sell teaspoons of sugar, and make much more profit. They sell two slices of bread, which is an amazing business technique, and they have come to dominate the informal market. Well, there may be something problematic about the way they sell things from a commercial crime point of view but it doesn't make them distinctively different from what the little shop around the corner in Mitchell's Plain is doing. So what I'm saying is, the presence of foreign nationals or legal or illegal immigrants' involvement in criminality is not distinctively different from what is there anyway. And second it does not reflect, to me, from what I've seen, any globalized kind of pattern. We do not speak about Somalian organized crime. Crime is crime.

In terms of our precinct the only transnational crime that we have picked up of late involves counterfeit cigarettes involving cross-border smuggling. This is a thriving business where syndicates operate. The dominant drug in the area, *Tik*, is locally made. You don't need to import methaqualone from China and all those things. When it comes to the profile of drug suspects we have pensioners, middle-aged persons with big families, and many others.

EVDS: In your depiction of the policing strategy in Mitchell's Plain, the emphasis is placed on the service aspect and on community consultation. What exactly is the role of force?

JV: Force should only ever be utilized commensurate with the force that you face. It is not a policing methodology. It's one of those tools used when the situation justifies it and requires it. The militarism part of it shouldn't be part of our contact with the public. The public should not respect me because I wear a gun on myself all day, or because I have military insignia upon my shoulders, or because I march in a particular way. They must respect me for the way I engage them. That's one of the things sector policing has changed. The Safer Schools Project in Mitchell's Plain took police officers totally outside of their normal role or the way they perceived the role to be. So when it comes to the use of force, there's a place for it commensurate with threat that you face. Of course there's a need for specialized capacities like the task force that might be more militarized in its approach so as to deal with hostage situations or bank robberies. There's a place for that. Practical police officers know that 9 times out of 10 you can get out of a confrontational situation by engaging psychologically and using your street sense, not by pulling a gun. If, however the situation is life threatening and I have to use this gun then I have to.

The culture is changing. At the station we don't believe in strutting around and looking dangerous. The macho or bravado part of the image is not really what is having an effect. What is affecting Mitchell's Plain is our community emphasis and improving service delivery—not looking more threatening.

What I can tell you in the beginning at most stations I worked at I reintroduced a culture of walking, of foot patrol. We all know foot patrol is not going to stop a hijacker. One of the reasons I engaged in foot patrol is because it is a technique to break fear—fear that is informed by a fortified mentality in the police service, in the police station. We get into this van and we drive out there and then we come back. You want to break that mentality. You put the police person on the street. You engage people, ask them how they are. The change shocks them at first. You are more effective than in 10 vans driving at 100 km per hour attending to complaints the whole day. It creates an important way of relating. Now in Mitchell's Plain, people come to our crime meetings. We put up our crime statistics. We discuss people we are looking for. It is normal now.

EVDS: How does this approach work with members of gangs? Does this approach extend to gangs?

JV: Gangs … there's a different type of policing that is required for people who constitute that particular type of threat. Gangs standing around in front of a *shebeen* or taking up posts, represent a paramilitary threat whether they are protecting a particular drug dealer or whether they are protecting themselves from another gang. You deal with that type of threat differently. You expect that the threat will be armed so the emphasis should be regular stop searches, regular disruption of activity. That's our approach because in the eyes of the community they look powerful as they stand on the street corner. Stop searches are standard where we are dealing with gangsters and drug dealers and are directed at disrupting their attempts to mark down their turf through loitering on a particular corner or manifest their presence to others in an intimidating fashion.

Gangs are a force of regulation among each other. I used to have meetings with gangs to make them understand how conflict is going to affect everybody's business. My line was if you are going to fight about turf we will remove all of your soldiers off the street. Who will then fight your wars? A third person will move in and take over. Those are the type of things that people understood. So the regulatory part is internal. I do not think it must be confused with thinking of gangs as informal social ordering structures. The new breed in the gang/drug world are people who steer away from tattooing their faces, steer away from only hanging out, driving

BMWs and selling cocaine, because if they sell cocaine, they need to sell in more affluent suburbs so they obviously have to look at this, their network, their identity has to be different. So you are dealing with a different type of person at the moment. So the gang identity is used more for business purposes rather than for traditional ones.

EVDS: What about the unspoken difficulties of policing—the things that make you lie awake at night?

JV: Not much. There were threats against me in the beginning when I came to Mitchell's Plain. But that threat you deal with. I think gangs are predictable, drug dealers are predictable. To me the most unpredictable criminal in Mitchell's Plain these days is your *Tik* addict. If you intercept a *Tik* addict, immediately after he or she has bought the fix the person fights and that's the difference here. The addicts, the *Tik* users are all unpredictable. The *Tik* profile comes with a whole lot of unpredictability. Then it often becomes an arrest involving the use of force. They fight to keep their *Tik*. Gangsters know where they stand with us. We know where we stand with them. They don't make threats against police officers. They understand. But *Tik* addicts don't fit the classical profile of addicts.

EVDS: What in your view is the definition of a good cop?

JV: I think it is one who understands that the solution to any form of crime and the prevention thereof in the majority of cases is determined by the relationship with the community as opposed to dependence on highly specialized technology. Most of our crime in this country requires that you need to go look for and engage people. It's not enough to only stand on the crime scene with the best technological tools of processing evidence. The approach needs to be people-centered. I personally found that through the street committees and neighborhood watches we increased our solving rate in Mitchell's Plain. The people constitute a resource in terms of information. The solution of any crime you know lies with an approach that engages people, including the hostile suspect and hesitant witness. You know, no crime takes place without something being seen. Witnesses often don't realize the significance of what they see. Now the approach is that nothing is invisible, something must be seen no matter how insignificant, whether it's a car driving too fast in the street. That type of approach changes the investigation practice to an approach that says I'm going to first do surveillance and study the pattern of sound, the pattern of movement in this particular area to identify potential sources of information similar to the time when the crime occurred. And that requires an intelligence-driven approach and method.

EVDS: What in your experience has made the profession of policing personally satisfying?

JV: You know with me, I was born in the Cape Flats environment where the police never serviced the community. To me part of the satisfaction lay in the opportunity to be part of transforming the police, to be part of a process that developed within a new creative space. The other part of it in terms of the community was to change community conceptions about the police. And to try and prove to the community that we are a different entity from what existed prior to 1994. It has been exciting to see that people are able to speak with us differently and not speak of us in the same terms as they've spoken of us before. Mind you, all police services in the world underwent a change in the post-Cold War era. Most police forces had capacities that also involved political policing which defined their perceived identity. The UK had its special branch, Northern Ireland its Royal Ulster Constabulary. In Latin America and in the United States each had different capacities that involved political policing at a centralized level. In South Africa after 1990 we became part of an international approach based on what Robert Peel intended us to be: protecting the community from crimes that affect their safety and security. I find it a creative environment. In this climate everything is new, somewhat unpredictable, and very challenging.

EVDS: Are there enough people like you?

JV: There are a lot of people. Even the recruits. We now have matriculants, others with degrees who are eager to join the police—in the context of unemployment. The recruitment pool includes much more educated people than what they were before. In the long term we will be able to produce more quality together with new approaches to management training. We are going to produce a type of police management with a community-centered corporate approach to service delivery. There's a new generation with a strong community ethic that thinks beyond the issues we had to struggle with in the past. We are growing into positions of management as opposed to political placement where Afrikaner *Broederbond* membership or Free Mason pedigree determined senior appointment. The process is much more positive.

EVDS: And pockets of resistance within the police organization?

JV: Not much now. Look, in the early 1990s, when we came in, it was battle after battle, mind games involving the media and out maneuvering inside the system. It's different now. Where you have elements of resistance it is more likely tied to people's personal ambitions rather than a politically hidden agenda. Even in the crime intelligence environment we've began to find each other as police officers. In the Western Cape police environment things have opened up. This used to be the home of colored police officers and white police officers. In the past recruitment used to be "local," that is, restricted to people in the area. The only people who were mobile were security police officers. Now it's changed. We get intakes from the Eastern Cape, from the Northern Cape, from Mpumalanga, and all those places. That's one important way in which we have changed. In the Western Cape in particular, the demographics of the police have changed dramatically, it is more diverse than any other province. So we are exposed much more to diversity and I think it has positively contributed to much more cultural tolerance.

EVDS: Thank you.

Glossary

Broederbond **(translated as Afrikaner Brotherhood):** An elite and secret society founded in 1918, which consisted of Afrikaner cultural leaders who had as their central objective the advancement of the cultural, political, and economic interests of Afrikaners.

CPFs: In terms of provisions contained in the South African Police Services Act of 1995, Community Police Forums became key institutional mechanisms for entrenching community policing at the local level.

Imbizo: A forum for dialogue and interaction. The origin of the word is Zulu meaning "a gathering" or "a coming together."

Shebeen: Informal drinking houses.

Tik: Local slang for methamphetamine.

Umkhonto we Sizwe (MK): Translated as "Spear of the Nation," MK constituted the military wing of the ANC. Launched in 1961, it became involved in guerrilla warfare against the apartheid state until the early 1990s.

Interview with Dr. Monica Bonfanti, Chief of the Geneva Cantonal Police, Switzerland

13

INTERVIEWED BY DOMINIQUE WISLER

Introduction

In the preamble to the interview with Geneva police chief Monica Bonfanti, a brief overview of the policing system and the history of Switzerland and Geneva will provide the reader with contextual elements to better grasp issues and concerns raised during the interview.

Switzerland, in broad terms, can be described as a progressive, locally based association of free territories which, once in the Confederation, remained jealous of their political autonomy. The 1848 federal constitution, never amended fundamentally later on, was born out of a compromise between modernism and conservatism. The new federal constitution left policing (the reproducing of order) and education matters (the reproducing of culture) to cantons while Switzerland became integrated economically as a single entity. The cantonal monopoly over policing was never seriously challenged in recent Swiss history. A federal layer crystallized nevertheless at the end of the last century, following pressure by Chancellor Bismarck and Prussian authorities on Swiss authorities to pursue anarchist and communist exiles in Switzerland and, later, by fears over propaganda efforts by European fascist countries. The federal police, created in 1935, was initially entrusted with the mission of protecting the state. The federal level of policing achieved more consistency in 1994 when responsibilities for organized crime were legally transferred to the federal police. Since 2002, the federal police has had its own investigative capacity in matters of organized crime. Despite these advances, the reality of policing in Switzerland remains one of strong cantons and a weak Confederation.

The Geneva cantonal constitution and its police have been heavily influenced by a short historical period of French occupation and annexation under Napoleon Bonaparte, from 1799 to 1814. At that time, Geneva became a French "prefecture." The French influence survived the defeat of Bonaparte and the recovery, sealed by the Vienna Treaty of 1815, of the sovereignty of Switzerland. Geneva is proud of being a "republic," and its institutions, modeled on the French republic, are highly centralized. While many other Swiss cantons have granted localities a high level of communal autonomy, this has not been the case in Geneva. While Geneva allowed the creation of municipal police services in the canton, their authority and competencies have been very limited. In contrast, other cantons, such as Vaud, Zurich, or Bern, granted their municipalities extensive policing competencies.

The French imprimatur can further be seen in the Geneva police institution itself. The gendarmerie created in 1799 in Geneva survived Bonaparte's defeat in 1814. French gendarmes were eventually rehired by the new Geneva authorities. A judiciary police (Police de Sûreté) was created only much later, in 1892. More recently, a major organizational reform took place in 2001 when a new division was created in the Geneva cantonal police: the International Security Police. The division deals with the security of diplomats, the European seat of the United Nations, and the airport. The Geneva cantonal police employ 1300 police officers and 400 civilians. It is one of the largest organizations among the 26 cantonal police forces in Switzerland.

There are therefore three levels of policing in Switzerland: the locality or communal level, the cantonal level, and the federal or national level. In recent years, a fourth level has been added through associations of cantons, the so-called concordats.

Monica Bonfanti was appointed by the Geneva authorities—the Conseil d'Etat—as Geneva cantonal police chief in August 2006. She had not applied for the job, but was hand-picked by the new cantonal Minister ("Conseiller d'Etat") in charge of the police. In the press conference announcing her nomination, the minister spoke of "fresh air," "a needed elevation of spirit," and "a rare person." The Geneva police had just experienced unusually turbulent times at the top of its hierarchy. The last two incumbents of the position had resigned after serving only short periods. Successively, the ministers in charge of the Geneva police had lost their reelection bids. In a few years, the police image had plunged, with only 57% of the public "satisfied" with the overall performance of the police in 2004, a level well below the national average of satisfaction with police services in Switzerland (67% "satisfied"). What could account for such turbulence in the otherwise quiet and bucolic city at the end of the lake of Geneva? One can only speculate over the factors at play, among these a rising criminality (in 2005, the rate of increase was 6.7%), recurring public controversies over abuse of police authority in the streets, public perceptions of racism within the ranks of the police, or the controversy over the preparation and the handling of the protest in Geneva during the G8 meeting at Evian.

Chief Bonfanti is the first female officer to occupy the position of police chief in Geneva. Chief Bonfanti is young. At only 36 years of age, she is the cadet (youngest member) in the association of the police chiefs in Switzerland. Unlike most chiefs in the common law countries, Monica Bonfanti did not start at the bottom of the hierarchy. She entered laterally when she was selected for the position as head of the forensic laboratory of the cantonal police of Geneva in 2000. After graduating from the School of Criminal Sciences in Lausanne, she wrote a PhD dissertation on ballistics, and subsequently became lecturer and substituted as an assistant professor at the University of Lausanne. Her list of publications is impressive. She has published several books, including a massive co-edited textbook in 2006 with the title *Forensic Investigation of Stolen-Recovered Vehicles and Crime-Related Vehicles*, published by the Academic Press, Burlington. In parallel to her academic career, she has worked for several forensic laboratories in Switzerland and the Netherlands. Chief Bonfanti is an accomplished sportswoman. She won the Swiss championship of synchronized artistic skating in 1989 and represents the French-speaking cantons in the commission overseeing skating at the famous Federal Sport School of Macolin, Switzerland. Chief Bonfanti is well versed in languages, speaking fluent Italian, French, German, English, and Dutch. Her vitae speaks for itself. She has a contagious enthusiasm, is highly energetic, and possesses a good dose of refreshing spontaneity.

The interview took place on January 5, 2007 in her office.

Managing Change

Given her still fresh nomination at the time of the interview, her vision over necessary "changes" and her priorities for the next 5 years is the first topic we focus on. In her diagnosis of the Geneva police organization, Chief Bonfanti identified productivity as an issue. The "machine," she observed, "gives the impression of being heavy and too slow." One of the main reasons is its overly vertical compartmentalization into three operational services.

> For over a century, the Geneva police has been comprised of a large gendarmerie and a judiciary police. We then added an international security police. Then, you have what has become the "poor parents" of the police, that is the general services which, among other tasks, provide the logistics for other services. The result of all this is a highly compartmentalized organization and, too often, it is simply forgotten that everybody works for the same organization, the Geneva cantonal police.
>
> This overly vertical internal organization of the police needs to be revisited. In addition, while past reforms have concentrated on public services or operational divisions, such as rapid intervention, community policing, or criminal investigation divisions, other divisions, the so-called support processes or "general services," have been neglected. They are the "poor child" of the organization. But more solid support processes are a key for productivity.

One also forgets very basic principles of management. If we want that the people at the front of the organization perform their tasks correctly, you need strong logistics to back them up. If you look at the Vietnam War, for one person operating at the front you had 10 others in support. At home, here, we have forgotten these lessons. We perhaps give the impression that we do a good job at the front, but, behind the stage, the reality is that all this gets a bit diluted because the support services are lagging behind.

We need to move in this new direction. This implies a change of vision, a change in our conception of basic training, an upgrading of courses, and, above all, we cannot forget the civilian personnel. Usually, these personnel are less valued by the organization despite the fact that they are essential to the quality of the services delivered at the front. A police service is the result of a successful, continuous, and coherent chain of activities. This is where I intend to concentrate my efforts.

Today, complains Chief Bonfanti, there is a "reflex" to put new problems into predefined operational "boxes":

What is too often the case is that when you want to introduce a change everybody starts to think about who is best suited for the job. Someone will say "Ah! This is a job for the judiciary police" or "No! This is rather something for the gendarmerie." From now on, we will start thinking more in terms of missions that all should carry out. This is the reflex that I am expecting.

Working strategically on shared visions and organizationally on developing the concept of task forces where units from various divisions collaborate closely together, that will become more of the mainstream in the future. The experiences with the "drug task force" and other task forces are mentioned by Chief Bonfanti as being models. Services, in particular perhaps support services, will become more integrated. With this philosophy in mind, she has already started a reorganization of the intelligence services. Intelligence has been compartmentalized along the main operational divisions of the police.

There are currently three intelligence groups in the Geneva cantonal police, one in each main operational division. Intelligence dealing with federal issues is mainly performed by the Judiciary Police (and more recently by the International Security Police) while intelligence regarding local events is dealt with by the gendarmerie.

In her opinion, however, "intelligence is a cross-cutting issue and needs to be coordinated." Consequently, "I have initiated the reorganization of the intelligence services at the Geneva cantonal police in order to improve internal coordination. As intelligence is gathered today by three services, I have decided to introduce a coordination mechanism with a senior officer who will head all three services." He or she will begin work on March 1, 2007.

Community Policing

Community policing, or as it is known in French-speaking countries, *police de proximité* (proximity policing), is another priority of Chief Bonfanti. Community policing starts with the analysis of the expectations of the public. A key instrument is the so-called Local Diagnostic of Security, an analytic instrument whose core is represented by a survey of public images of the police, day-to-day security of residents and their expectations with regards to police services.

> It is clear to me that the so-called Local Diagnostic of Security is among the instruments that allow us to identify priorities. They are very important. The LDS allows us to collect information on the social demand on security issues and to analyze the image of the police.

Paradoxically, she observes, community policing might not translate operationally into more neighborhood police stations. Indeed, in the Local Diagnostic of Security:

> We learn that when confronted with a problem, the public wants rapid intervention by the police whether it comes by foot, on the back of a horse, or on a bicycle. This observation has led us to revisit the concept of local police stations. What is more important? A local police station? A rapid, highly mobile intervention mechanism, so as to provide a response to a call for service without delays? These reflections will guide our discussion about the future of policing in Geneva given our ultimate objective to improve our performance on the ground and ensure a better fit with the expectations of the public.

Consequently, Chief Bonfanti is currently working on a model where the two main parts of Geneva city, the right and the left banks, will be serviced by one main police station, open 24 hours, with "proper waiting rooms" and most specialized services at hand. "We already respond to most calls for service in a highly professional manner," she adds, "let us not be afraid to be effective in our approach." At the same time, experiences with so-called "policiers de proximité" or community policing officers has been highly successful. There is no intention to dismantle this service:

> We have several local police stations and in these stations we have community policing officers. This deployment has proven its value. In these local police stations, a high number of issues can be dealt with. Without this service, here, at the headquarters, we could not decrease the size of "minor dispute services" by a factor of 10 or 20. It is necessary to maintain this linkage with the public. I find this important.

The Dynamics of Federalism

The Local Level

Coordination is a permanent concern for a cantonal police chief in the Swiss policing system. A first level deals with municipal security agencies. Currently, she recalls, the "Municipal Security Agents (MSA) [police employed by local communities] as they are known in Geneva, do not have the status of police officers, which requires they be accredited by a federal certificate." "There are many discussions around the very notion of municipal police," she confesses. This discussion involves "chapel quarrels" around issues such as "whether they should carry weapons or not." The real questions are of a more fundamental character. It is an issue of "leadership," "coordination," and "efficiency." Coordination is limited by day-to-day practical factors which, she argues, have operational implications and create misunderstandings and dissatisfaction within the ranks:

> Otherwise, we will have again silos of competences, organizational divisions, and we see that when there are joint operations, well, each silo has its own rotation shifts, its own imperatives, and all this creates a sense of dissatisfaction among the collaborators. Officers do not understand the reasons for these differences. They are with a partner; now this partner goes back to his or her office and can write 10 extra hours, the other only 5. For the first one, the bus is paid, for the other not. As supervisors in the police, possibly these things may appear marginal. However, they can have important effects on the level of satisfaction of officers with their job.

For all these reasons, she considers that an intelligent solution is the absorption into a cantonal structure, as this seems to be the path followed by a number of Swiss cantons such as Bern, Neuchâtel, or Vaud:

> We see that in other cantons there is the reverse trend. One wishes rather to create a single cantonal structure, strong, and efficient to coordinate all this. I would find it more clever and more coherent to have one single cantonal police strong enough to coordinate and federate other institutions.

While absorption or, at least a more integrated system, seems reasonable for practical reasons, Chief Bonfanti emphasizes at the same time that, at the policy level, the collaboration with municipal security agencies is excellent and that the cantonal leadership has never been challenged:

> We have the same doctrine. We have the possibility to move jointly towards the same goal, toward the same mission. I can picture myself easily defining the mission and all of us will implement it. In this context, I can mention joint campaigns promoting road safety like the "Foresee" campaign which

involved the Municipal Agents of Security (MAS). The MAS have fewer competencies than our gendarmes. However they are there, they do what they are expected to do in the same spirit as the cantonal police. What is important is that everyone accept one single leadership. It goes without saying that if one says that this is important and others deny this, we will never be efficient on the ground. I would say that collaboration is working well. The leadership role of the cantonal police is well accepted and we have a single chain of command. Mentally, this allows us to reach common goals.

The National Level

Chief Bonfanti expresses more impatience with the federal level of coordination. In some areas, such as intelligence, the daily collaboration with federal agencies runs "smoothly":

> It is clear that we have intelligence services at the cantonal police of Geneva. These services work in close collaboration with the federal level and it is the federal level that maintains contacts internationally in Europe and in the world. We evaluate the local security situation. In my opinion, if we discuss the collaboration with the federal level in this regard, it works well. We are satisfied with the work done at the federal level. If they are contacted at the European level, they immediately transfer the information to our cantonal services.

In other areas, such as the fight against crime, this is not the case. She identifies a number of problems. Although (some) criminal databases have been integrated nationally and are maintained by federal agencies, a corresponding national service of data analysis and investigation coordination has not been created. The full "revolutionary" potentiality for criminal investigation of the DNA profile national information system—a system created in 2003 and managed by the Confederation—to take one example, is therefore left unexploited:

> The federal structure will issue enthusiastic statements on the usefulness of the DNA database. It is truly an extraordinary and revolutionary instrument. Now, the reality is that most of the time all we do with the instrument is to input into the database the profile of a person and, once a trace is found, search for matches. And everybody seems happy with that. It is truly useful. However, with this instrument, there are a number of other procedures that could be undertaken. Think about a "trace-trace" search! I recall that I was once able to find 48 hits in a trace-trace search. This means that instead of using the database to find a match between a trace and a profile, which obviously allows you to identify and arrest that person, something that everybody would applaud, well, you use the database to observe that the trace that you found here can also be found in Schaffouse, in Neuchâtel, and in Jura. At the end, you may have 50 traces that are identical in terms of DNA structure and

have been left on crime scenes in various places in Switzerland. And then, what do you do with such a finding? You have the archaic way to start calling your colleagues in other cantons: the police officer in Geneva calls his colleague in Schaffouse; in Schaffouse, the police officer calls his colleagues in Basel; in Basel they call Bern, and so on. Using combinatory calculus, we end up with about 3000 phone calls that need to be made; or you have the possibility that all this is coordinated and taken care of at the federal level.

She concludes: "it is a waste, and it is a pity." The Confederation should develop its service function to cantonal police forces. Why is that not happening?

The federal structure tells you that it is competent for organized crime only and the case you are dealing with is not an organized crime case. And this despite the fact that these cases are of high concern to us. We have to recognize that the cantonal structures cannot deal appropriately with these cases.

Do we face a fundamental limit of federalism? Could concordats fill the gap? Associations of cantons could indeed, perhaps, create structures to undertake the job, if legal issues prevent the Confederation from dealing with nonorganized criminality? Or could the Confederation use more proactively, courageously perhaps, her coordination mandate as the basis for such activities? She replies:

A responsibility to coordinate? But we have tried. We had once a case—a case that had a media twist—which involved several cantons as well as persons of old age. We were told that these cases were not organized crime cases. If we ask what is the definition of organized crime, well, they remain more or less silent. Thefts are important. It is the most frequent infraction and above all is of high concern for the public. I am glad that in our police we respond to calls for service in these cases; elsewhere, in some cantons, the police have stopped intervening in these cases. For me, this is important and a good barometer of the professional standards of the police.

Beyond the legal issue at stake, Chief Bonfanti believes that the federal institution suffers from other handicaps. It is a young institution and there is obviously room for progress:

All is not lost, I think. But I observe that this structure has been left dormant for some time. In the Ruth Metzler [former justice minister] period the Confederation was busy building up a structure.

But, for the moment, it is bureaucratic, technocratic, displays poor understanding of practical policing issues.

If I make a phone call to obtain information, well I am not sure I will receive an answer to the question asked. No responding officer. This is a bit difficult. Staff rotate quickly. And above all police are mostly operational institutions.

We have the impression that they are on another level, a bureaucratic level, and when we want to mount an operation, well they are busy with legal matters, constraints, and above all it will take us 3 months to be up and running. This is a little bit the impression we have in the field when we work with the federal level. Most of the staff working at this level have not received police training, they know little about the police institution and we do not see really … They, they have competencies in matters of financial crimes, terrorism, etc., OK, well they can keep them and we keep our competencies. But we could do much more if only there would be a common vision, a common ground.

… and [they] need to listen to cantons and to consult if the goal is a shared vision, a shared understanding of issues, and a practical and efficient cooperation:

… and there are decisions taken [by federal agencies] that are not well understood by cantonal police. If they want to consider us as partners, well it will be necessary that at a certain point of time they … our local partners consult us! You know, the big options, what do you think? Things like that.

Policing and Expertise

How policing and science interact together is a favorite topic of Chief Bonfanti. This is a field where her tenure is already palpable in the organization. Expertise, she believes, has revolutionized policing. In criminal investigation, she states:

Confessions were the queen of the proof. Today, they are just the "fruit on the pie." If we have them, the pie will be tastier—perhaps! If we do not have them, then we will need a maximum of proofs. It is true that we have fewer and fewer confessions. Given this new situation, our defense system has become virulent.

The perverse effect, however, of this practice sanctioned by the judges is this:

What is perhaps annoying is that there are a number of cases where we do have material traces; there is a perverse effect of this fact. The absence of traces does not mean ipso facto that the person is not involved. The person could be even if we lack material traces. By insisting too much on material traces, there is a perverse effect to that. We need to emphasize also material witnesses and other elements of proof. The courts need to be able to make decisions even if there are no available material traces.

Experienced criminal investigators cultivate a condescending discourse and attitude when they see a new entrant joining the ranks from the universities:

The truth is somewhere in between; when someone comes from an academic institution and starts dealing with real cases, his or her colleagues will let that person know that she comes from an academic environment and things here are different.

Her message to these officers is, however, that the justice will not indulge officers who—for whatever reason—make their investigation too hastily:

It is necessary to find a balance that is indeed delicate and difficult to find. But we need to never forget that we operate for the justice and we transmit our products to the justice. And indeed it is the justice who evaluates the quality of what we give to her. I cannot tell the justice that I did not take this trace because it was rainy or because I needed a ladder in order to climb, or because I was called somewhere else. Therefore, it requires that we keep our heads cool. Yes, some concessions need to be made in order for our work to retain its meaning. We need to be academic in what we do; we need to be analytical, approach problems as we are taught at the university. The aptitude that we have to look at a problem, see the risks, take a rational decision involving a risk analysis. In practice, given the volume of files that are piled on our desks, we are tempted to take shortcuts, and sometimes, this proves a false calculus as it will have negative consequences on the final quality of what we deliver.

To keep up-to-date with innovation, new best practices, new techniques require reading and spare time, two things that prove somewhat incompatible with a full-time job as investigator. Yet, it is crucial for the job. Her solution to the dilemma? One of them is part-time jobs for academics:

In 2002, we put into place a mechanism that allowed a link between practice and theory. That year, I hired two PhD students who worked 50% in the university and 50% in the police. This gave us the possibility at any time to tap into innovations at the university and that could be applied in our work at the police; it also allowed us to introduce in our services innovations we considered practical. This is something I consider important. Once in operational work at the police you realize that you do not have the time to keep up with information and have no time to read scientific journals such as the *Forensic Science International*, the *Journal of Forensic Science*, and others. You have even less time to introduce these new theories into our daily practices. This was therefore the response we gave to this observation.

Another strategy is to require new entrants to keep their ties to their academic network:

We have also officers who have an interesting CV for us. We have for instance a good number of engineers and have requested that they do not cut the umbilical cord to their academic institution. Most of the time, we are talking of the Federal Polytechnic High School in Lausanne or the engineer school in Geneva. I have always requested that they keep that linkage and, when I need it, when I am confronted with a particular problem, we talk and I describe the type of expertise I need, ask for their opinion and we discuss where the appropriate technique can be found. They have their network in their academic home institutions.

For instance, I had two female investigators who were archaeologists. When we have to dig to find corpses somewhere, well these two investigators with the help of the university can give us a hand. While digging, they can easily tell us by looking at the stratification of the ground where it was excavated recently. There are a number of persons with a career who have access to specialized networks that they are requested to keep. We have to call for expertise in our work that is sometimes quite unexpected. I can quote this example when we needed to identify the blood of a bird ... Now with the issue of dogs, dog bites, we need to know more. Some one of us needs to meet with specialists of animal behavior, we need to have an understanding of genetic analyses of dogs, we need to have a knowledge of quite a number of things. Now we have a canine brigade and when we face a problem they are the ones contacting the animal behavior experts we need, etc.

Yet another strategy, initiated by one of her predecessors in 1996, is an in-house analysis capacity. The police of Geneva was the first Swiss cantonal police to establish a Strategic Analysis Service, based on the Royal Canadian Mounted Police model. With the new centrality in police organizations of problem-solving approaches, community policing, and partnership with nonpolice agencies, social sciences have moved closer to the core of policing. The service seemed to have been somewhat neglected by the two last Geneva chiefs of police; with Chief Bonfanti, the service becomes a priority as it is aligned with her vision of stronger support processes and better productivity through analyses. The service is directly attached to her and, she insists:

I have almost daily working sessions with the Strategic Studies. I believe that the Strategic Studies are very useful because they are in a position to interpret field data and process that data so that it can be useful to mount operations in the field as a response to the field observations. This is this aspect of the analyses that I want to develop.

For Bonfanti, however, the operational character of data analysis needs to be developed in the future. The service should combine strategic and operational analyses. This requires that data is collected more methodically by field police officers; in return, field police officers should be able to see the value-added character of the data analysis in their daily activities. More operational analyses will feed a virtuous circle: field officers, encouraged by useful operational analyses will take more seriously the data collection task and this, in turn, will augment the quality of operational analyses:

> This implies that to be able to make valid analyses the data is collected in a reliable way, as precisely as possible, so that patterns and causal relations can be detected. It is also necessary that the officers who collect the data see the value of the analyses. These analyses need to get back to them in the field. Only if they understand the value of these analyses will they be ready to collect data with the required precision. The whole chain is at stake. I would like that this becomes much more systematic in the future.

Interview with President Ing-Dan Shieh, Central Police University, Taiwan, ROC

14

INTERVIEWED AND EDITED BY MARK M. CHEN

INTERVIEW RECORDED BY CHENG-FENG LI

Background

President Shieh was the 12th director-general of the National Police Administration, Taiwan, the highest rank of police in this nation. His previous experience includes director-general, Taoyuan County Police Department (1995); deputy commissioner, Taiwan Provincial Police Administration (1996); director-general, Kaohsiung City Police Department, the second largest metropolitan area in this nation (1997). In 2001 he was promoted to deputy director-general, National Police Agency, the second highest position in the police force. In 2004 he was appointed director-general, National Police Agency, the highest rank in the Taiwan police force. Since 2006 he has been president of Central Police University. President Shieh has had experience in police operations and police education. His almost 40 years of experience in police work has produced many innovations that are now important resources for police management and operations in Taiwan.

The Interview

This interview was conducted on September 7, 2007 in the office of President Ing-Dan Shieh, Central Police University. This university is the highest learning institute for police education in the nation; it operates under the Ministry of the Interior, with supervision by the Ministry of Education. As a result, the education offered by this university must not only meet the requirements of college education but also the special demands of education for police cadres. Concretely speaking, the main missions of this university are to study advanced police academic subjects and to cultivate special police personnel. Right now this university has 13 undergraduate police-related departments,

195

12 graduate schools, and 3 doctoral programs. Totally, this school has a student body of about 2000 and around 340 faculty and staff.

MC: Tell us a little bit about your career: length, organizations worked in, movements, specializations, etc. What about how your career developed surprised you? Did your work prove as interesting or as rewarding as you thought it would?

[In places, President Shieh's remarks are paraphrased by the interviewer; his direct remarks are in quotation marks.] President Shieh was the 12th director-general of the National Police Administration, Taiwan, the highest rank of police in this nation. He had various experience in police work and received a lot of praise not only from his commanders but from his subordinates and the public as a whole. In 1971 he graduated from the Department of Police Administration, Central Police University, and earned a degree of Bachelor of Arts. In 2004 to 2006 he served as the director-general, National Police Agency, the highest rank of police force in Taiwan. And since 2006 he has been the president of Central Police University. So he has had police experience in administration, investigation, and education in three different areas of police work.

The president admits that he had the great luck to interact with various levels of society and people, and from this experience he developed a deeper insight into the basic issues of human nature. He thinks that the most meaningful job of police work is to come into contact with and assist every level of people—whether president, elite, or indigenous people, even extending his concern to animals and plants. He said that he never insisted on a particular job change or promotion, but that he put his whole heart and effort into any job assigned. Therefore he solved almost every kind of crises during his work and received his commanders' and subordinates' praise and support.

MC: What do you see as the most important changes that have happened in policing over the course of your career (philosophies, organizational arrangements, specializations, policies and programs, equipments, personnel, diversity etc.)?

After 30 years served in the police, President Shieh thinks that the democratization and development of checks and balances in government is the most important change. He experienced the transformation of Taiwan during the democratization movements, the protest activities, the street riots, the partisan conflicts, and the shift of power based on elections. As a police commander, he had the responsibility to deal with all of those profound changes. From this experience he thought about the police role in a democratic changing society. He concluded that a police strategy should be "customer oriented," providing better quality services to all of the public.

Motor Theory as the Vision of Policing

"Society needs support from different groups and perspectives; otherwise, it will soon collapse," said President Shieh. As for police power, he offers the "motor theory," which is to let the police become one of the crucial elements of this social support.

He assumes that the police organization is a giant machine, with every police officer playing an important role within the organization, no matter whether he or she is in the rank and file or in a leadership position. The public as a whole is the resource or energy of this machine. Therefore, we need every part of society to join hand in hand and work together to run this motor. When the motor is activated, then every element, police or public, has a duty to perform. In a rapidly changing society the police must maintain a good quality of service by having a proactive, sensitive, and comprehensive management strategy. This means the police have to be very responsive to the needs of the public and pay full attention to the needs and satisfaction of civilian thoughts about the enforcement of the law and good communication and dissemination.

"Furthermore, the commanders of the police need to have a commitment to a democratic society. Whatever the changes of the political entity, shifts among the ruling parties, or conflicts based on politics, the police need to play a solid role in enhancing social stability. They need to disseminate the idea to politicians and the public that staying politically neutral makes police power more beneficial to the society and public as a whole. During a big change in politics, as happened in Taiwan from authoritarian-oriented to democratic politics, there may be some normless phenomenon and periods, what Emile Durkheim called anomie, but there will be no bloody revolution. That is due to the neutral enforcement of police power. This Taiwan police experience may become an example for developing countries as they evolve into more democratic forms of government."

MC: What changes in external conditions (support from communities, legal powers, judicial relations, relations with minority communities, resource provision, political influence, etc.) have had a significant impact on policing?

ID-S: After the lifting of martial law, human rights, the right of privacy, and other basic rights have been demanded by the public. The right of public protest and petition has increased enormously. The application of the criminal procedural code and the due process model from the common law system, especially the cross examination by the defendant and plaintiff (or prosecutor) equally, changed the position and the way that the civil law system had granted more power to the prosecutor. By the same token, the public pays more attention to police performing their duty in investigating cases. With this criminal justice evolution the police not only have to offer better service to the public but need to execute their duty more cautiously. While discrimination never becomes a problem here in Taiwan, the police have to stay neutral and alert in order to prevent any incidence of police discrimination relative to any ethnic group.

From Professionalism to the Resource Integration Model

"To receive more support from the central and local governments and also the legislature, police work needs to touch the hearts of the public by performing better service, on one hand, but the police also need to receive more public support, on the other hand. The partnership between the public and police is a crucial idea of the integration police model. But coercive enforcement of the law has been the ordinary practice of policing, so it is not easy to create a partnership relationship between the public and the police. The following experiences provide some examples of this kind of strategy."

First Example: Yi-Lan County Police Department

"When I was the director-general of Yi-Lan County Police Department, some of the citizens were obsessed with the lottery and various kinds of gambling, and juvenile delinquents caused many crime problems. To curb these issues we initiated a project called "Love Association" in March 1990. The police encouraged Buddhists monks to give speeches to the jail and prison inmates; programs were designed to assist the elderly who did not have any family members to care for them; and children who were without parents were adopted by citizens who were willing to offer their assistance. At the end of the school day, volunteers offered assistance to control the traffic at school crossings. My idea was that integrating the resources of the Buddhism associations of the county helped to execute my integration model of policing. At that time in this county we had 18 elementary schools with "Mama Traffic Control Guardian Teams" of almost 300 volunteers. This successful experience has been duplicated nationwide. This demonstrates what I have said that if the police change their strategy to the integration model then the public will be moved to cooperate in this police initiative. This is what the global trend towards 'community policing' is all about."

Second Example: Kao-Hsiung Metropolitan Police Department

"When I was the director-general of the Kao-Hsiung police department, the citizens of Kao-Hsiung and the police did not have a good relationship. So I promoted the 'Volunteer Project' for public involvement in police work. This created a forum for a partnership between the public and police. This project not only enhanced the security of the society but decreased citizens' fear of crime.

"The volunteer project included services to citizens when they reported a case to the police station, assistance services to victims, especially in domestic violence and rape cases, and assistance to traffic accident victims. Volunteers also assisted officers in public security surveys, disseminating crime prevention strategies and techniques, and the execution of community policing projects. In 2004, Prime Minister Chang noted that this public and police partnership policy was a better strategy, not only for better service to the public but also as a better crime control strategy. He ordered that this policy should be extended to the whole nation. Until now almost 13,000 civilians have joined this project. This is also following the global policing trend of the partnership strategy."

MC: Overall, has the quality of policing improved or declined (street work, specialized units, managerial capacity, self-evaluation, interagency cooperation, etc.)?

ID-S: After democratization had gone on for several decades here in Taiwan, the traditional police use of coercion to enforce the law may have caused more conflict between public and police because of this democratic evolution of society. Furthermore, lack of new and appropriate legislation may have impeded the development of a better quality of police service. Although 90% of students of Central Police University (CPU) have passed the national universities admission test, they choose to enroll in CPU instead. The programs here in this university need to be enhanced in a more flexible way in order to educate better quality officers to deal with this more complicated police job. Besides, we need to reach out to the community and create partnerships with the public so that we can deal with the security issue more effectively.

In ancient times police took the security issue as one for their own shoulders only, but the results were not so good. I think that it is not a good strategy for police to deal with crime independently. They should work hand in hand with other sectors of government and create partnerships with the community as well. For instance, in telephone fraud cases it will not be a good strategy to use traditional investigation skills to curb this new type of crime. We need to integrate the new technology and intelligence systems to deal with this crime more effectively. I think the following two approaches may be applied to this new police strategy: (1) disseminate prevention skills to the public and community; and (2) create an antifraud forum among the different government sectors, including economic, financial, transportation, telecommunications, banking, justice, education, and security departments, etc., to integrate all aspects of intelligence and resources to curb this new type of crime.

With this idea in mind, I recommended to the prime minister to use this strategy to solve telephone fraud and other economic fraud cases here in Taiwan, and received successful and marvelous results. Now, we can also extend this strategy to other types of crime, such as auto theft, professional gambling cases, etc.

MC: In general, is it more or less difficult to be a police officer (street, manager) now than in the past?

ID-S: After the lifting of martial law here in Taiwan, coupled with the democratization process, the public wished to have more freedom. However, the legal system was slow to catch up with the rapid transformation; consequently, law enforcement is tougher to execute than ever before. For good quality police work we need not only to enact suitable new laws, but we need to enhance our quality of enforcement, promote technology, and develop better quality police officers as well. As the computer system needs to be upgraded from time to time, the police also need periodically to inspect and promote their own capability.

The Taiwan police force has an in-service training institution, but because of the complexity of police operations it is very difficult to find a suitable schedule for all officers. Right now we have several policies to solve this problem. The training requirement and certificate system may become an incentive for training. Also, changes in recruitment practices will emphasize recruiting more capable and representative ethnic groups. Reasonable police operations systems and reasonable police work hours may also improve the working environment and job efficiency of the police.

MC: What do you think should be the role of the police in society?

ID-S: Social security is needed to provide consistent and long-term efforts to attain quality-of-life goals. In the future, security surely will face more stringent challenges. The police need to adjust their role, not only for a better strategy of enforcing the law, but for providing better quality services to the public as well.

The police may be seen as the symbol of justice, just as the Japanese police see themselves not only as law enforcers, but as "moral examples" for the community. Police also need to look at themselves as the catalysts for community cooperation. The duty of the police is not only to be a means for crime investigation, but also for safeguarding a peaceful community environment and solving community problems.

MC: How should policing be performed? What should be the preferred priorities and strategies; hard-edged crime control, prevention, services, order work, what mix for which types of problems; proactive-reactive; community policing-law enforcement, etc.?

President Shieh was the director-general of the National Police Administration for 11 months; the important initiatives during his tenure included setting up the police duty death pension fund and system; demanding and receiving 4% of the central government's fiscal year budget to subsidize the police; and initiating an e-case reporting system, etc.

He thinks that the "fixed police beat" is the foundation for social stability, even though crime investigation is the key issue for maintaining social order and security, but that the "community policing" strategy is also an effective and efficient way to curb crime and the public fears of crime. Taiwan currently has 1500 police boxes, small police stations or what the Japanese call *Kobans*. These police boxes are further divided into 15,000 fixed beats nationwide. But even with this strategy, the public still is not satisfied with the police service. The reason for this is that the police in the fixed beat system have too great a workload so they find it difficult to spare time or energy to focus on a community-oriented strategy.

ID-S: During the martial law era the government assigned too many functions to the police, so the police were too focused on law enforcement. It was very difficult to create good relationships between the public and the police. When martial law was lifted, initially the conflict between the public and the police increased. So it was not a good situation for executing a community policing strategy. But when I was the director-general of Kao-Hsiung Metropolitan Police Department in 1997 I showed my enthusiasm and honesty to the officers and citizens and it was decided that it was the right time to execute "Community Policing" and "Love Your Own Home" projects for the creation of partnerships between the public and the police. Crime control and prevention had excellent results under those projects.

The Kao-Hsiung police strategy aroused public cooperation and increased support for the police. The strategies included projects to protect students and safeguard the elderly, police mini-service posts within gas stations and stores, and a civilian neighborhood patrol project.

The above description of the Kao-Hsiung police experience was an initial fundamental effort for community policing. This new trial was an integration model of government, to involve schools, businesses, and civic associations in local security matters.

The traditional wisdom of assuming that all security-related matters are the responsibility of the police and the police only can create too much pressure and work overload for the police. The solution to this dilemma is to change the social security assumption to a more integrated model, creating a partnership among various public and private institutions. The community policing strategy can become a more effective way to deal with crime and social order.

The fixed beat officer needs to integrate the resources at the community level. The quality at this basic level of officer actions can be promoted in the following three ways: (1) professionalism, by improving the fundamental education and in-service training facilities to promote the quality of human resources; (2) a service-oriented philosophy and disseminating this philosophy to the officers, changing their belief of policing into a more service-oriented operation; (3) humanism, creating a more humanistic organizational culture and environment, enhancing the officers' abilities in communication, persuasion, consulting, and in the "restorative justice" skills, that is, mediation and arbitration techniques.

MC: In your experience what policies or programs have worked well and which have not? And can you speculate for what reasons?

ID-S: I have dealt with lots of critical social issues. For instance, after the 2004 presidential elections, Taiwan was filled with partisan protests on the street and around the president's office. As the director-general of the national police I had to solve this social disorder. My viewpoint and policy was to persuade the public to realize that maintaining good social order was a benefit to them. Because good social order and quality of living are the real top priorities of the public, they must trust the police to maintain order based on the rule of law only. As a developed nation and progressive society we need to keep political influence away from these public common interests.

Each nation has its unique system and culture, but as for Taiwan we just transitioned from an authoritarian to a democratic system. We need to upgrade and change the ways of police education and focus on the core values of democratic policing. The police in a democratic society have to show their capability and determination to maintain security for the public good, and then they can receive their trust and support in return. We have to insist that the police role is neutral; that we only follow the rule of law and the interests of the public. As for internal communication, we need to insist that the police must be loyal to their duty and need to remain politically neutral whenever they execute police work because this is what advanced policing is all about.

MC: What would you consider to be the greatest problem facing the police at this time?

ID-S: Too great a population density in Taiwan, a small island nation, coupled with the rapid change of the economy, culture, and way of living create so many paradoxes and conflicts that cause social security problems. This may be the greatest issue right now here in Taiwan. This is of course a challenge for the police but, on the other hand, it is also a good chance for the police to evolve. As a matter of fact, the government and politicians have to pay more attention to police suggestions, because the officer is the one who has the closest and most frequent contact with the public, who knows the public's needs and the trends of that community. If national policy makers can carefully listen to police recommendations on how to manage the society then that will pass on a lot of information and be a great help for their administration.

Traditionally, the politicians did not pay much attention to what police knew about the community. But the society changes so fast that this is a quick and easy channel to collect information on the public's real needs. President Shieh strongly emphasized that "if the politician and society as a whole can use the police in the right way, then security of the society can surely prevail.

MC: What problems in policing do you find are the most difficult to deal with? What would be easy to change? Internal problems (culture of the organization, managerial deficiencies, allegations of corruption, or gender related problems, etc.) or externally generated problems (resources, community support, etc.)? Is anything easy?

ID-S: At present, the major police issue here in Taiwan is that politicians use injustice in a way to humiliate the police. For instance, the city councilmen may ask for a "grounding punishment" [standing still for several minutes while the councilors ask questions in the council hall] for not obeying their individual wishes; or they ask officers to exercise their discretion for the good of politicians; or they humiliate the police by leading the public to the police station and accusing the officer or protesting in front of the station. These unreasonable actions may damage police reputation and in turn decrease their incentive to execute the law. The inappropriate behavior of the politicians presents a wrong model for the public to follow. Police in this situation will face the dilemma of whether they are doing their jobs right whenever they deal with an issue related to these people. The bad guys then will have no fear when committing a crime because some key person will back them up for their wrongdoing. This is the worst damage to security and is also an inevitable negative development to democratization. That is surely a good lesson for government, police, and the public as a whole to learn so we can finally reach our democratic vision and dream. This precious experience in Taiwan may become a useful resource or reference for other developing nations.

MC: What should be the relationship between theory and practice? What can practitioners learn from theory, and what can theory builders learn from practitioners?

ID-S: The mission of the police should be to develop a comprehensive approach to serving the public. Police decision making and job design already have their theoretical foundation. They utilize existing theories and principles and are the important strategies to execute complicated police practices.

But police practice is so complicated that there is, inevitably, a gap between police theories and practices. Police work has its urgent nature and serves very different communities. A consequence of this is that there is no unique panacea, treatment, or theory to fit all police forces. So one must utilize the existing theory but pay attention to the local differentiation and local special needs to make police work more effective. For better police policy making, therefore, we need to combine theory and practical experiences.

MC: What is the relationship right now? Does it exist? Does it work? What holds collaboration or interactions back?

ID-S: In Taiwan right now the relationship between theory and practice still needs a lot of improvement. The reason for this is because social change is so rapid that the existing relationships are not changing fast enough to achieve effective policy and operational goals. These obstacles include the political issue caused by the legislative department's inability to enact appropriate legislation. During this situation, I think my school, the Central Police University, can play a key role in integrating the theorists and practitioners.

MC: What kind of research, in what form, on what questions would you find most useful for practice? If not very useful, what could or should theory builders do to make their products more useful to you?

ID-S: At the present time, research on the legal aspects of policing is a great help and is important for police practice. Because police are authorized to enforce the rule of law they have always to follow this rule. Especially in a democratic nation, due process of law is as important a core value of justice as the control of crime by the substantive law. Therefore, amending inappropriate laws or regulations will be a crucial activity for the academicians to focus on.

Also, the academicians, right now in this country, pay attention to homeland security protection, police strategy, crime prevention, police morale, and citizen satisfaction with the police. All of these studies can assist practitioners in dealing with these new issues or problems. We have a unique organization, the Central Police University. It is equal in level to the National Police Administration (NPA) in our organization chart. Therefore, we have an equal position of cooperating with each other and balancing power, if you will, between these two highest police agencies. So our university prepares the best quality of officers for the NPA, and the NPA, whenever faced with new issues, can hand those issues over to our university for the development of correct solutions. This allows academicians to have direct access to collect first-hand data for feasible and invaluable studies, while, on the other hand, the practitioners can find solutions to new problems.

MC: Where do you find theory-based information? Where do you look? What journals, books, publications, reports?

ID-S: In Taiwan we have the Central Police University providing a 4-year bachelor's degree and Taiwan Police College preparing the rank and file with a 2-year junior college degree education. Through these two institutions we can hold the seminars, conferences, and special training and workshop programs so necessary for the continued improvement of the police. Also, we publish many journals and conference documents for police use. Faculty members in our schools, through strategic cooperation programs with the other universities, offer police-related classes.

Usually, I will first use the "police data bank" of our school library to find needed resources. This data bank includes the journals of our university and of other educational facilities from all over the world, including theses and dissertations from criminal justice-related disciplines. Therefore, it is convenient and easy for me to find the needed resources. Police agencies in Taiwan right now encourage their officers to enroll in higher degree education programs. Many of them learn up-to-date police knowledge to apply to their work. For example, the so called "Police White Paper—the Annual Strategic Plan" is a cooperative program between academicians and practitioners. Through this integration we can find a more feasible and effective approach to deal with crime and social disorder.

MC: Does the organization do research on its own? On what types of issues or questions?

ID-S: As for the issue of the police organization conducting research on its own, our police force would like to apply cutting edge technology and theory to their work. For instance, successful business management practices, such as total quality management (TQM) or quality control circles (QCC) has been applied to the police administration. A research task force will execute these new approaches and sometimes uses quasi-experimental approaches to test whether they are suitable for Taiwan's police environment. If the result is positive then that treatment will be promoted to every police force nationwide.

Also, the promotion of an "entrepreneur government" has become the main theme of Taiwan's government. Citizen satisfaction is one of the crucial factors of this new strategy. Therefore, the police force just applied the ISO 9001 model from the International Organization for Standardization to their managerial innovation procedures. From 2001 to 2005 the ISO 9001 has been successfully applied to all the police headquarters and police stations islandwide. For further development we may utilize a "problem oriented policing" model to promote community involvement and the police service marketing system, etc.

In addition, the "police network service" is also an effort to increase innovation. This service innovation, or so-called soft power, can shorten the distance between the public and police and it also can provide police services easier and faster to the public. The e-case reporting system, the ISO, the Corporate Identification System (CIS) for redecorating the police station, and customer-oriented policing are all based on this new idea or philosophy of redesigning police work.

The National Police Administration also conducts lots of research on current security issues. For instance, juvenile crazy driving activities, riot incidents, and human trafficking problems; all of these issues are complicated social phenomena. We need a special task force or project to conduct a study in order to figure out a feasible way to solve the problems. In addition, studies pertinent to police morale, police computer system construction, police officers' consulting system, community policing strategy, crime trends and prevention, police law and regulation, comparison of police systems, and public satisfaction surveys are usually contracted to the Central Police University or other universities for in-depth study. The police in Taiwan just wish to keep up with new police developments from all over the world and research is one of the crucial vehicles to reach this goal.

MC: Have you been affected, and how, in the work of your organization by developments outside the country (human rights demands, universal codes of ethics, practical interactions with police from other countries, personal experiences outside the country, new crime threats, etc.)?

ID-S: Righteousness and evil are all imbedded in the nature of human beings. Therefore, it is inevitable that each society has its own crime and social problems. Some nation's successful experience in dealing with these common issues of the human being can become an example for other nations. Coupled with the globalization trend of the twenty-first century and the fast development of transnational crime, international cooperation becomes a necessary approach to deal with these global problems.

The influential leadership of the international cooperation associations, and nongovernmental organizations (NGOs), recognizes that international crime needs international cooperation to curb or prevent it. If Interpol (or the ICPO, International Criminal Police Organization) did not follow the core value of international cooperation and assistance without political interference then it surely would cause some disadvantage or sometimes even harm to some regions. Taiwan as a nation has been expelled, because of mainland China, from the United Nations and the ICPO. This has caused many obstacles to cooperation and the exchange of intelligence with other nations. This is not only a betrayal of the spirit of international organizations but also impedes the international cooperation needed to investigate or prevent transnational crime. The result is that both the international community and Taiwan lose in their crime fighting efforts.

Although across the Taiwan Strait, we and China have different ideologies of politics and separated sovereignty, but cross-border crime is a common concern for both sides and all the international community as well. This is a tremendous harm not only to both nations but also to their citizens, including businessmen from Taiwan who invest in mainland China—investments that will become the basis for benefits to China's social and economic development. But because of political reasons, or by discretionary enforcement, there are unsolved crimes pertinent to Taiwanese businessmen. As a result, the final damage will inevitably go to both sides of the Taiwan Strait.

MC: Have those interactions been beneficial or harmful? What kind of external international influences are beneficial and which ones less so? How have developments post September 11 affected your work?

ID-S: Transnational crime has no national boundary; especially for terrorists who utilize another nation as a channel to attack their main target country. Therefore, international cooperation is a must for safeguarding a nation's security.

There is an old Chinese proverb that "Whoever wishes to get the benefit for himself will have to offer the benefit to others in the first place; whoever wishes to have an achievement for himself has to assist others to achieve their goals first" [attributed to Confucius, from about 2500 years ago]. The police all over the world have to think about how to create a forum for intelligence cooperation and for sharing their information and resources and keeping the transnational criminal away from their territories. It is also true that the police in developed nations need to enthusiastically assist the lesser developed nations to enhance their police capability and provide technology where needed. From this kind of international cooperation we may improve the efficiency of police and their efforts to curb transnational crime.

The source of power for the police is the righteousness of the society, so the role of the police is to keep politically neutral. It is unlike the military or national defense, which has to be concerned with competition among other nations. The police have the common good and core values of all human beings as their responsibility, which is to maintain justice and safeguard the social order of whatever nation they may be part of. To attain this common goal we do not have to compete with each other or hide any intelligence that is valuable to crush crime. The police all over the world should have this kind of elegant vision and dignified set of values.

MC: Are you basically satisfied or dissatisfied with developments in policing? What are the most likely developments you see happening and which would you like to see happening? What is most needed now to improve policing?

ID-S: In general I wish to show my gratitude and respect to all the police officers around the world who have devoted their efforts to the development of the police system. Because the function of policing is to protect human beings, safeguard personal property, and to maintain justice and order in the society, we all owe a debt to our sister police organizations. We also wish to learn about the more progressive police systems in the developed nations. We found that not all the public understands the real functions and principles of policing. We need to push policing and its academic development towards a new era in which the police will become a symbol of justice and a moral example for society and for the public. This is what we must devote our entire life to if we are serious about police career development.

Generally speaking, the public imagines that the police function is only to enforce the law, but ideally, police have to be involved in the community and work hand in hand with the public on a daily basis. Therefore, the officer is the one who knows the community the best. Unfortunately, the public traditionally thinks that the police are not very well-educated people, as Dr. David Bayley of the University of Albany put it. The public believes that there is no need to consult with the police whenever it faces a problem. It is a pity that the public does not know that the police have improved their quality over time. We have the responsibility to change the credibility of the police image and leading the police to become a more professionalized and respected career.

In a developing nation the image and integrity of police is not so good; therefore, it is more difficult to receive the public's respect and the authorization of appropriate power from the government. The appropriate authorization of police power and the suitable management of that power is also a very crucial policy decision for the government. If too much power is authorized and the officers can carry lethal weapons and they execute this power in a manner not in accord with the due process of law, then the police may become a disaster to the public and society. As educators we have the responsibility to develop and prepare a better police personnel in order to promote the quality of police all over the world. We also have to emphasize that the police play a key role in the social development of a nation. This is the core value of what ideal policing is all about. With the proper development of the police they can then become a significant factor for the social stability of that nation.

Concluding Comment

President Shieh has both practical and educational police experience. He has devoted his life to police innovation and development in Taiwan. Many projects involving community policing, problem-oriented policing, and e-policing strategies have been set up and completed in Taiwan. Currently, as president of the Central Police University, he has enthusiastically devoted his energy to the reformation of the higher police education system. His experiences and ideas for new police development are a very crucial knowledge base for police development everywhere.

Glossary

Martial law: When the Republic of China, not the Peoples Republic of China, transferred from mainland China to Taiwan in 1949, Taiwan was governed in a way based on martial law. In 1987 Taiwan lifted martial law and evolved into a normal democracy.

Koban: A small police station; usually fewer than 10 police officers work in this small police station. It is also the name Japanese call their small police stations.

The National Police Administration: Taiwan is a centralized police system. The NPA is the national police headquarters. Taiwan has a total of around 70,000 officers.

The Corporate Identification System (CIS): A new initiative for Taiwan police to use this enterprising managerial approach to redecorate their office or station. Using more brisk or animate appearances to remodel the building and their equipment in order to refresh the traditional police image from the paramilitary model to one that hopefully receives more acceptance and support from the public.

The Taiwan Strait: The strait, 130 to 250 kilometers wide, between China and Taiwan.

ISO 9001: The standardization of police administration in Taiwan and certified by the International Organization for Standardization. ISO 9001:2000 is one of the products of ISO specified requirements for a quality management system.

Service network, e-case reporting system: Using computer science and network technology to enhance police services to the public. Using these new systems, citizens can apply for police services or report a crime from their home through the Internet or at the police station by using police computer terminals or be assisted by the police on duty.

Interview with David Coleman, Chief Constable, Derbyshire Constabulary, UK

15

INTERVIEWED BY BONNIE ARMBRUSTER

Structure of the Police Service of the United Kingdom

At the top of the police structure in England and Wales is the Home Office, one of the largest government departments and responsible for a wide range of responsibilities. The person in charge is the home secretary. Within the Home Office a number of police units have been established to support the police and pursue a variety of crime reduction initiatives, such as the Office for Security and Counter-Terrorism, and the Crime Reduction and Community Safety Group. Three delivery agencies provide directly managed frontline services from the Home Office: the UK Border Agency, the Criminal Records Bureau, and the Identity and Passport Service.

There are 43 police forces in England and Wales, including over 140,500 police officers, nearly 75,000 police staff, and over 13,400 police community support officers.

These 43 forces are grouped into six regional or territorial police forces, referred to as constabularies or county forces and headed by a chief constable, which is the highest level of achievement in UK policing. The constabularies are controlled by a "tripartite" structure. One pillar of the tripartite is the chief constable, the other two being the Home Office and the Police Authority, an appointed body, which controls how local police services are delivered (set budgets, monitor police performance, and set police priorities by consulting the people who live and work in the constabulary or region).

Introduction

David Coleman graduated from Manchester University in 1975 and then joined the Derbyshire Constabulary as an officer on the beat in Shirebrook in that same year.

After serving in numerous and varied positions, including uniform and detective roles, he became divisional commander at Derby in 1995. The following year in 1996 he transferred as assistant chief constable (Operations), Leicestershire Constabulary. This would be the only period he spent outside his home county of Derbyshire. Mr. Coleman began his service as chief constable of Derbyshire in January 2001.

As his career progressed, he served in investigative roles but the majority of his time was spent on frontline operations. While leading the Derbyshire police, Mr. Coleman saw overall crime fall by 21% between 2003 and 2006, and he was honored with the Queen's Police Medal for distinguished service in 2004.

An ongoing theme for Mr. Coleman is meeting the needs of the people he serves and he is a staunch believer that neighborhood policing is a good way to fulfill that goal. As a result, he has left an impressive legacy of strong community neighborhood policing. When he became chief constable his police force had about a dozen people doing neighborhood beats; when he left his service they were approaching 400.

Most interestingly, the UK has an organization, the ACPO (Association of Chief Police Officers), which is strictly voluntary for its chief officers, yet has a high level of responsibility in the UK police organization. David Coleman spent an extraordinary amount of his time fulfilling responsibilities within this organization, including 3 years as a member of the Standing Sub-Committee on Emergency Procedures; 4 years as a member of the Race and Community Relations Committee and lead officer on stop/search issues; 3 years as lead officer responsible for forensic science; 6 years on the Terrorism and Allied Matters Committee, and the last 3 years of his service he was lead officer for forensic procurement. When asked how he found time to devote to all of this work and still meet his responsibilities as chief constable, he said he realized when he took the job as chief constable it would place great demands on his time. "There were long hours, many nights away from home, lots of weekends when I worked. That's the nature of the beast. I enjoyed the work and I was passionate about it."

This interview took place over several phone calls between the United States and the UK, during December 2007. Mr. Coleman conducted his interview from the book-lined study of his home in the Derbyshire countryside. Both an academic and practitioner, he expertly and interestingly spoke on topics ranging from science and technology to management philosophy and principles, extensive knowledge gleaned from his 32-year career span in the police service.

BA: As your career developed, has anything surprised you?
DC: Ha! That's a difficult question with no easy answer. From a personal perspective, a pleasing surprise I have found moving into senior ranks

is that I have easily adapted to them. And I've probably been better at them than I may have thought. So that's kind of a nice thing. In terms of looking outwards, I do not think anything surprised me really. I mean I've been around a long time and I guess it's difficult to be surprised when you're familiar with the environment.

One thing worth mentioning, when I became chief constable, which in UK policing is the ultimate rank really, is the amount of time spent on things other than the operation of policing; in terms of dealing with politicians, finances, organizational development, and so on. I think many people, moving into the rank, perhaps really do not appreciate that breadth of it before they actually get into it.

BA: Has your work proved as interesting or rewarding as you thought it would?

DC: Yes it did, always. I was fascinated by the job. I got into policing, sort of by accident really. I didn't start out as a kid with an ambition to become a police officer. But having joined it and now looking back on that career, it was a fantastic, worthwhile, enjoyable, rewarding career. I wouldn't say I enjoyed every minute, because that wouldn't be true. But I enjoyed the vast, vast majority of the work and I was very passionate about it. So hugely rewarding, yes.

BA: What do you see as the most important changes that have happened in policing over the course of your career?

DC: Speaking purely from a UK perspective, I think accountability, transparency, openness of the service to the public, and the amount of scrutiny the service is under from government and other bodies, has been a huge change. In public service, I am sure we are now the most scrutinized and one of the most open public services in the UK.

The other major change organizationally is the way the finance has been internally linked to what we do. Again in the UK, chief officers are very preoccupied with the finance that's available for policing, developing efficiency measures, and so on. And it takes up a lot of time. It is very clear to most chief officers that you can achieve only what you are financed to achieve.

I feel the organizational climate has changed dramatically, for the best. I go back to the 1970s when there was a huge amount of sexism, racism, and so on in the UK police service. Malpractice was normal business, but because of the leadership of service, politics, and the openness of the various laws that have been passed, much of that has been swept away. I am not suggesting it is all gone, but it has dramatically improved.

In terms of operational policing, clearly the onset of huge IT support, forensic science support has made a major difference in the UK. One major system, the Police National Computer, is a very successful and an excellent tool. Even in the last 5 years, when I was the lead officer for the Association of Chiefs of Police Officers (ACPO) on Forensic Science and Developments, there has been massive added value to crime investigations due to the National DNA Expansion Program and the Automatic Fingerprint Identification Systems, and so on. In terms of scientific support and forensic investigations, I think there is a general acknowledgment that we are probably the leading country in the world, certainly the leading police service, in terms of the use and the development of forensic science.

BA: Do you feel UK police are well financed?

DC: I think you always have the dilemma with policing, because you could always make the case for having more. I think in broad terms, there is a need for the finance to match the mission that the government expects the police to achieve. I think there is a mismatch between the two at the moment. The force I've been in command of has had financial restrictions for some time because of the way that it is funded by the government. And it is not funded to the level that it should be, even by the government's own assessment of its funding needs.

I have a particular view of finance. I think generally speaking, one has to be careful about listening to police chiefs cry for more money. But when all said and done, if they are using their existing finances as efficiently as they possibly can, the only way they can achieve more in terms of service delivery, is to get more money. That's where I sit on it.

In terms of spending from a local perspective, despite financial stringency, my officers had, I thought, the best possible equipment, the best possible vehicles, best possible communication systems, and there have been massive improvements in all of those issues, certainly in my time in the police service.

BA: What changes in external conditions have had a significant impact on policing?

DC: I think legal powers. Since I joined in 1975, there has been a massive influx of new legislation, particularly under the current government. Over 10 years, they have brought something like 3000 more offenses to the statute books in the UK. The civil libertarians would suggest that some of that is pushed too far, and there are certainly some senior police officers who feel that that is the case.

Relations with minority communities have had an impact and tend to be headline stuff when things go wrong. So you get a jaundiced view of relations when you look at the headlines. But when you look at what's going on, on a day-to-day basis on the streets with police officers who are working in the community, relations are generally excellent.

I think the other important thing is the number of members of the ethnic minorities actually joining the UK police services. This has made a difference; internally, to the way that colleagues view members of ethnic minorities, and externally to how the police actually look. They look more representative of the community. For example, in the Muslim community in the UK, there are tensions between elements of the Muslim community and the police service. However, after the recent bomb attempts at Glasgow airport and in London, because we have made such efforts to communicate with the Muslim community, there has been a very positive response from the Muslim community around the country to the appeals made by the police.

BA: Overall, has the quality of policing improved or declined?

DC: I think it has improved massively, I really do. Police officers in general are better qualified, they are better trained, their behavior is better, they are much more professional. Maybe they are not as free and maybe they are not as entrepreneurial, because their behavior is now codified and it is more restricted. So they don't feel free to bend the rules or break the rules like they used to do, even in a noble cause.

Overall, we have been an organization that has continually improved over the years. And we have been proud of the fact that we are responsive to change. There is a view that the police service is a little bit reactionary and conservative. I have never found that. I have always found people wanting to do things better. And I think that is a sign that people are very well motivated and want to succeed.

I think the great thing that has happened over the last few years has been a kind of the resurgence of the local neighborhood cop. And we now have a national strategy to deliver neighborhood policing. People like myself have been working hard to try and deliver this for many years. The politicians have caught on to it in recent times and it now seems to be presented as something that the current government invented. It is certainly a policing philosophy that many senior officers have been aware of for a very long time, and quite often just not had the resources to do properly.

I still don't think that UK policing has cracked the nut of developing managers as well as it could. I think we have some excellent managers. But we also have a lot of excellent police officers who don't, for one reason or another, make as good managers as they are police officers and I think we got some work to do there.

BA: Is there interaction between the police service and other agencies?

DC: Interagency cooperation I think is a really interesting one, because we have a massive philosophy of partnership working with other agencies. There are some glowing examples in the UK of police working with government, with other agencies such as the immigration service, local authorities, and housing associations. I can give you an example of the county I work. We have the Derbyshire Partnership Forum, which has probably 60 or 70 members from a very wide variety of agencies. There are such people there as the Council for Voluntary Service, the people from the National Park, all the different local authorities, the Probation Service, the Fire and Rescue Service, etc. We have a climate of working together. Each individual agency in the UK, in terms of public protection, community safety crime reduction and so on, now almost never tries to solve the problem on its own. We will always look for partners, to try and share the burden and bring all the resources to the table and other skills to the table so that the problem is more easily solved. That is the way of life for policing in the UK now. That has changed an awful lot, since the 1970s when we almost never talked to any other agencies and we were very insular and tried to manage on our own.

BA: What caused agencies to begin forming partnerships?

DC: Well, going back an awful long way in the UK, there was a report called the Morgan Report which set out the philosophy of partnership working. And 2 or 3 years following the Morgan Report which the government picked up and ran with, there was something called the Crime and Disorder Act, which is one of the major pieces of legislation over the last 20 years, which now, in legislative terms, requires certain people or agencies to be responsible partners. There are various provisions in the act which require various agencies to sit around the table together and formulate plans and so on. There were many of us who felt that that was probably one of the best pieces of legislation that the government implemented in the last 20 years. Again, there were a lot of us that had actually adopted the philosophy of partnership working, but the legislation underpinned it and forced some of the more reluctant people into partnerships. And I think it's probably got into its stride over the last 10 years and it's really started to become very effective.

BA: And the impact of this legislation?

DC: We have seen the crime levels dropping quite dramatically in the last few years. There is no doubt in my mind that part of that success is partnership working and getting people who previously didn't think that crime and disorder were their problem, to actually acknowledge that they can contribute to solving that problem. If that could be replicated elsewhere, it would work very well. I am sure it is replicated to an extent in many countries but probably not in legislative terms.

BA: In general, is it more or less difficult to be a police officer now than in the past?

DC: I think it is more difficult. On the street, there is much less deference to police. We don't carry the authority that we used to carry in the UK. People are more inclined to challenge police. And it's more violent. I am not suggesting the overall level of violence is greatly higher, but the degree of violence is greater. Firearms are more prevalent than they were. Drugs are far more prevalent than they were. When I joined, you almost never arrested anybody in possession of drugs. Now, most people arrested have some involvement in drugs, so that has changed to a great extent.

And technology has actually created difficulties. For example, police officers going into situations now regularly come up against people with camera phones who film what they are doing. Photos can be posted on the Internet or used as the basis for a complaint. Officers are sometimes deliberately provoked so that they can be filmed.

So there is very much a need to go out on the street realizing that your actions are highly visible, and very likely to be subject to challenge. You've got to be much more professional these days, and use your coercive powers in a much less physical way than perhaps we used to.

BA: Do you find it to be more or less difficult to be a police manager?

DC: To be a manager, it is more difficult. When I joined, if the sergeant said jump, you said "how high?" on the way up. If the sergeant says jump these days, police officers are more likely to say, "well, why am I doing it?" They will question and challenge the managers. And employment laws have had a bearing on the way the organization runs because people are inclined to go to employment tribunals if they feel they have been badly treated.

It is a more difficult job than it was in the past; in broad terms, society has changed. It is much more complex. Communication is instant, transport is rapid, and people can move around a lot. The actual make-up of society in most countries now, certainly in most Western countries, is very diverse. You are likely to meet, even in my provincial city, someone speaking any one of 60 languages in a day. So you have the difficulty and complexity to handle. Inevitably, therefore, it's more difficult.

BA: What do you think should be the role of the police in society?

DC: I believe the police service belongs to the people. Of course we are an arm of the government to the extent that we are funded by government and we have to enforce the laws and we have to meet government targets and so on. I always wanted to police with the consent of the people. So I always wanted to involve the community in what kind of policing they wanted and engage it in the debate about what could be afforded and what could not. I think people deserve to know.

Citizens often have misconceptions in terms of what is possible and what is not possible given the resource levels available. You have to temper public expectations so that their expectations are something like what you are capable of delivering. Because if not, they expect you to do a lot more than you are actually capable of doing, which inevitably leads to disappointment, and then they don't feel you give a good service. For example, on a night shift in the city of Derby, they may think there are 200 police officers on duty, when in actual fact there's probably less than 50.

There is frustration in not being able to get across to the public a lot of information about policing. You know, we did an exercise recently where we asked members of the community, how many burglaries they thought took place in Derbyshire every day, and bear in mind this is an area where about a million people live. The answers were quite astounding. People thought there were up to 1,000 burglaries a day. In actual fact there was an average of seven. They were very pleasantly surprised when they realized that crime was nowhere near as bad as they perceived it to be.

BA: Overall, how do UK citizens view the police service?

DC: The British public is quite cynical about its police service. They don't like us getting too big for our boots! There is a large element of the public that is very supportive of the police service, and thank goodness. But there is also an element of the public that thinks the police service is, you know, a bunch of time wasters. So there is a need for the service to set and maintain the highest values and therefore be a kind of example to the community, something the community can be proud of, and not something the community condemns or feels uncomfortable with.

BA: Personal policing philosophy. What do you think should be the role of the police in society? What should be their job, functions, and roles?

DC: I have always taken a view that the role of the police is to create the climate that allows people to live their lives as they want to live them. And not to restrain them from doing so. My view is, if somebody is doing something that is not illegal and it's not bothering anybody else, then why do the police need to get involved? I believe very much in a police service that tries to maintain a state of tranquility where people can go about their business, unhindered. But inevitably there's also got to be a role for the police in terms of setting the boundaries. A permissive rather than restrictive mindset among officers creates a different, more citizen-friendly policing style and a different relationship with the community.

The police service itself has got to be beyond reproach. So again, officer behavior, conduct, and integrity have got to be of a very high standard, because you are expecting those officers to go out and cast judgment on other people's behavior. I like to be in a position when I am telling somebody they can't do something or they shouldn't do something, they're not able to point at me and say but you do that yourself (laughs). And I think the whole service should practice that.

BA: What organizational arrangements work and which do not?

DC: There is an interesting debate on that. As I say, that sets out the broad structure of the Tripartite; it is kind of a three-legged stool. That works when the power is balanced. It works when each of the three parties does its own job and doesn't try to do the job of the other two. And of late, there's been a little bit too much of the home secretary trying to do the job of the police authorities, and the police authorities trying to do the job of the chief constables. And to some extent, the home secretary trying to do the job of the chief constables. And so it has become a little bit centralized in the UK. There has been a little too much power drawn to the Home Office and decision making.

I believe, as the chief of my county, I have a responsibility to ensure that I understand what the citizens of my county want me to do. And to explain to them, whether I can do it or if I can't do it, why not. I don't think you can do that from a remote bunker somewhere 100 miles away. To me, that doesn't work.

What works very well is a geographically based structure, where a senior officer will have responsibility for a particular geographical area. And they, in a sense, are simply allowed to get along with policing and not interfered with. I've always found that if you give people a responsibility for time, that is, if they simply cover the shift, that they come on and when they go home, they tend to be less committed, than if you give them the responsibility for an area. Because they will, my officers who were working in neighborhood policing, will give their private cell phone numbers to local citizens. You can call anytime. You know the officers are working on the response units, they come on at a particular time of day and go off at a particular time of day, and they might cover any neighborhood, don't develop that relationship with citizens. So that is something to me that works very well, where citizens and cops have that sort of relationship.

BA: How should policing be performed?

DC: (laugh) That is a huge question! It should be performed sensitively to the needs of the community. It should be performed visibly as far as it can be and there are elements of police work that can't be done visibly, covert criminal investigations and so on. It should be performed with integrity to the highest standards. And it should be performed in harmony with the community, not against the community. Should do it with the community and not to the community, if you see what I mean.

BA: In your experience what policies or programs have worked well and which have not?

DC: In terms of a program that has worked exceptionally well in the UK is the National DNA Database Expansion Program, which I had personal experience with because I was the lead officer on forensics at the time it was running. That is where the government made a large sum of money available to allow police forces to take DNA samples from a much wider range of people who came into police custody and we expanded the National Database. It is approaching four million profiles now. There is a controversial debate around it because there are people on there who have not been convicted of any crime. In terms of a policy that united the police service in the UK and that focused it on developing a very important crime investigation tool, it worked exceptionally well over the 5 years or so that it ran. And the database went from something like 300,000 up to three and a half million. So now, I would say the vast majority of the criminal population in the UK has a profile on the database. Therefore, people who continue to commit crime, after having been DNA profiled, always have the risk that they are going to be identified. And it does, daily, yield very good protections and has increased detective ability considerably. That is a very fine example of a program that has worked very well.

BA: What would you consider to be the greatest problem facing the police at this time?

DC: I think it's got to be terrorism. It's got to be the current Islamist, as opposed to Islamic, terrorism. I would argue that this terrorism is not really about Islam. In a sense it is anarchical. It is nothing to do with Islam in its purest form which is a religion which is against violence. The problem from a police perspective, the difficulty is, that we have a new dimension of thinking the unthinkable. I mean, 9-11 has changed the face of the world. We must start to think about things we have never thought of before that might happen, and therefore start to change the way we work, and the preparations we make for the future. I don't think we are through that. To quote Churchill, "It may be the end of the beginning, but it is definitely not the beginning of the end." We have a generation at least and probably two generations of it to cope with.

The new dimension of it is that the perpetrators want to die. Where we have a long experience in this country of terrorism, over 30 years of Irish terrorism, they did not want to die. In many cases, they actually did not want to kill people. They just wanted to blow things up and make a statement. Islamist terrorists, however, Al Qaeda and their acolytes, are finding a ready supply of willing people who want to die, and want to kill as many people as they possibly can. That is a massive new dimension to counterterrorist policing.

It is a great thing from the U.S. point of view, that since 9-11 there really haven't been any more terrorist attacks. For U.S. police agencies, counterterrorism has risen up their agenda very rapidly, but I still don't feel it is as high on their agenda as it is on ours. We feel the immediacy of it, and I don't think the States does yet.

These people are extremely difficult to detect as we have found in recent years. Inquiries into the 7-7 (2005) London bombings in the transport system have shown that although some of the perpetrators were known, there was nothing to suspect that they were going do something of that magnitude. And so, this is a hugely difficult problem to deal with. It is going to need an awful lot of resources. It is going to need the development of very close relationships with Muslim communities, a development and a trust.

Also, to be frank, it's going to need the Muslim community to get its own house in order. You know, right thinking Muslims who don't support Al Qaeda and the Islamist Fundamentalist approach, have got to stand up and make sure that their young people, particularly, understand that it is the wrong way. And police services around the world have got to understand the need not to alienate the mainstream Muslim community, but actually to work with it, and understand it and develop trust with it. So we're in a long-term battle here. And there's a need to know—who do these people represent? They are an amorphous group. They don't represent a state; it's even difficult to see what philosophy they represent, quite frankly. What do they want? We don't really know what they want. All of which adds to the difficulty of defeating them.

BA: You have said terrorism is our current biggest challenge. What would be easy to change?

DC: Well … (laughter) I never really found anything easy to change. I think all change is potentially difficult.

BA: What should be the relationship between theory and practice?

DC: I have given thought to this, actually, and I think there's quite an unsatisfactory relationship at the moment, and I think this is one of the tensions around the IPES (International Policing Executive Symposium; at www.ipes.info) symposiums. There isn't always an understanding between theorists and practitioners as to what's needed. There is a need generally, for practitioners to express their needs more clearly, and for theorists to seek to focus their areas of research on things that the practitioners will feel most useful. I'm not sure that always occurs.

It is quite understandable because of course academics will tend to have a particular interest in a particular field, and may not always take account of whether the practitioners feel they are useful or not. And you know, one would not want to try and constrain academics to particular types of work if they weren't interested in that. But if the relationship between the two is to be improved and enhanced, then I believe that both parties have to see the benefits of close liaison with the other.

BA: What can practitioners learn from theory, and what can theory builders learn from practitioners?

DC: I think it is much along the same lines, really. In my experience, I have on a number of occasions come across good pieces of research that have made me think about policing in a different way. And I have benefited from that. So there is very definitely something to be gained from a liaison between the two sides. In terms of what theory builders can learn from practitioners, quite often something that has been in the abstract, in the quiet kind of isolation of the study facility, can appear to work on paper but doesn't necessarily work in real life. Therefore, when theories are postulated, it ought to be a regular occurrence that when the theory is put into practice that feedback is given at last. The theory can then be amended to accommodate what the real world situation actually demonstrates in practice. And I am not altogether sure that happens in a systematic way. I mean, what I am saying in broad terms is, it is essential that practitioners have access to theoreticians, and vice versa. And I don't think the communication between the two is as good as it could be.

What we've tried to do for (the 2008) IPES meeting in Cincinnati, if I can give you an example, is we were trying to achieve a better balance between police practitioners and academics. It has proved extremely difficult to do and the balance is still quite heavily

weighted in favor of academics. Because I guess, police practitioners are anxious to get on with the job, rather than spending time
reflecting on what they do and how they do it, and how successful
it is. They live in the moment. I think that a problem with policing generally, internationally, and then certainly nationally, is that
we don't spend enough time thinking through what we are doing
and training for it, and so on. We are actually delivering real-world
services in real time and that tends to often prevent us from quiet
reflection.

BA: What is the relationship right now?

DC: It is improving. I think particularly in the UK. You know there are a number of institutions in the UK that have very close links to their police
practitioners and in fact involve police practitioners in elements of
their research, and to that end, I applaud that. It's extremely useful
that that happens and I believe more of it ought to happen. Then
again, you would probably find it is not a widespread practice.

BA: Is there a specific thing holding back further collaboration?

DC: I think one of the things is finance, actually. I think we often find that
academics are willing to do research, providing police forces are
prepared to pay. And quite often police forces aren't prepared to
pay. Or if academics receive funds from other sources then the
other sources often dictate the academic research ought to be in
a particular area, which may not be entirely useful to police practitioners. So it doesn't quite fit strategically somehow. You know,
they are not quite like a jigsaw piece that fits together. They are
kind of off-center with each other. And I do think finance has quite
a lot to do with it.

BA: What kind of research, in what form, on what questions would you find
most useful for practice?

DC: My kind of background is fairly general and a lot of the research I have
found very useful in the past has been around the neighborhood
policing, community policing arena. I found that extremely helpful, particularly in terms of problem-oriented policing. This has
been quite a vibrant theme in the UK over recent years, with quite
a number of Home Office publications, Home Office research. And
the Home Office has a series of research papers that are among those
that are actually more closely aligned to real world policing needs.

There is an awful lot of good research around. I think one of the
problems is, with active police officers, they simply don't have the
time to sit and read lengthy research papers, so you tend to look for
abstracts. And perhaps in getting the abstracts, you don't always get
the essence of the research. You don't always fully understand the

rationale, and maybe you don't therefore attach so much credibility to it.

And most police officers aren't academic, it has to be said. And so they will not tend to occupy their private time in detailed research about their profession. So theory has got to be accessible. Reports of theoretical investigations have got to be very clearly and simply written, in an easily digestible style. So that people who aren't academic, but who are practical, can (a) understand what is being proposed, and (b) put it into practice. And I don't think that is always the case. I am kind of half-way between an academic and a police officer [laughs]. I hope, a reasonably well-educated police officer who finds the reading of academic papers interesting, but I don't have the time to do it. I know where to look if I want it.

BA: Where do you look?

DC: We have a National Police Library at the Police Staff College at Bramshill. There is a vast array of academic research there, both physically and online.

BA: If not very useful, what could or should theory builders do to make their products more useful to you?

DC: There is more of a dialog to be had. As an example, I was a member of a group that sat in the Home Office which looked at the Home Office Police Science and Technology Strategy, which was about a kind of a futurist look at what policing might need in the future by way of science and technology. As part of that we have a lengthy debate about how we would deploy any sort of research that became available, among academia, in order to generate the sort of research that we would find useful. If that kind of debate were ever to reach fruition in terms of having a recognized system from a national perspective in the UK, I think there would be great benefits in doing that; for identifying what research might need to be done, for prioritizing that research, and for actually giving out grant funding to academics to carry out the research.

BA: You have stated, "the values of developing a clear vision and having a relentless focus to achieve it" have characterized the remainder of your service. Can you explain?

DC: Yes, I've got this way of expressing the importance of leadership really, in that you are not actually much of a leader if nobody is following what you are doing. You can go off in a direction, for a while, and if they don't understand what it is you are trying to achieve, if you turn around and look behind you nobody is there, that's generally what will happen. So when I took my last job as chief, I spent a lot of time with people right through the organization, developing a vision that we could all share. It was essentially a statement of what our organization was about, and what we were trying to achieve. We got a large scale buy-in to that, and people understood what it was about because it was in fairly straightforward language. And once I felt that everybody understood it and everybody had bought into it, I felt then we really could sharpen the focus on achieving the vision, and do that consistently across the whole organization, over a whole range of activities. People would understand why we were doing certain things, because they could see the link to the vision. The vision statement was written down and used on all sorts of publications, and a constant for seven years.

You know, so often we will spend time developing a vision, and then it is stuck on the wall as a sort of a yellowing, curling piece of paper [laughs] and nobody makes it come alive. And then a few years later, people say what was all that about? I wanted to have the vision that people could share, and we would then make it live.

BA: Where do you find theory-based information? What journals, books, publications, reports do you read?

DC: As I mentioned the Bramshill Library has a very extensive collection of journals, and books and articles. On a regular basis, I read police publications. In the UK, we have the *Police Review*, the *Police Professional*, and the *Police Journal*. Also, there is of course, the IPES journal, the *International Journal of Police Science and Management*. Some of the papers presented at the IPES conferences are published here.

BA: Does the UK do research on its own?

DC: Yes. I mean, in most forces it would not be academic research, in the typical sense. It is research from the point of view of organizational management research around the way we organized and deployed resources and the impact of particular operations and we call it operational research. To establish how we might improve services, how we might deliver better results, how we might find efficiency savings, and things like that. It is a constant corporate development process, and most forces in the UK will do some form of research. It may not always be academically rigorous, but it is usually practically useful.

BA: Your background states you are an enthusiastic supporter of Jim Collins' Good to Great philosophy?

DC: Yes, actually it is an approach to leadership, more like a theory than a philosophy. It has a practical application, and I have practically applied it over recent years.

The Good to Great philosophy, which is to get the right people on the bus, get them in the right seats, and develop this kind of momentum, on the big flywheel. I came across Jim Collins only in the last 2 years. What immediately struck me was that Jim Collins articulated precisely exactly what I had been trying to do for years. It was the only time really that I've read a management theory or a management philosophy that I almost entirely agreed with and could relate it to my own practical experience.

My philosophy is very simple. When you go into any organization, find the 25 people who are going to help you change it. The first thing you have got to do when you go into any organization is to find out who are the group of people who you are going to build around to take that organization forward. You will inevitably find, in any organization, there are some people who are never going to change, there are some people who are not going to change for you, and there are some people who want to make changes that you don't want to make. As a leader, usually the best way of dealing with them is not to make them your key players. [laughter] If you have a team full of people who want to be individuals, and play in different directions, it is very difficult to mold them together and take them forward on a single direction.

What I tried to do when I took my last job, was I made changes in the early stages designed to persuade various people to move on, and to allow various other people to have opportunities they otherwise wouldn't have had. I perceived them to be the right people for the bus, as it were. And it took me probably, 2 years to get the right people on the bus. And another year, or 18 months, to get them in the right seats. And then, for the last 3 years, the organization was performing absolutely out of its skin. The performance improved tremendously. A major part of that was a product of getting the right people on the team and getting them on the right places in the team. So that's why, when I picked up Jim Collins, I felt, that's exactly what I've been doing although I never articulated it in that way.

BA: Have you been affected, and how, in the work of your organization by developments outside the country?

DC: The UK is certainly not unique in terms of international migration both for economic and other reasons. We are hugely affected by it, and there has been a massive influx, obviously because of the European Union. The freedom of movement within the European Union gives unfettered access to the UK to all nationals of member states of the EU, both from the point of view of travel and from the ability to work here.

So our communities have changed quite considerably and are incredibly more diverse now and policing is more difficult than it was. What also comes with that is organized crime, people trafficking, and trafficking for the sex trade into the UK. It demands that policing tactics and operations adapt in order to cope with it and resources need to be put to it.

It has also brought a need for more close cooperation between ourselves and policing in other countries.

Relations with other European countries, I think have improved significantly and contacts with other European countries in policing terms have increased exponentially.

BA: Have those interactions been beneficial or harmful?

DC: I cannot say I can think of anything that has been harmful. International relations almost always benefit from dialog and cooperation. I think if you can bring police from different countries together focused on what we have in common rather than what differences we have, you can almost always find a way forward to cooperate. But you understand that policing problems are pretty much the same the world round.

BA: How have developments post September 11 affected your work?

DC: I think tremendously. While a member of the Association of Chief Police Officers (ACPO) the Terrorism and Allied Matters Committee (TAM), post-9-11 we had to completely rethink the international approach to counterterrorist work, and really redesign our whole response to terrorist activity. That work goes on and there is a huge amount that needs to be done. So over the last 5 years, as the lead chief officer in my region, the East Midlands Representative, on TAM, we had to review absolutely everything, from the training we got to the amount of resources available, to the call-out procedures, right through to the way that we deal with community and the way we gather community intelligence, and so on and so forth. It has been a very detailed and intense effort, which has taken up far more time than it ever did pre-9-11. And quite rightly, because in a democratic society it is an absolute priority that such things aren't allowed to defeat democracy.

Very much of what we've done over the last many years, pre 9-11, but certainly more intensely since, is we have tried to develop very strong peace-time links. Very strong community links, in normal running circumstances, where we develop trust and dialog between ourselves and as many of the minority communities as possible.

BA: Are you basically satisfied or dissatisfied with developments in policing?

DC: Well, I am basically neutral [laughter]. There are some developments I am satisfied with, and some I am dissatisfied with. I am concerned that there is an undercurrent in the UK which is seeking to exert stronger political control over the police. I think that is a retrograde step, because in the previous 10 years or so the police have been less tightly controlled by party politics. And I certainly don't want to see a situation where police chiefs are put under political pressure to do or not to do particular things for the benefit of a particular side of the political spectrum. My ideal situation would be that the police are politically neutral, seen as politically neutral, and respected as politically neutral. And not drawn into politics.

BA: What is most needed now to improve policing?

DC: I'd like the community to have a greater in-depth understanding of policing and the difficulties and practicalities of delivering comprehensive policing services, and the cost. And I would like to see greater understanding by politicians of what is possible and what is not possible. So to me, it is understanding and knowledge of police service by the community, that's what is most needed now to improve policing. If people understand what you can and cannot achieve with the resources and the skill levels and the legal framework that is available to you, then surely some of the problems that the police face will be addressed.

Conclusion

Mr. Coleman retired from police service in September 2007. In addition to consulting work, he plans to devote his time to local organizations, including the Derbyshire Association for the Blind, community social services, and sporting organizations. He sums up his policing locally and internationally: "There isn't a massive difference between the problems that police face in the UK, the problems in the States or the problems the police face in China. It's about maintaining law and order and tranquility in society, for the most part. So we all have lots in common, and it is important that dialog continues."

Glossary

Association of Chief Police Officers (ACPO): An independent, professionally led strategic body, in the public interest and, in equal and active partnership with government and the Association of Police Authorities, ACPO leads and coordinates the direction and development of the police service in England, Wales, and Northern Ireland. In times of national need ACPO coordinates the strategic policing response. *http://www.acpo.police.uk/.*

Automatic Fingerprint Identification Systems (AFIS): As a biometric technology, can provide absolute identification of an individual by processing the image of a fingerprint.

Derbyshire Partnership Forum (DPF): The countywide Local Strategic Partnership (LSP) responsible for developing the Derbyshire Community Strategy. *http://www.derbyshire.gov.uk/council/ partnerships/derbyshire_partnership_forum/*

Morgan Report: ("Safer Communities: the Local Delivery of Crime Prevention through the Partnership Approach"—Home Office Standing Conference on Crime Prevention, August 1991) introduced the concept of "community safety" and emphasized that crime reduction should be "holistic" covering both situational and social approaches. The Morgan Report identified six elements crucial to multiagency crime reduction work: structure, leadership, information, identity, durability, and resources.

National Police Library: Membership is free for all serving UK police and police staff. Membership arrangements are also available for non-UK police researchers. For information on joining the library: *http:// www.npia.police.uk/en/5218.htm.*

Neighborhood policing: Provided by teams of police officers and police community support officers (PCSOs), often together with special constables, local authority wardens, volunteers, and partners. Neighborhood policing teams are also known as safer neighborhoods teams or safer stronger communities teams. They are all working with local people and partners to deliver solutions to issues that people say make them feel unsafe in their neighborhood. These can include crime, antisocial behavior, disorder, speeding, and environmental issues such as street lighting. *http://www.neighbourhood-policing.co.uk/.*

Operational research (OR): The discipline of applying appropriate analytical methods to help make better decisions. The OR Society, with members in 53 countries, provides training, conferences, publications, and information to those working in operational research. The society also provides information about operational research to interested members of the general public. To learn more about OR, visit *www.scienceofbetter.co.uk. http://www.orsoc.org.uk/orshop/(sax-ny0blgfv4iifludc1fcy2)/orhomepage2.aspx.*

Police Authorities: A police authority is an independent body made up of local people that sets the strategic direction for the force. *http://www. apa.police.uk/APA/About+Police+Authorities/.*

Police community support officers (CSOs): Police authority support staff, intended to be used on high-visibility foot patrol, providing a strong anticrime presence, and focus predominantly on lower-level crime. *http://police.homeoffice.gov.uk/community-policing/community-support-officers/community-cso-faq/.*

Police National Computer (PNC): Updated in 2007, holds information about people, vehicles, property, and crimes, which can all be accessed electronically by officers 24 hours per day. A report can be found at: *http://police.homeoffice.gov.uk/publications/operationalpolicing/Police_nat_comp.pdf?view=Binary* .

Vision statement: for the Derbyshire Constabulary can be found at *http://www.derbyshire.police.uk/who/10.html.*

Interview with Harold L. Hurtt, Chief of Police, City of Houston Police Department, Houston, Texas, USA

16

INTERVIEWED BY DR. ELIZABETH H. MCCONNELL

The Interview

Chief Hurtt and Dr. McConnell met in Chief Hurtt's office on three occasions, September 9, November 11, and January 14 to complete the interview. Dr. McConnell wrote Chief Hurtt's responses as well as tape-recorded the sessions. Once each session was completed, the notes and tapes were transcribed and both parties worked together editing the interview. The process was more lengthy than anticipated; however, we believe that the process produced the best product. I am deeply appreciative of Chief Hurtt's contribution to the project and hope that we can work together in the future.

Chief Hurtt's Career

Harold L. Hurtt serves as the chief of police in the City of Houston Police Department (HPD) and has since March 24, 2004. As chief, he reports to the mayor and is responsible for the effective and efficient operation of the police department in the fourth largest city in the United States. He is in charge of a staff of 6,300 sworn and nonsworn officers and an annual budget of $606 million. He describes his duties in much the same way that many major metropolitan police chiefs do, for example, "planning, leading and facilitating the activities of the department personnel in preserving order, preventing crime, protecting life and property, and enforcing laws and municipal ordinances" and "cultivating good community relations." Of the varied duties he acknowledged, good community relations is the glue that bonds the chief to those he serves, whether department personnel, civic leaders, or members of the community.

Hurtt is a chief who came up through the ranks. He began his career in policing on June 22, 1968 when he accepted an early discharge from the

United States Air Force to join the Phoenix Police Department (PPD) in Phoenix, Arizona. His first 7 years in policing were spent assigned to the Patrol and Community Relations Bureau. Hurtt is one of the few U.S. police officers who walked a beat as well as served as a youth-resource officer for elementary and high schools at a time when the community policing model was in its infancy in the United States. It is through these experiences that Hurtt developed an appreciation for community policing and an understanding of the power derived from good police-community relationships.

Hurtt understands the need for and supports higher education in policing and it can be said that he leads by example with regard to higher education. For example, he attended Arizona State University while a patrol officer and received the Bachelor of Science degree with a major in sociology in 1977. Additionally, while serving in staff-command positions he attended the University of Phoenix where he received a master's degree in organizational management in 1991.

Hurtt seized the opportunity to lead a police department in 1992 when he accepted the position of chief of the Oxnard Police Department (OPD) in Oxnard, California. He returned to the PPD as chief in 1998 where he served until 2004 when he began his duties as chief at HPD. To date he has led three police departments as chief and has over 39 years experience in police work, 15 of which has been as chief.

Hurtt is a staunch proponent of innovation and change in policing as reflected by substantive changes in the police agencies he managed. Central to the diverse innovations he implemented is the community policing model. For example, he played an integral role in the enhancement of the youth and crime prevention programs in PPD's Community Relations Bureau and in cultivating good community relations by interacting with government, fraternal, and community members. Innovations that reflect community policing efforts by Hurtt while chief in Oxnard include opening the first police storefront, starting the Police Activities League, increasing Neighborhood Watch Patrols, enhancing the police department's cable television program, Street Beat, and co-founding the Ventura County Leadership Program.

Hurtt talks about his impact on policing in broader terms, acknowledging the importance of changes in the routine day-to-day operations of police departments he administered. For example, he has a record of significant accomplishments in the following areas: community policing, department operations, personnel management, policy development, the budget process, labor relations, and community relations. As a chief, he believes it is necessary to develop a broad perspective of policing and this is done by being assigned to all police divisions rather than through specialization.

EHM: Did you always know you wanted to do police work?

HLH: Not really, I think what got me interested in police work was the 1960s and what was happening in America. At that time, I was in the air force and I watched the civil rights demonstrations on television. I knew I had to play some role to bring about change. I knew I did not want to march, throw rocks, or whatever, so I decided I could change the system from the inside doing police work. That was the impetus for my career in law enforcement.

EHM: What about how your career developed surprised you?

HLH: When I began police work I wanted to be a homicide investigator, I did want to specialize at that point. Because I also wanted to affect changes in civil rights, I knew my career path in policing needed to include every job I could possibly obtain. I began in patrol, moved to walking the beat, and then was chosen for an assignment in the Community Relations Bureau. That is where the PPD was focusing on police community relations. That is also where I was assigned to schools as a youth-resource officer. Being on a walking beat, working in the schools and in community relations is where I developed my philosophy of community-based policing. The walking beats were in the neighborhoods and schools, and around the bars. We did not have a car, in some cases we were literally dropped off by an officer. This in essence forced you to develop positive community relationships because you were there for 8 hours. So that is where I developed problem-solving skills and learned the importance of good community relationships. I realized that the police get most of their information from the public and if you are not approachable then you do not get information. I had a very successful experience as a patrol officer because people (from the neighborhoods I patrolled) would call me and tell me who committed offenses. Detectives would call me and give me descriptions of a suspect and because of the people in the community I knew, I could assist the detectives with their cases. Putting the emphasis on developing positive relationships with people in the community, government representatives, led to my success in promotional processes including becoming police chief in Phoenix. Some of these people often were on boards that influenced decisions made by police managers and city officials. The positive relationships I developed with people in the community paid off, not only in the apprehension of offenders but also in the advancement of my career.

EHM: Did your work prove as interesting or rewarding as you thought it would?

HLH: Oh yes, definitely!

EHM: How is it interesting?

HLH: We make the news; we know what the news will be tomorrow. People get up (in the morning) and read about what is happening. We already know what is happening, either if it is what is internal to the police department or external in the government or community, at some point in time someone will have contacted the police department. They will be calling for assistance for things that are happening next week, or with immediate problems, or just to inform the department about what is going on. Also, being out in the community people tell you things if they trust you. So you are a day or two ahead of the rest of the world.

You learn a lot from children. When you are working in the schools, you hear a lot about what is going on, about what will be played out on the weekend. You learn that the east side may be feuding with the west side. You share that information with the department so that it is prepared for the conflicts that are likely to occur.

EHM: Surely one of the most interesting aspects of police work is the people you come in contact with?

HLH: Yes, that is true. They range from the people you may have arrested to those you have helped to those who have helped you solve some major crimes throughout your career. They even include one young man who was a community activist who was sometimes on the opposite side of the law. So when I went back to Phoenix as chief, I ran across him on the street and I recognized him although he was much older. He says, "hey dude, I made you a success."

I can recall one day when I was a captain with PPD there was a shooting in a housing project and it turned out that an Anglo officer shot a young African American man in the back. This incident caused a tremendous uproar, from the state government down through the community. I can recall working throughout those next few days, meeting people that as an officer I did not think I would ever interact with, from the governor's office to legislators, the city manager and mayor, and community leaders. All of them wanted to know what we were going to do about it, how did we let it happen, what were we going to do to keep it from happening again? You experience all of the things that as a police officer on the street you had no idea you would experience. As a result of my many police experiences I have been elected president of the Major Cities Chiefs, have traveled to Israel and sat at a table, like this, and talked with Prime Minister Ariel Sharon about terrorism. It has been an outstanding career as far as expanding my horizons, from being a beat officer to looking at threats from an international perspective, such as terrorism and homeland security issues. These are not things that I ever imagined I would do when I began my career.

Changes Experienced

EHM: What do you see as the most important changes in policing over the course of your career?

HLH: What will always be the most important element in policing are personnel. The skills that are required for police officers today have significantly changed. Considering the skills needed to be able to take advantage of the technology and forensic science, such as DNA, crime analysis, all of which support police work. It is also important now to be able to forecast where crime may occur in your city. The new recruit needs to be able to take advantage of all this new information and resources.

Politics is another element that has changed. Officers need to be able to understand and survive in the political arena. I can recall as a young captain or major attending a staff meeting to deal with a critical issue occurring in the police department. One of the more senior members of staff said, "you know we were never involved in politics and there is no reason for us to start now." I think that we have learned that we must develop partnerships and resources that in the past were not as important as they are now. As a police chief, if you are not politically savvy you will soon be a former police chief. Another aspect of politics is police unions, which were almost unheard of when I began police work. Now police unions have considerable impact on police policy and the management of police departments.

It is mandatory now if you are in middle management you must have a minimum of a bachelor's degree. The lifeblood of any organization is its finances and to be able to sit down with city managers and mayors and negotiate for the financial resources that are needed requires an understanding of finance. Police managers must be able to communicate using the language of business and understand budgets and financial forecasting. Many mayors are very successful businesspeople and they expect police chiefs to run the police departments as a business.

EHM: What do you see as the most important changes in policing philosophies over the course of your career?

HLH: We can no longer operate on the "just the facts" philosophy. Progressive police philosophy must integrate community policing, based on partnerships, with high-tech policing. One must consider threats beyond our border, so you have now integrated "global policing" into progressive police philosophy. Our officers now must have a good understanding of what is going on around the world in order to effectively interact with people on the street. Houston is one of the most diverse cities in the United States. It has more than 250,000 Muslim residents, a Latino community that outnumbers the Anglo community, a significant Asian population, and a large African American community. Police officers in Houston must have a global perspective and appreciate diversity to be effective.

EHM: What do you see as the most important changes in policing specializations over the course of your career?

HLH: One of the components of policing where we got caught short 25 or 30 years ago was that we had no idea who we would be providing police services to in the twenty-first century. Most cities during that time were relatively Black, White, and Latino with some Asians and most of these residents could communicate in English. In Houston, we are constantly being challenged with understanding the language and being able to communicate with the people we serve. And more importantly is the necessity to understand the cultures of the people we serve.

EHM: What do you see as the most important changes in policing policies and programs over the course of your career?

HLH: I think that the model that helped us be successful as we adapted to change was community policing. We were fortunate that we did take that model very seriously and expanded it to those communities that were more challenging.

EHM: What do you see as the most important changes in policing personnel/diversity over the course of your career?

HLH: I believe that the personnel of a police department should reflect the community it serves in terms of diversity. To accomplish this employment policies have certainly changed in the last 30 years. Not only should community diversity be reflected among patrol officers, the same should be so for the command staff. It took the riots in the 1960s to demonstrate the need for the police to reach out to the communities they serve, especially during critical times. There was a time, I recall, while attending community meetings when I heard a minister say that minorities fear the police and the police fear minorities. Of course this begs the question, how do you have partnerships between groups where no one trusts one another? Racial, ethnic, and gender diversity has been a difficult objective to achieve; however, we are closer to making necessary changes today than we were 20 years ago; but understand, there is still much more to achieve.

EHM: What do you see as the most important changes in policing equipment over the course of your career?

HLH: I think the police, just like the rest of the world, have been significantly impacted by computerization. Having the ability to gather
and analyze data that we use in making decisions about resource
allocations and goal setting has helped us immensely. Today most
police agencies are capable of making data-driven decisions.

EHM: What changes in external conditions have had a significant impact on
policing, for example, support from communities?

HLH: We could not have calm and peace in communities without community support and people being willing to stand up and be involved,
especially at times when the police use deadly force against members of the community. Some of the critical moments that require
community support are when questions of excessive use of force
arise, questionable use of Tasers, and the police handling of the
mentally ill. The chief's response to this is to make sure that the
officers are following policy and trained to handle themselves as
professionals. I applaud the fact that we were smart enough to
reach out to the community (when these situations arose) and to
take advantage of the community resources that were there. The
faith-based community has been tremendously helpful.

EHM: What changes in external conditions have had a significant impact on
policing, for example, changes in legal powers?

HLH: I used to walk the beat where the incident occurred that resulted in the
Miranda decision. But you know that was a needed change in the
way we conduct police business. I think in some cases the Supreme
Court decisions helped us make the changes that made law enforcement more professional. These decisions mandated more training
that prepared officers how to do their jobs and how to do it legally.
I believe that the legal decisions have been supportive of police professionalism rather than a hindrance. The question of whether the
courts have handcuffed the police, ones view on that depends on
who is on the giving and who is on the receiving end of the service.
I believe most community residents, when involved in interactions
with police, would say that they are treated more humanely as a
result of the changes.

EHM: What changes in external conditions have had a significant impact on policing? For example, changes in relations with minority communities?

HLII: I think that the schools and social service agencies have helped us.
I was a school-resource officer in two of the toughest schools in
Phoenix and I was able to establish some very positive relationships with young people at the high schools. I was successful in
collaborating with the community, especially the Boys and Girls
Club, to work with young people. And I know that this approach
works because there are several individuals that I worked with who

are now command staff members in major police agencies. They have told me that the relationships they had with me are the reasons for their success.

EHM: What changes in external conditions have had a significant impact on policing? For example, political influence?

HLH: At the local level, I believe policies concerning immigration enforcement by state and local agencies are currently the hot issue. In the past most police administrators were not concerned with things beyond their jurisdiction. Now police managers must have a global perspective, one that encompasses both national and international concerns. Today it is not enough to just be concerned with traditional public safety, now homeland security must also be considered. Policing has become more global in nature.

EHM: Overall, has the quality of policing improved or declined in terms of street policing?

HLH: Due to the level of training and skills that recruits have they are not as myopic. They are more broad minded, they have access to the world through the Internet and television. They are more informed about the local, national, and international issues that play out in our cities. Street policing has changed since the attack on the World Trade Center on September 11. An example of how the focus of street-level policing has changed is that we are now concerned about national and international gangs and terrorists rather than just the local youth gangs in cities. Policing now reflects an international perspective.

EHM: In general, is it more or less difficult to be a patrol officer now than in the past?

HLH: I think that it is, the officer is dealing with a more educated public, cop shows on television, legal decisions, and the public's access to this information makes police work more difficult. The officer is often admonished for not reading a suspect's rights or the suspect demands to see a search or arrest warrant. The other thing that is more challenging is the increased use of drugs and the availability of guns. Another thing that compounds this problem is that there is little reluctance by perpetrators to use guns and other weapons against the police and the community.

EHM: In general, is it more or less difficult to be a police manager now than in the past?

HLH: I believe that it is more difficult. Accountability has certainly increased for police managers. Police managers are accountable to mayors, community members, courts, police unions, and numerous external watch groups that monitor the criminal justice system.

Personal Policing Philosophy

EHM: What do you think should be the role of the police in society?

HLH: I talk about this a lot. We have a responsibility to maintain an environment where people can be successful, in other words a safe environment. A place where residents can start and maintain businesses, have families, where schoolteachers can teach because they are confident that there are no weapons in the schools. This includes crime prevention, apprehension, investigation, and educating the public about their safety. Because policing is very expensive, we cannot afford to hire enough officers to maintain a safe environment by ourselves. As a result we look to the community to participate in the process and educate them about how they can protect themselves and their property.

EHM: What policies on relations with the community work well?

HLH: The community is our strongest partner in our efforts to provide public safety and we need to continue to enhance that relationship. When I talk about the community, I am not just talking about the residents and the neighborhood groups. I am also talking about the businesses, the media, and other areas of government. The community is anyone that can help us in achieving our public-safety goals.

You have to understand that community empowerment can get messy. For example, partners may decide that they want more of a role influencing decision making in the department. They are in the room, they are at the table, and they want to have the opportunity to set policy. It is really time consuming for police managers to work with community partners, making sure that they understand their limitations in a way that does not hinder the partnership. It has been my experience that members of the religious community and media are key players as community partners. They have the ability to deliver the message to the largest segments of society on a regular basis.

EHM: How should policing be performed? For example, what should be preferred priorities and strategies, should they focus on hard-edged crime control, prevention, services, or order?

HLH: The most important priority is crime control. However, communities want and expect police departments to be full service agencies. Police agencies should assist the community with the prevention of crime and safety issues, such as providing assistance to businesses and private citizens about making businesses and homes safer and resistant to criminal victimization.

I believe that it is important to communicate with the community, even when it appears that the community does not need the police. This is the opportune time for officers on the street to establish personal relationships with members of the community; thus, providing them with opportunities for input regarding their needs and expectations. Officer contact with members of the community goes a long way in limiting the levels of fear of crime on the part of the community. The community becomes more confident that the police are there making their communities safer.

EHM: What types of problems do you consider appropriate for the following styles of policing: proactive-reactive, community policing, and law enforcement policing?

HLH: The style of policing used depends on the situation. Some of the most important aspects of policing are catching criminals and responding to calls for service in the community in a reasonable amount of time. There is a great deal of value in being able to stop and talk with members of the community to determine their expectations. If serious crime like gang activity or crimes of violence are prevalent, then the residents in these neighborhoods expect a hard-edged style of policing, which is associated with proactive-reactive policing. Prevention and service are expected in areas experiencing lesser types of crime.

Chiefs have to be flexible. Their job is a balancing act when meeting the needs of diverse groups in the community as some groups expect and need crime control where other groups are more concerned with crime prevention or services. One of the great dilemmas for police administrators is providing all that the community expects, especially if resources are limited. The chief has to understand what is most important and prioritize the use of resources to meet the needs of the diverse groups in the community.

Problems and Successes Experienced

EHM: In your experience, what policies or programs have worked well and which have not?

HLH: I think that the policies that have worked well for me, especially recently, are policies that have allowed us to take advantage of cutting edge technology, for example, using cameras to monitor traffic lights and high crime areas, use of the Internet for online offense reports. Use of this technology allows the department to maintain the maximum number of police in the neighborhoods where they have more opportunity to build relationships with the people they serve.

One recent HPD policy that has not worked well was a pursuit policy. Although I successfully implemented the same policy in two other cities where I was chief, the policy generated considerable controversy in Houston. The policy significantly limited police officers' authority to engage in automobile chase pursuits of criminals. The basis for the policy was my concern for the safety of innocent citizens as well as the safety of police officers engaged in the pursuit. One thing I was reminded about by the controversy is the importance of consulting all stakeholders for input. I implemented a policy that I thought was good for the community and the police and was supported by both to find out that was not the case. Even though similar policies were accepted in other cities where I worked, as well as other major cities, there was opposition to it in Houston.

EHM: Can you speculate about what makes a policy successful?

HLH: Successful policies are those that reflect the wishes and needs of the people that are affected by them.

EHM: What do you consider the greatest problem facing the police at this time?

HLH: Recruitment and hiring of qualified candidates is the greatest problem we face at HPD and around the country. We are competing with the military and the private sector for the most marketable youth. In a robust economy such as we are currently experiencing, the private sector offers more opportunities for young people beginning their careers. Additionally, increases in the number of youth attending college have resulted in making them more marketable, thus more desirable by the private sector. Our competition for recruits is not just the military anymore, but now includes the private and public sectors.

Another issue that hampers recruitment is the drug culture in America. Drug use standards set by police departments eliminate large numbers of police recruits; even so the policing profession must maintain the drug standards. Policing is a very complex job and not everyone is suited for police work. So, it is incumbent on police management to maintain standards such that people who are suited for police work are the ones that are hired.

EHM: What problems in policing do you find are the most difficult?

HLH: The ineffectiveness of the criminal justice system is, I believe, the biggest problem in policing. Since we are considered the "gate keepers," there is the expectation that the police are responsible for making the community safe. However, law enforcement is only one component of the system. A safe society depends on the success of all components of the criminal justice system, for example, policing, courts, corrections, and juvenile system. Because law enforcement is the most visible part of the criminal justice system, it tends to receive more criticism for the system's failure.

The juvenile justice system has not kept pace with treatment demands of delinquent youth. As a result, many delinquent youth become adult offenders and this makes the job of policing much more difficult. In fact, we have very few successful treatment programs for juveniles and adults; this means law enforcement, as the gatekeeper, continues to arrest the same people repeatedly. Our ineffectiveness in changing criminal behavior is what I regard as the biggest challenge.

EHM: Which of the following would be the easiest internal problem(s) to change, culture of the organization, managerial deficiencies, allegations of corruption, or gender-related problems?

HLM: Management deficiencies are the easiest of the four to change. Chiefs appoint their command staff and these appointments impact the other internal areas. These appointments guide police departments. The most difficult of these to change is the culture of the organization as police organizations tend to be very traditional, often characterized by family links and unwritten informal agreements between management and labor.

One strategy for addressing gender problems in police organizations is to appoint a command staff that reflects the gender of the department. I have made it a point to see that HPD's command staff is representative of the department in terms of diversity.

The best way to address all of these internal problems is to set high expectations.

EHM: What would be the easiest externally generated problems to change, resources or community support? Is anything easy?

HLH: Community support is key as resources depend on support from the community. If the police department loses the confidence of the community, it is difficult to get it back. The Los Angeles Police Department's loss of community confidence has created a very difficult situation for that police department as they are continuing to struggle. Community support is essential. Support by the community provides the resources needed to pay salaries, purchase equipment, and to function day to day. And community support is not limited only to money; the officer on the beat would not be very effective without assistance from neighborhood residents.

It has been my experience that nothing in policing is easy, especially when it comes to change.

Theory and Practice

EHM: What should be the relationship between theory and practice?

HLH: When I was a university student, I was most impressed by two business professors who were both businessmen and professors. The thing that impressed me was that they tested business theory in their businesses and would then share their findings with their classes. These practitioners were also academicians. This real world approach left a lasting impression on me and I believe is a good model for theory and practice. Academicians should have an understanding of the practical aspects of organizations. The least effective approach is someone delivering a lecture on abstract concepts, yet has no understanding of the practical application of those concepts. This is especially relevant when applying theories to management of large police departments.

EHM: What is the relationship between theory and research?

HLH: Theory and research go hand in hand. Academicians with practical experience tend to have more credibility with police practitioners than researchers who have never worked in the field. Practitioners believe that researchers who also have field experience truly understand the nature of police work. Researchers who have least credibility with practitioners are the researchers who do not have practical experience because these researchers do not understand what it takes to make changes in a police organization, to develop programs, or to sell ideas to the city manager or the mayor.

I was disappointed with the research findings regarding the DARE [Drug Abuse Resistance Education] program. Although I was never a DARE officer, I believe that many positive outcomes resulted from DARE. I also believe that the researchers evaluating DARE did not ask the correct questions and that these questions were not asked because DARE practitioners were not part of the evaluation process. I believe that the evaluation did not consider the relationships between DARE officers and youths or how these relationships influenced youths' decisions about using drugs, especially at earlier ages. Parents became more knowledgeable about drugs due to DARE as children educated their parents. Parents have told me that they learned about drugs from their younger children and that they used this information to help them deal with the teenage children in the family, that they learned what signs to look for, what drugs looked like and smelled like.

Prior to DARE there were no police in the classroom; children would see officers on the beat, which is not the same thing as having them come to class. DARE was successful in changing community perceptions of the police, elevating the level of trust by the community of the police. I know that DARE did much more than impact decisions about using drugs, it provided opportunities for positive police interaction with families that the police had not developed before.

EHM: Does a relationship between research and practice exist?

HLH: Yes, there is a relationship between research and practice and there should be. I encourage police managers to cultivate this relationship as researchers provide valuable information for policy and program development. I believe that professors and graduate students are great resources for police managers. They are particularly helpful with special projects and can be called upon as consultants. They can partner with police management; for example, we are currently involved in two outstanding projects with Northwestern University. One of the projects is an analysis of HPD's calls for service and the other is an analysis of traffic citations. The findings from these projects will assist HPD management in allocation of resources as well as provide factual data upon which to justify the need for additional resources. This is especially important when justifying additional personnel as nothing seems to impress funding sources more than academically sound research.

EHM: What kind of research collaboration would you find most useful to police practice?

HLH: One type of collaboration that had been most helpful to HPD is with working with other police managers to identify and prioritize items that require funding by the state legislature. What we have discovered is that individual department needs share similarities to other departments. By working with others, for example the Texas Police Chiefs Association, we have been successful in convincing the legislature to fund things that are important to most departments.

A type of collaboration that, I believe, has not been tapped is private security. There are 45,000 private security employees in the city of Houston who could provide immense assistance to HPD. Can you imagine what would happen if you could get HPD information regarding stolen property or people being sought by HPD to these employees? I believe that private security is an untapped resource that could increase the effectiveness of police departments. One thing I have learned in my attempt to engage private security is that they too are setting their employment standards higher and that they tend to have more financial resources than police departments. I believe that this is something that we need to consider, that is public-private partnerships and collaborations for sharing information.

EHM: What kind of research would you find most useful to police practice?

HLH: A national formula for staffing police departments that works is needed. HPD and similar large police departments are expected to use the same staffing/funding model used by New York City where relatively small areas are saturated with police officers. We need researchers to establish funding models for law enforcement agencies; models that reflect differences such as size of jurisdiction and tax revenues. This also relates to crime rate data. Crime rates in Houston are compared to crime rates in places like New York City without taking into account the differences in the two locations that influence the crime rates of each. For example, NYPD spends significantly more money on law enforcement and has greater ability to reassign officers to target crime-ridden areas than does HPD. A more holistic approach in the development of crime rate data is needed.

How we deal with the mentally ill needs further research. We need to determine if the handling of the mentally ill by the criminal justice system is as cost effective as mental health agencies providing treatment for them. Using criminal justice system revenues to respond to the needs of the mentally ill is not a prudent use of public funds. It results in significant costs, for example, costs associated with arrests, criminal prosecution, and incarceration. In the end it does very little in addressing the treatment needs of the mentally ill, which means that this group, like the criminal, becomes statistics in the revolving door of offender populations. We need research that analyzes the criminalization of the mentally ill and its economic impact on the criminal justice system.

Transnational Relations

EHM: How have you been affected by transnational relations?

HLH: I have had the unusual privilege of being a chief in three states that have international borders: Arizona, California, and Texas. Illegal immigration was and continues to be problematic in the three states. In the next 3 to 5 years, how the criminal justice system deals with illegal immigration will be problematic because the public is polarized about the issue. We expect U.S. cities to become more diverse as immigration increases. Several years from now when immigrant populations become the voting majority criminal justice policies for responding to illegal immigrants possibly will change. Immigration is the next most critical issue that we in this country have to address.

The big question that the United States has to address with regard to immigration is who do we close the doors on? We are seen as the police of the world as we have been advocates of human rights. However, our approach now seems to be more related to the availability of oil and the U.S. economy rather than human rights.

I am reminded of a conversation I had several weeks ago about immigration when someone said that the United States opened its borders to people providing cheap labor. When this happened laborers came with their families and their needs. The business community in the United States wanted the cheap labor; however, no one was prepared to handle the social problems associated with immigrant populations and we continue to be unprepared.

EHM: Have transnational demands on human rights affected the work of HPD?

HLH: HPD changed some of its policies. A policy that comes to mind is the policy that requires HPD officers to determine the residency status of all arrestees. This policy was implemented following the shooting death of HPD Officer Rodney Johnson by a felon who was in the United States illegally. According to policy, residency status is noted in arrest records and residency status statistics are reported to ICE (Immigration and Custom Enforcement). Further, if it is determined that the arrestee is in the United States illegally, ICE personnel are notified because they have jurisdiction in immigration matters. Another change is that HPD welcomes ICE to visit its jail to pursue immigration cases. Prior to this change, ICE inquiries were made through the Harris County Jail.

HPD actively supports the funding of federal agencies that are responsible for immigration matters. We recognize that these agencies do not have the resources needed to adequately handle the deportation and illegal immigration of illegal immigrants. We encourage the federal government to provide the funds needed by ICE to enforce immigration laws. HPD has also made it clear that "Houston is not a sanctuary city." If you are involved in criminal conduct you will be arrested and prosecuted.

EHM: Have transnational demands for universal codes of ethics affected the work of the HPD?

HLH: No, I do not think so. The greatest impact by transnational issues has been in the area of terrorism, specifically, how law enforcement agencies approach terrorism since the September 11 attacks in this country. There is a greater degree of cooperation in the law enforcement community; this is true across all levels. For example, prior to September 11, there was minimal sharing of information among law enforcement agencies, except for the few task forces that were appointed to handle special criminal conduct. The attack on the United States made it clear that everyone, public service agencies and agencies in the private sector, must work together for the safety of America.

Use of force is one human rights issue that generated correspondence from Amnesty International. HPD received numerous letters encouraging the use of Tasers, rather than guns, in situations requiring deadly force. HPD's Taser policy encourages the use of Tasers, prior to having to resort to using deadly force. The policy also discourages the use of Tasers unless their use is necessary to bring a situation under control.

EHM: Have practical interactions with police from other countries affected the work of the HPD?

HLH: Yes, interactions between HPD officers and police officers from other countries are different compared to how they were before the September 11 bombings There is a greater willingness to share information. I believe that this change resulted from the success we have had in addressing terrorism. September 11 created the necessity for public service agencies to work together for the safety of society. Cooperative relationships were established and everyone agreed that it was for the greater good; even when the crisis was over, cooperation and collaboration continued. The threat of terrorism will bound law enforcement from this point forward.

EHM: Have personal experiences outside the United States affected the work of the HPD?

HLH: I have made official visits to Israel, China, and Costa Rica with visits to the latter two resulting in recommended changes to their law enforcement practices. I believe that the United States has benefited greatly from law enforcement practices in the United Kingdom, particularly with regard to terrorists. For example, the British have successfully demonstrated the use of security cameras in public places. The American public, always vigilant about privacy, has been reluctant to support the placement of security cameras in public places; however, I believe we are witnessing a growing trend by Americans to support this use of security cameras. Further, I believe growing support by Americans is associated with England's success in identifying terrorists with the use of security cameras. HPD and other law enforcement agencies in the Houston area are experiencing a growing use of security cameras, particularly for purposes of traffic enforcement, and public safety in public places.

EHM: Have new crime threats affected the work of the HPD?

HLH: New crime threats that have significantly affected work at HPD are computer-related crimes such as child pornography and abuse, terrorism, and financial crimes such as fraud. In many cases, offenders in these crimes reside in a different state or country, thus making these offenses difficult to investigate and prosecute. Successful prevention or apprehension in multijurisdictional crimes requires collaboration among law enforcement authorities and governments.

Another new crime-related threat that affects HPD officers is the weaponry used by street criminals. Although HPD policy supports the use of quality firearms, the standard police firearm is often no match for the automatic weapons used by violent street criminals such as drug and human traffickers. This has been a continuing problem, as it seems that when law enforcement agencies upgrade officers' weapons, street criminals raise the stakes higher by using something more deadly. Further, HPD's employment of higher caliber weapons, body armor, and other new technology has budget implications as these are more costly and require additional training.

Lastly, human smuggling is another new crime threat. The significant profits associated with human smuggling coupled with demand for cheap labor are driving forces behind increase in human smuggling offenses. The lucrative nature of these offenses, as well as drug trafficking, has resulted in the escalation of violent behavior. To protect their financial interest, criminals committing these offenses are using higher caliber weaponry and are willing to do what is necessary as they have little regard for human life. As a result, police work has become more dangerous.

EHM: Have transnational interactions been beneficial or harmful?

HLH: Transnational interactions have mostly been beneficial, as we have bridged the gap that existed prior to September 11 attacks. We now have a common enemy, terrorists. Our common enemy has provided the impetus for our working together.

EHM: What kind of external international influences are beneficial and which ones less so?

HLH: I believe policing successes in the United Kingdom, France, Canada, and Germany have been most beneficial to policing in the United States. For example, the United Kingdom's successes in identifying terrorists have directly affected the American public's support for the use of security cameras in public spaces. Policing in the United States has benefited from advances in training and use of experimental equipment by all our international colleagues.

General Assessments

EHM: Are you generally satisfied or dissatisfied with developments in policing?

HLH: I am generally optimistic about developments in policing, especially with regard to the quality of personnel seeking careers in law enforcement and advances in technology. I believe the personnel we are hiring are better educated and more sensitive to cultural diversity; as a result, they have a more stabilizing effect on law enforcement and the community. Modern technology is a "force multiplier"; for example, the technology used to track criminals is beginning to equal having additional personnel in the field. One possible negative effect of technology is a decrease in the human side of law enforcement. It is important to maintain a balance between high tech and high touch.

EHM: What are the most likely developments you see happening?

HLH: The most likely developments in policing are international bridging and increasing amounts of violence. This is especially true with respect to the growth in international banking crimes. With regard to violence, we are seeing an escalation in violence intensity among our citizens, for example, road rage. It seems that there is a growing desensitization to violence; this increases citizens' willingness to engage in violent attacks for the most minor reasons.

EHM: What would you like to see happening?

HLH: Coordination between local, state, national, and international agencies is an area where much improvement has occurred, yet there remains room for improvement. Instantaneous sharing of information among the various groups would enhance crime prevention and apprehension.

Society would benefit greatly from improvements in other components of the criminal justice system. For example, if the corrections component were successful in the treatment and rehabilitation of offenders, there would be considerably less crime as repeat offenders commit many crimes. This is not a criticism of corrections agencies but more an indictment of society's unwillingness to provide the resources required for the rehabilitation of offenders.

EHM: What is most needed to improve policing?

HLH: A good start in improving policing is to begin with personnel. Departments need to hire personnel that reflect the communities they serve. We need personnel who understand the culture of their citizens and can speak their language, as their work requires them to deal with people in the community every day. Equipment and technology that facilitates officers' instantaneous access to information is important. This would result in officers being able to view, analyze, and respond to crime as it is happening. Of course to accomplish both of the above, police departments must have the resources to employ the quality people, purchase equipment and technology, and to train its personnel.

Conclusion

Chief Harold Hurtt is a dedicated chief who leads by example. For example, his view that the police should mirror the community is reflected in the diversity of HPD's command staff and line staff personnel, even though not everyone at HPD supports this commitment. His vow to engage the community in policing is exemplified by the numerous programs and projects that Houston-area communities have to interact with HPD. Nothing embodies his dedication to policing as a profession more than HPD's policies supporting higher education and training for its officers. Chief Hurtt's engaging manner and ability to put one at ease resulted in an interview that seemed more like a conversation with a colleague than an interview with a chief executive officer of a police department in the fourth largest city in the United States.

Interview with Chief Gary L. Vest, President of the Ohio Association of Chiefs of Police, USA

17

INTERVIEWED BY BONNIE ARMBRUSTER

The Unique Structure of Law Enforcement in the United States

The model for policing in the United States is very different than any other country in the world. Each large city down to the smallest town has its own law enforcement agency or police department (PD) which is led by its chief. A term commonly used to describe this type of policing structure is "home rule." Each police department is focused and predominately supported financially by the community in which it serves. Local departments are unique in the services they offer to residents to prevent crime and promote safety. The concept of community policing[1] is widespread and popular across the country.

The United States has approximately 18,000 police agencies, which are dispersed across 2,042 counties. Unlike countries with a national police, there is no single leader of these agencies. Each state is divided into counties and only 60 to 65 counties in the United States incorporate large cities. Ohio has over 900 law enforcement agencies, which includes towns and villages, highway patrol, and state law enforcement agencies. Each county has a sheriff who usually also operates a county jail. Ohio has 88 counties, thus 88 sheriff offices, and within each county, there are police departments led by a chief for each town, large and small. The federal law enforcement agencies are basically involved with laws that have a national interest or cross state jurisdictional lines. The federal government does not provide basic police services, so fighting crime, drugs, terrorism, etc., in the United States involves the cooperation of federal, state, and local agencies.

Higher education for chiefs, as well as for police officers, has been a focus of policing in the United States for years. It is not uncommon for a chief to hold a bachelor's or master's degree and many police officers have attended college-level programs. A minimum of hours is often required by state governments for in-service training, and these minimums are often surpassed by the chief's own requirements of his or her officers. This has resulted in more highly trained, professional, and culturally sensitive law enforcement agencies in Ohio, and across the country.

251

Background

Gary Vest is the chief of the Powell Police Department and president of the Ohio Association of Chiefs of Police (OACP). In suggesting Chief Gary Vest as the police leader to be the focus of this article, Todd Wurschmidt, PhD, executive director of the OACP, believed Chief Vest serves as an exemplary example of many of the 18,000 chiefs across America. Small towns such as Powell, Ohio represent 80% to 85% of the police agencies in the United States. Thus, the vast majority of geographic area is served by these smaller police agencies. Todd Wurschmidt said, "Chief Vest and thousands of chiefs and sheriffs like him represent the influencing force of U.S. policing. I know of few police leaders who can match Chief Vest in his creative power in influencing the profession of policing and in his unbridled passion."

Chief Vest began his career in law enforcement in 1976, shortly after serving 4 years in the United States Air Force. He received his undergraduate degree in criminal justice and followed with a master's degree in public administration and has made higher education in policing a main focus of his career. In the Powell Police Department his officers receive between 40 and 80 hours of in-service training annually.

Chief Vest was an active member of the Ohio Association of Chiefs of Police (OACP) for many years before being elected president. The OACP is the organizational "think tank" through which Ohio chiefs collaborate to create highly regarded educational programs, some of which retain a waiting list of several years. Local police departments allocate funding to train new officers, but rarely can afford training for leadership and skill training for department managers. The OACP fills the need for management and leadership training very efficiently and with a high degree of excellence.

The Interview

Two interviews took place with Chief Vest in May 2007, at the offices of the Powell Police Department.

BA: How does the Ohio Association of Chiefs of Police (OACP) advance policing?

GV: The OACP is a unique blend of law enforcement executives, with the organizational structure consisting of two major components. The first is the most critical part: the practitioners, including the law enforcement personnel, the police chiefs, the command officers, some sheriffs, the Ohio State Highway Patrol, and other state and federal law enforcement agencies. They set the direction for the

OACP by prioritizing critical issues, establishing needs for the profession, and then defining effective solution-oriented programs. Overall, the OACP is a means by which upper-level law enforcement managers and leaders, through collaborative relationships, address problems we face in our communities.

The other component of the organization, and equally as important, is our administrative staff. We have an executive director, Dr. Todd Wurschmidt, who is an excellent business manager and for the past 23 years has guided the process of all staff operations. Obviously the chiefs do not have the time or resources individually to research and develop quality educational programs; therefore, it is the staff that actually moves the process forward—they are the engine of the ship and the practitioners are at the helm. Through our association, Ohio law enforcement is able to achieve higher levels of competence and educational standards throughout the state, and improve policing within our communities.

BA: What do you offer in the area of higher education for law enforcement?

GV: We offer many excellent educational opportunities for police managers. The STEP program (Supervisor Training and Education Program) is for first-line supervisors; the PELC program (Police Executive Leadership College) is designed to meet the needs of upper-level supervisors, for command staff and chiefs; and the CLEE program (Certified Law Enforcement Executive) allows law enforcement to become credentialed, having been able to demonstrate through examinations, tests, and study of leadership principles, a mastery of knowledge essential to the highest levels of executive performance. We also have in-service training and individual classes in specific areas.

BA: What do you see as the most important changes in policing?

GV: I think technology has been the major change in my career in law enforcement. We now have the ability to capture information with video cameras and other forms of surveillance, the ability to pinpoint geographical locations of a cell phone call, etc. Police cars in many agencies including ours, are outfitted with videotapes, and the cameras come on at the same time as the emergency lights. The ramification for policing is that cameras change conduct, just as it would for the average citizen.

In the past, an officer on the street operated with a sense of autonomy with the citizens and when a crime was committed the officer would be the only witness. Should the officer be called upon to testify in court, he or she would be regarded as more truthful than the citizen.

A shift occurred in the public perception of police, when on March 3, 1991, in Los Angeles, California a citizen videotaped Rodney King being repeatedly struck by the police, forever changing the image of law enforcement and trustworthiness of officers. As a result, technology has changed the way the public views law enforcement.

The media has impacted public perceptions of law enforcement. The capturing of actual law enforcement events on television and the increase of television programs depicting crime scene investigations is another issue that wreaks havoc for prosecutors and police departments across the country. Today when a crime is committed and DNA is not found, it is difficult to prosecute because public perception is that DNA is necessary to prove a person's guilt. However, DNA is not left at every scene. But the expectation from the public is that science will solve all things. The police are being held to a higher standard, in the area of collecting evidence and the preparation of their cases. Our media and the availability of DNA have raised the expectations and complexities in our investigations.

Other advances in technology are tools like the Taser electronic device. Although the use of the Taser device has met with controversy, its actual usage has been found to reduce injury to both the suspect and the officer. Studies and opposing views will be presented for a number of years on this subject. As long as there continues to be advanced tools available to the officer there will be a greater expectation that the officer will select the appropriate tool for the situation which is what we call the continuum of use of force.

Laws have become more complex. Twenty-five years ago statutes that consisted of one paragraph today cover multiple pages. Complex laws are more difficult for police officers to learn and uphold.

Labor laws and unionization have brought significant changes to policing. About 25 years ago in Ohio, police departments began collective bargaining, which is simply the right of police officers to negotiate. And because police are not allowed to strike, they may take their case before an arbitrator and obtain a ruling as to whether or not their position should be upheld in this negotiation process.

Unions also have an impact on the discipline process and the removal of an officer. Should an officer be found to have been dishonest, there have been times when an arbitrator literally put them back to work. So the union involvement has been both a positive change for raising the quality of life for police officers, and a negative change when it allows officers to keep their job when they shouldn't.

BA: What changes in external conditions have had a significant impact on policing?

GV: World events clearly have had a significant impact on policing in the United States. We had our eyes opened as a country after September 11, 2001. We saw a shift from the mid-1960s through the early 1990s, because during that time the biggest issue facing local law enforcement was biased-based policing, in other words, racial profiling. It was a concern that the police were targeting minorities. The events of September 11 took the issue of profiling off the radar screen.

BA: How have the developments post September 11 affected your work?

GV: I see an attempt to shift the focus of local law enforcement to terrorism prevention. The primary role of law enforcement is the same after September 11 as it was before. That is, to keep the streets safe, to protect human life and property. We want to protect property and human life regardless of the motive. Terrorism or the threat of terrorism is an ever present danger but remains a front page story only until some other newsworthy incident captures the headlines. Vigilance is essential to the extent that officers continue their normal activities and are mindful of the relationship between terrorism and other traditional crimes. Terrorism may be motivated by religion or politics, but from a crime standpoint, it is still classified as an assault or homicide or a theft or other designated crime. I think initially after September 11, people were very cautious, more alert, more vigilant. This seems to be waning somewhat as time goes on and as there are other priorities.

BA: Are the police treating Muslims fairly?

GV: I think generally speaking, the police are only delivering the expectations of society. After September 11, we did not know who the enemy was, so the face we began painting on terrorism was unfortunately the face of Islam and Muslim countries and cultures. That was the dreadful downside of the tragic event.

The fact is that we have good, honest, hardworking Muslims in our communities who have been here long before September 11. However, after September 11 we instantly began to equate a Muslim from the Middle East as being opposed to the American way of life. In fact, the American way of life made it possible for Muslims and people of other faiths to live here in freedom in the first place. The role of the police is to uphold equal protection for everybody. We need to make sure we are responsive to everybody, irrespective of public perspectives or misconceptions. These issues are more an act of humanity within our country for the profession, that is, how do we respect the rights of all people to practice any faith they choose?

In Ohio, through our cultural diversity initiatives, we have created an extensive guide, *Ohio's Collaborative Effort to Enhance*

Homeland Security 2003–2006, in cooperation with the Ohio Department of Public Safety, to spread awareness of pertinent cultural issues and detail practical solutions and programs.

BA: The OACP has established relationships with international law enforcement agencies. What has been accomplished?

GV: In 2006, I traveled with other members of the OACP to many cities and countries in the Middle East and elsewhere: Bishkek, Kyrgyzstan; Dubai, United Arab Emirates; Islamabad, Pakistan; Manama, Bahrain; Amman, Jordan; and then Istanbul, Turkey, which I have visited three times. Universally, police officers are people who have committed their lives to a public service, realizing they would never be greatly compensated. We all realize this profession is a willingness to put our lives on the line for other people. Policing is a service, not unlike the military service. Also, the police are the most visible form of their government and if there is dissatisfaction with the government there tends to be dissatisfaction with the police. And the opposite holds true, if there is an appreciation of the government, there tends to be an appreciation of the police. I see a lot of commonality with policing across the international community.

We have a great program with the Turkish National Police. For the past 6 years the OACP has had an ongoing exchange with the Turkish National Police, hosting educational exchanges in both countries for the purpose of learning about their culture and religion, and to nurture a relationship of mutual trust and respect. An estimated 250,000 Arab-Americans and Muslim-Americas live in Ohio, primarily in Columbus, Toledo, and Cleveland. Since many of their homeland cultures have dictatorial governments, the only way for Arab and Muslim immigrants to learn that the American police are not the same as those from the countries they left is through contact—informed and consistent outreach. The outreach done in Ohio was received with skepticism by many in the Arab and Muslim communities here, and we were told by our multicultural affairs officer that it would take at least 6 months to develop productive partnerships. He admitted to being pleasantly surprised that it took only 2 to 3 months to make significant progress, because we followed our words with action. We made consistent contacts. We "walked our talk." We have been told by federal government officials that our program of outreach in Ohio is unique. We have the Turkish National Police working with us. We go to the various communities and ask them to explain their faith and customs to us. And we develop educational programs for our officers. It is something that is ongoing. It is a priority. This relationship between the TNP and OACP is founded on a memorandum of understanding (MOU). We also have a MOU signed with the State of Beara, Brazil, and expect to sign a MOU in the coming months with the Jordanian National Police.

Our ultimate goal is to attack extremism and radicalism in Ohio, which is a shared goal across the country. When we do not communicate, some cultures can become isolated, turn inward, and become radicalized. I believe that 98% to 99% of the population consists of good people.

And if we reach out to those good people, they will help us identify the 1% to 2% of those who want to cause harm. This is a common theme running throughout our organization.

BA: What has been learned or brought back from your meetings with international police?

GV: We have learned a great deal. I would say, the most important lesson learned is that we have more in common than we do differences. Second, we have an ongoing mutual learning process that we are all interested in continuing, and have all benefited from greatly.

We, as an organization and individually, have thoroughly benefited from mutual learning and exchanges with the IPES. In particular, Dr. Dilip Das, IPES [International Police Executive Symposium] president, does a masterful job of providing leadership and expertise to the organization, and the OACP has greatly benefited from being involved with the IPES. It is wonderful network of police leaders, police executives, and academics from all over the world with which we have been honored to participate.

BA: Have any programs specifically been developed as a result of your international relationships?

GV: A program that the OACP has developed as an offshoot of the TNP (Turkish National Police) project is a first responder training program that addresses outreach to Muslim-Americans and Arab-Americans living in Ohio. The OACP, working with Ohio State Highway Patrol and Department of Public Safety, formed a committee to study concerns raised by police officers, firefighters, and sheriffs' deputies in their interactions with people from Ohio communities with a predominance of citizens of the Islamic faith. This group created a comprehensive DVD that can be used either as an 8-hour training course or as a reference tool to answer specific questions about interaction with people of the Islamic faith. This DVD has been sent to every law enforcement and fire agency in Ohio. In June 2006, the DVD first responder training program was demonstrated at the IPES meeting in Ayvalik, Turkey. In September 2006 the DVD was presented at a NATO conference sponsored by the Turkish National Police in Washington, DC.

Personnel from the Department of Homeland Security told our executive director, Dr. Todd Wurschmidt, that Ohio is second to none in helping our first responders understand the dynamics of the Arab and Muslim culture and religion.

Through our many exchanges with the Turkish National Police, the advice of Director General Aydiner of the TNP, now retired, was to "be proactive in understanding the needs of the Islamic community in Ohio." We continue to do that, and at the same time we continue to expand our relationship with the TNP. We created a memorandum of understanding between the OACP and the TNP that encourages continuing cooperation with each other. In the fall of 2006, the TNP and OACP added an addendum to the memorandum of understanding that names the OACP as the International Center for Applied Policing and Training (ICAPT).

BA: Overall, has the quality of policing improved or declined?

GV: I think police work has improved. I think that law enforcement as a profession has a conscience and because of the feedback we have gotten through the media, through people attending our council meetings and so forth, citizens are more likely to question the conduct of police officers today. They challenge their government more.

BA: In general, is it more or less difficult to be a police officer, now than in the past?

GV: It's a much more complex world today. People are learning things sooner in life, and the level of sophistication in society has gotten higher, so we have a higher level of expectation in the people seeking to be police officers. Therefore, it is increasingly more difficult for police officers to meet higher expectations in an increasingly more complex and culturally diverse society.

BA: Have standards in hiring changed?

GV: The OACP and an organization called I-O Solutions, from Chicago, Illinois, have developed a core attribute test which is being used in hiring police recruits. This test not only tests for initial cognitive skill levels (e.g., reading, writing, math) but also measures police candidates on 16 core personality traits (e.g., teamwork, compassion, communication skills, public service, etc.).

BA: What do you think should be the role of the police in society?

GV: Sir Robert Peel said the police are like normal citizens, both having a duty to protect their communities and to be vigilant. My sense is that our neighborhoods will only be safe if the responsibility for policing is a shared responsibility; whether it's shared with other law enforcement agencies, departments of government, or with private citizens.

BA: What should be their job, functions, and role?

GV: A police officer acts much today as a protector, a keeper of the peace, a counselor—a beacon in a storm. If someone needs to be redirected to a social service agency, the police officer should be able to do that. If the issue at hand extends beyond local concerns or resources, the officer needs to be able to collaborate with other entities in order to be able to solve that problem.

BA: What organizational arrangements work?

GV: I find that delegation is effective because I try to keep my worldview, my perspective, at the 30,000-foot level. I try to see how things fit together and then through relationships, assign tasks to appropriate groups. I feel as though I accomplish more by orchestrating the event than I do by physically putting it on, whether it is people in my internal staff and/or if I am encouraging a police chief or sheriff to help us move a project forward. Being able to link talented people together with a shared goal has proven to be a successful formula for me.

BA: How should policing be performed?

GV: Professionally. This means we set high standards, for example, through organizational programs like CALEA.[2] We also train constantly and consistently—not only in police tactics, but in such issues as police ethics and community service.

BA: What should be the preferred priorities and strategies?

GV: I believe law enforcement must carry the role of authority in a community. So the first priority always has to be to sustain order. When control is lost, you have martial law. We must keep people from getting hurt; prevent loss of life and loss of property. I consider those as the top priority. But in the next breath I would say, it is also essential to put out a fire while it is just a flickering flame, whenever we are able. I am saying if we invest in our children from the very youngest, and give them opportunities to grow in a safe environment with good role models and using the system to support them; if they can be competitive in this world, I believe we are less likely to see as many people in the criminal justice system. This is an underlying philosophy behind the prevention programs and many educational programs at the OACP.

BA: In your experience what policies or programs have worked well and which have not?

GV: Plans that involve more people tend to be more successful. If I develop a plan on my own and try to deliver or "sell it" to other people it tends to never have the same success as when solutions are based on open discussion and programs are built around the collective response.

BA: Do you have an example of something that has worked especially well?

GV: Yes, our OLLEISN (Ohio Local Law Enforcement Information-Sharing Network) program. I have been credited for OLLEISN because of my vision to connect information systems. Every police chief and sheriff throughout Ohio and the United States realized the many disparate software vendor systems did not provide for sharing information between local law enforcement agencies. The challenge was how to get around that and the answer was evident—each vendor had to change his software. Independently, local agencies did not have enough influence to change the vendor. Each department was merely one customer, but collectively and through the OACP, we were able to influence change. By offering a solution, and even alternative solutions, we created a main network through which all vendors were required to follow prescribed guidelines in order for their customers, the local law enforcement agency, to have access to the data from other contributing agencies. OACP's approach to information sharing allows local agencies to remain with their existing vendor and still share data with other law enforcement agencies.

BA: Is this a national problem, the lack of information sharing across jurisdictional lines?

GV: Yes. In fact, information was sometimes not shared within the same community. Should an incident occur at an intersection in any one given city in the state of Ohio, any number of agencies could have taken a report, including the city police department, the sheriff, and the highway patrol, without the capability to share information. Recently, Central Ohio experienced several shooting incidents that took place within 5 miles of each other which involved several different jurisdictions. It was not until a citizen was killed that we became aware all the other shooting incidents were related. The importance of linking systems is obvious; if we don't know there is a pattern of crime and if we don't have all the pieces to the puzzle, by linking systems we are enabling any agency to look at the other pieces, even though they occurred outside their jurisdiction, and see how they fit together.

Actually I think the model would work as a world process, particularly as it relates to Internet crimes, identity theft, child pornography, human trafficking, and drugs. Our chances of stopping these activities would increase if we didn't create havens for criminals because we don't share information.

BA: What would you consider to be the greatest problem facing the police at this time?

GV: Many structures put into place many years ago are not valid today. One example is the situation with immigration control, which is a federal issue. However, when the federal government cannot perform proficiently, it creates a local burden. We now have the situation where local police departments and sheriff's offices are dealing with undocumented persons who don't fit in the normal criminal justice system. How do you issue a ticket for speeding or driving without a license to a person who should not be in the country in the first place, and then expect them to show up in court? The federal policies on this issue are placing a tremendous burden on local government.

The increasing concerns about privacy are an issue. We are seeing much more video surveillance of open public areas used to identify criminals and meeting with success. And although there is a desire to not have Big Brother looking over one's shoulders, the public wants Big Brother to see if someone is going to hurt them. The issue is finding that balance between how much intrusion society is willing to accept, and what's appropriate.

BA: What would be easy to change?

GV: Philosophy is probably an easy one at the leadership level, to set new direction. However, the larger the ship, the harder it is to get it turned. It is most helpful when an organization chooses to be transparent, we use the term "walking the talk." In other words, they are actually doing what they say they are doing. People look for consistency in the police department and if the police department is holding itself accountable, that goes a long way.

BA: Is anything easy?

GV: It's easy to stay on the course that you are on—until the train wrecks. Many agencies are able to continue with old patterns and practices and have not yet experienced a disaster. When the disaster occurs and is published on the front page of the newspaper, the police chief or sheriff is out, and the new person comes in offering change. It's a pretty simple process—change now or change later.

BA: What should be the relationship between theory and practice?

GV: We must analyze where crime occurs and use that information to allocate our resources. For example, let's say we respond to burglaries in a given neighborhood. We then record incidents, analyze data, and allocate resources in the neighborhood. We then reapply that information to see if there is a reduction in crime in that neighborhood. The measurements we took are documented and applied to the theories. I feel theory should be applied in practice and then reevaluated as part of a circular pattern of doing business.

BA: What is the relationship right now? Does it exist?

GV: I think it exists. New York City met with great success using the broken windows theory—that is, if you clean up neighborhoods (fix broken windows, clean up trash, and get rid of graffiti, etc.) those actions will raise a sense of pride in the community. People will feel less likely to put graffiti on a wall that's cleanly painted or litter a park that does not have trash strewn all over. So I think we do it, it is just not applied as much as it should be.

BA: What holds collaboration or interactions back?

GV: The lack of trust; that is, we question the motives of others. If someone tells us they are a Democrat or Republican, we have preconceived ideas about possibly their faith, about their beliefs in the welfare system, their position on abortion, taxation, etc. These assumptions are based on past experiences and generalizations because we do not take the time to get to know the individual. For example, it is common for a police officer to generalize about a "social worker" and think they coddle citizens when discipline is needed to solve the problem. Of course, this is a generalization about social workers; however, it is probably a label frequently attached. Collaboration therefore is held back because of a generalized mistrust.

BA: What kind of research, in what form, would you find most useful for practice?

GV: I would like to see research done as a more multidimensional approach to problems, involving different disciplines. If a truancy problem exists in the schools, then the research would involve certainly the school counselor, it may involve the teacher, should involve the law enforcement officer, particularly if there is crime being committed during the time these truancies are occurring, and some type of family counseling may be appropriate. The more we collectively look at who our stakeholders are in a problem, and the more research that is done to show that systematic approaches are more effective. Too often problems are segmented as either a police problem, a health care problem, etc. We are finding many problems in society are blending into other areas with collaborations between agencies resulting in greater success.

BA: Are you basically satisfied or dissatisfied with the developments in policing?

GV: I am very pleased. Police officers are more accountable today. As mentioned earlier, through technology, through public expectations, and the role of the media. We scrutinize ourselves more so than any other time. The general education of law enforcement has continued to increase. We have more access to critique and review, and I use the example of Columbine, the school shooting, and more recently, the Amish school shooting[3] in Lancaster, Pennsylvania. Law enforcement officers are sharing experiences involving critical incidents and as a result I think there is a greater sense of professional accountability today than what we might have had.

BA: What are the most likely developments you see happening and which would you like to see happening?

GV: I think interagency cooperation is improving, particularly in the United States. The exchange of information between agencies is relatively simple when everyone is under the same roof. As with the Turkish National Police, they are literally connected all the way down to the street officer. In the United States, particularly in Ohio, we have 900 plus law enforcement agencies in the state, so if we are not collaborating or sharing, through technology, through communications, then every agency functions as a small island in and of themselves. Not only do they suffer from not having the benefit of exchanging communications or data, but there is not the peer or organizational relationships, that can dictate the training or direction of the organization. Through the ability to network in an association, I think that's where law enforcement in the United States is able to accomplish much of what can be done in other countries that operate under one unified law enforcement agency.

BA: What is most needed now to improve in policing?

GV: We need to have professional standards. Today, there are voluntary standards, like CALEA (Commission on Accreditation for Law Enforcement Agencies). These voluntary standards have been around for 25 years, and yet, still only 10% of American law enforcement has chosen to voluntarily submit to these standards. Without somebody defining what a profession is, it's subjective to that community. How do you define your organization if you have no standards by which to measure? So I think professional standards continue to be an important aspect.

BA: What can be done about those agencies that do not comply?

GV: Part of how we are policed is by the media. As much as media is a frustration to law enforcement sometimes, they provide a vital service as checks and balances of a free press. They possess the ability to say, "You are not doing your job" or "You are doing your job." There is always a resistance by law enforcement to accept that from the media, but I think the media is probably the greatest tool to help manage law enforcement.

BA: Is there anything else you see that needs to be improved?

GV: Yes, salaries commensurate with authority and responsibility. The reason I say that is in this country or other countries, when pay is extremely low there does tend to be some level of corruption. And when it is so imbalanced that corruption pays so well and when legitimate police service is difficult for a person to feed their family, then we are certainly placing our law enforcement agencies at risk of corruption. That is certainly my concern.

As I have traveled internationally with the OACP, I have seen agencies where an officer is making $100 per month. In the United States, for instance, a police officer in the South might earn $20,000 or $25,000 in a year. At the same time a person doing that same job in one of the northern states might be making $50,000 or $70,000 in a year. Since we hire from the environment, local young people are going to gravitate toward a more living wage. In the area of the country where I'm at, the pay is appropriate but as a profession it's not where it needs to be and we suffer when that happens.

Conclusion

The police structure of law enforcement in the United States is unique in the world. Each agency operates on its own, which results in better relations with each community, but leaves collaborative efforts a challenge that is being addressed. The concept of policing is local, changes are local and knowing this provides better service for local residents.

Of the 18,000 American chiefs he represents, Chief Vest is an exemplary example of today's educated, professional police chiefs. The Powell Police Department he heads is an example of the many professionally managed police departments across America, due to the high level of training hours required by Chief Vest, and the high standards and ethics that guide his leadership. As a visionary president of the OACP, he has developed programs of national significance and led OACP delegations to the Middle East for the purpose of building lasting international relationships, to learn and understand cultures and share policing theories and practices. His legacy at the OACP will have a lasting impact.

Endnotes

1. *Understanding Community Policing, A Framework for Action*. U.S. Government, Department of Justice, Bureau of Justice Assistance, August 1994, http://www.ncjrs.gov/pdffiles/commp.pdf.
2. CALEA, Commission on Accreditation for Law Enforcement Professionals. http://www.calea.org/Online/AboutCALEA/Commission.htm. CALEA provides a long set of standards to judge and evaluate the professionalism of police agencies. Participation by police departments in this evaluation process is voluntary, and expensive.

3. Both the Columbine (in Colorado) and the Amish school (in Pennsylvania) incidents refer to shootings at two schools in which a number of students were killed by fellow students (in Columbine) and by an adult (in the Amish school shooting). The incidents generated much media attention and led intense discussions among police and criminal justice professionals about why such shootings occurred and how they could be prevented in the future.

Appendix
Suggested Guidelines for Interviewers

General Remarks

The general goal of the interviews is to present the views and interpretations of policing developments and current issues *by experienced practitioners.* What do they see happening in policing in their countries and internationally, and how do they evaluate or interpret developments? We have many analyses and interpretations of policing by scholars and policy makers from outside the police organization. What we would like to have are views and interpretations from within the organization. What do police leaders who do the work see happening in policing: what are the issues they consider important? What changes do they see as successes or failures? What is likely to last into the future and what is a passing fad?

The basic goal of the interviews is to capture the views of police officials. Your role should not be to be too critical or to interpret what the officials meant to say, but to write as accurately as possible what the officials told you. It is their views, based on their experience and thinking, that we are interested in. We know what scholars think about policing; but we know less what the people who do policing think about and how they evaluate trends, developments, and issues in policing. That is the important goal.

The basic reason for doing the interviews in the first place is our firm belief that police officials know a lot; that practitioners can make significant contributions to our understanding of the prospects and problems of policing today. It is that knowledge and their judgments of policing that we are after. But that knowledge is not easily captured.

The practical reason for the interviews is that police leaders do not have the time to write and reflect on their experiences, views, opinions and perspectives. We think interviews are one means to capture that knowledge and that is why we are requesting researchers like you to record their views.

We want to reemphasize one major point. We *do not want the official rhetoric (or the official success stories)* that high-level people sometimes fall back on during interviews; we want their *personal views and thinking.* If you have the sense that you are getting the formal language and official views of policing and reforms, see if you can get the officials to go beyond that and push them for their own views. The interviewer should seek to get the person interviewed to move beyond simple answers, and get them to analyze and reflect on their experiences and knowledge. That takes skill on the part of the interviewer—but that is why you were asked to do an interview.

Topic Areas that Should Be Covered

These are the basic areas we would like to cover. In some cases there may be other areas of importance in "your" country or community and you should ask about those areas as well. For example, questions of police leaders in transitional countries will likely deal more with changes in policing philosophies and organizations than question for leaders in stable democracies. We know, when asking you to conduct an interview, that you are quite familiar with the policing situations in "your" country and that you will tailor your questions toward the dominant local issues that have had to be dealt with by the leaders. Be creative but not overly so.

We have listed a number of topics that should be covered in the interview. Please try to cover the topics mentioned below as the conduct and flow of the interview dictates. And add, elaborate, follow up as you see fit and necessary to clarify points, expand on ideas, or pursue an insight offered.

All the topical areas should be asked, but the specific questions listed below for each topic area are suggestions. Interviews have their own dynamics. Follow them down their most fruitful avenues. Since each of you will be interviewing officials within different organizations the list and sequence of questions will have to be adjusted in any case.

The wording of questions is, of course your own. In follow-up questions, try to get specific examples or details of generalizations made. (Examples are probably among the most useful pieces of information to readers.)

Career: Tell us a little bit about your career: length, organizations worked in, movements, specializations, etc. Basically standard stuff.

Other possible questions (add other questions at your discretion):

What motivated you to enter police work?
What about how your career developed surprised you?
Did your work prove as interesting or rewarding as you thought it would?

Changes experienced: What do you see as the most important changes that have happened in policing over the course of your career (philosophies, organizational arrangements, specializations, policies and programs, equipments, personnel, diversity etc.)?

What changes in external conditions (support from communities, legal powers, judicial relations, relations with minority communities, resource provision, political influence, etc.) have had a significant impact on policing?

Overall, has the quality of policing improved or declined (street work, specialized units, managerial capacity, self-evaluation, interagency cooperation, etc.)?

In general, is it more or less difficult to be a police officer (street, manager) now than in the past?

Personal policing philosophy: What do you think should be the role of the police in society?

What should be their job, functions, and roles? What should be left to other people or organizations?

What organizational arrangements work and which do not?

What policies on relations with the community, with political groups, with other criminal justice organizations work well? What hampers cooperation with other agencies and groups?

How should policing be performed? What should be the preferred priorities and strategies; hard-edged crime control, prevention, services, order work, what mix for which types of problems; proactive-reactive; community policing-law enforcement, etc.?

Problems and successes experienced: In your experience what policies or programs have worked well and which have not? And can you speculate for what reasons?

What would you consider to be the greatest problem facing the police at this time?

What problems in policing do you find are the most difficult to deal with? What would be easy to change? Internal problems (culture of the organization, managerial deficiencies, allegations of corruption or gender related problems, etc.) or externally generated problems (resources, community support, etc.)?

Is anything about policing easy?

Theory and practice: What should be the relationship between theory and practice? What can practitioners learn from theory, and what can theory builders learn from practitioners?

What is the relationship right now? Does it exist? Does it work? What holds collaboration or interactions back?

What kind of research, in what form, on what questions would you find most useful for practice? If not very useful, what could or should theory builders do to make their products more useful to you?

Where do you find theory-based information? Where do you look: journals, professional magazines, books, publications, reports?

Does the organization do research on its own? On what types of issues or questions?

Transnational relations: Have you been affected by, and how, in the work of your organization by developments outside the country (human rights demands, universal codes of ethics, practical interactions with police from other countries, personal experiences outside the country, new crime threats, etc.)?

Have those interactions been beneficial or harmful? What kind of external international influences are beneficial and which ones less so?

How have developments post September 11 affected your work?

Democratic policing (there has been much discussion of what that phrase means and how it can be achieved): How would you define democratic policing? What practices would bring democratic policing to life? Can democratic policing be achieved in your country, or not, and what obstacles stand in the way? Should democratic policing be the goal of reforms?

General assessments: Are you basically satisfied or dissatisfied with developments in policing? What are the most likely developments you see happening and which would you like to see happening? What is most needed now to improve policing?

What to Do Before and After the Interview

Before

Get a sense of how much time you are likely to have and what questions you can get to during that time. In no interview will you be able to ask all the questions you want. And, when you write up the interview, you will have space for about 6000 to 8000 words (on the average). Choose your priorities. The top priorities for us are the reflections by the officials interviewed on changes experienced during their careers, how they evaluate those changes, and the interrelations of theory and practice. These are high priorities for the interviews.

After the Interview

1. Please write a short introduction to the actual interview. The introduction should:
   a. Briefly describe the basic structure of policing in your country. You have to be the judge of how much an informed reader is likely to know about the country and how much should be explained.
   b. Describe, briefly, the interview itself. Where and when it was conducted; how long it took, or multiple sittings; how honest and open you feel the discussion was.

2. You should, if at all possible, tape-record the interview. For publication, edit the interview to bring out the most important discussion and answers. Chances are you will have much more information than we will have space for your interview in the proposed book.
3. Write a short conclusion on your impression of the interview. What the major themes were, how well the views expressed accord with the known literature, but do not be overly critical on this point, please. Again briefly.
4. Write a glossary of terms or events mentioned in the interview a reader might not be familiar with. For example, if interviewing a German official and *Bundeskriminalamt* is mentioned describe very briefly what that is; or if in interviewing a South African official SARPCCO is mentioned, describe that. Just select the most likely items inexperienced readers might not know.
5. We have had two basic styles in writing up interviews. Both are acceptable, but we prefer the second style. One style is to simply transcribe the interviews—questions asked, answers given. The second style, which requires more work, is to write short statements about the topic of a question and then insert long excerpts from the interviews. The main point is to have the voice and views of the leaders being interviewed, not your own.
6. Send the completed interviews to me and Dilip.

The total interview, with intro, conclusion, and glossary should be about 6000 to 8000 words.

International Police Executive Symposium (IPES)

The International Police Executive Symposium was founded in 1994. The aims and objectives of the IPES are to provide a forum to foster closer relationships among police researchers and practitioners globally, to facilitate cross-cultural, international, and interdisciplinary exchanges for the enrichment of the law enforcement profession, and to encourage discussion and published research on challenging and contemporary topics related to the profession.

One of the most important activities of the IPES is the organization of an annual meeting under the auspices of a police or educational institution. To date, meetings have been hosted by the Canton Police of Geneva, Switzerland (Police Challenges and Strategies, 1994), the International Institute of the Sociology of Law in Onati, Spain (Challenges of Policing Democracies, 1995), Kanagawa University in Yokohama, Japan (Organized Crime, 1996), the Federal Police in Vienna, Austria (International Police Cooperation, 1997), the Dutch Police and Europol in The Hague, The Netherlands (Crime Prevention, 1998), and Andhra Pradesh Police in Hyderabad, India (Policing of Public Order, 1999), and the Center for Public Safety, Northwestern University, Evanston Illinois, USA, (Traffic Policing, 2000). A special meeting was co-hosted by the Bavarian Police Academy of Continuing Education in Ainring, Germany, University of Passau, Germany, and State University of New York, Plattsburgh, USA, to discuss the issues endorsed by the IPES in April 2000. The Police in Poland hosted the next meeting in May, 2001 (Corruption: A threat to World Order), and the last annual meeting was hosted by the Police of Turkey in May, 2002 (Police Education and Training). The Kingdom of Bahrain hosted the annual meeting in October, 2003 (Police and the Community).

The 2004 meeting in May of that year (Criminal Exploitation of Women and Children) took place in British Columbia in Canada, and it was co-hosted by the University College of the Fraser Valley, Abbotsford Police Department, Royal Canadian Mounted Police, the Vancouver Police Department, the Justice Institute of British Columbia, Canadian Police College, and the International Centre for Criminal Law Reform and Criminal Justice Policy.

The last meeting (Challenges of Policing in the 21st Century) took place in September, 2005 in Prague, The Czech Republic. The Turkish National Police hosted the meeting in 2006 (Local Linkages to Global Security and Crime). The Fourteenth Annual Meeting was hosted in Dubai on April 8–12, 2007 (Urbanization and Security) by the Dubai Police and the Ohio Association of Chiefs of Police and the City of Cincinnati (Ohio) Police hosted the last meeting in Cincinnati (May 12-16, 2008) on the theme of "Police Without Borders: Fading Distinction Between Local and Global." Ohrid, Macedonia (June 9–14, 2009) will be the venue of the 2009 meeting with the Government of Macedonia as the host and the theme will be "Policing, the Private Sector, Economic Development and Social Change".

The majority of participants of the annual meetings are usually directly involved in the police profession. In addition, scholars and researchers in the field also participate. The meetings comprise both structured and informal sessions to maximize dialogue and exchange of views and information. The executive summary of each meeting is distributed to participants as well as to a wide range of other interested police professionals and scholars. In addition, a book of selected papers from each annual meeting is published through Prentice Hall, Lexington Books, Taylor and Francis Group and other reputed publishers.

Closely associated with the IPES is the *Police Practice and Research: An International Journal (PPR)*. The journal is committed to highlighting current, innovative police practices from all over the world; providing opportunities for exchanges between police practitioners and researchers; reporting the state of public safety internationally; focusing on successful practices that build partnerships between police practitioners and communities, as well as highlighting other successful police practices in relation to maintaining order, enforcing laws and serving the community. For more information visit our website, www.ipes.info.

The IPES is directed by a board of directors representing various countries of the world (listed below).

IPES Board of Directors

The IPES is directed by a board of directors representing various countries of the world (listed below). The registered business office is located at 6030 Nott Road, Guilderland, NY 12064 and Registered Agent is National Registered Agents, 200 West Adams Street, Chicago, Il 60606

President

Dilip Das, 6030 Nott Road, Guilderland, NY 12084, USA, Tel: 802 598 3680 Fax 410 951 3045, Email: dilipkd@aol.com

Vice President

Tariq Hassan Al Hassan, P.O. Box 13, Manama, KINGDOM OF BAHRAIN; Tel: (973) 17 756777, Fax: (973) 17 754302 Email: Ropac@batelco.com.bh

Treasurer/Secretary

Terri Canterbury, 7017, Suzanne Lane, Schenectady, New York 12303, USA, Tel: 518 935 4657 terri.a.canterbury@us.hsbc.com

Directors

Rick Sarre, GPO Box 2471, Adelaide, 5001, South AUSTRALIA; Tel: 61 8 84314879 (h), 61 8 83020889, Fax: 61 8 83020512 Email: rick.sarre@unisa.edu.au

Tonita Murray, 73 Murphy Street, Carleton Place, Ontario K7C 2B7 CANADA; Tel: 613 998 0883 (w) Email: Tonita_Murray@hotmail.com

Mark Chen, Kwei-Shan, Taoyuan, 333 Taiwan, Tel 886 3 3282321, Ex 4755, Cell 886 920 915966 mark@mail.cpu.edu.tw or markchen53@yahoo.com.tw

Snezana (Ana) Mijovic-Das, 6030 Nott Road, Guilderland, NY 12084, USA, Tel: 518 452 7845, Fax: 518 456 6790, Email: anamijovic@yahoo.com

Andrew Carpenter, Chief, Strategic Policy and Development Section, Police Division, Office of the Rule of Law and Security Institutions, Department of Peacekeeping Operations, United Nations, Room S-2280C, 405 East 42nd Street, New York, NY 10017, Tel 917 3672205, Cell 347 721 1104, Fax 917 367 2222, Email, carpentera@un.org

Paulo R. Lino, 111 Das Garcas St., Canoas, RS, 92320-830, Brazil; Tel 55 51 8111 1357, Fax 55 51 466 2425 Email: paulino2@terra.com.br

Rune Glomseth, Slemdalsveien5, Oslo, 0369, Norway, E-mail: Rune.Glomseth@phs.no

Mustafa Ozguler, 1849 Algonquin Place, Kent, Ohio 44240, Tel 330 389 0187 (USA), E:mail: Mustafaozg@hotmail.com

Maximillian Edelbacher, Riemersgasse 16/E/3, A-1190 Vienna, AUSTRIA; Tel: 43-1-601 74/5710, Fax: 43-1-601 74/5727 Email: edelmax@magnet.at

Etienne Elion, Case J-354-V, OCH Moungali 3, Brazzaville, Republic of Congo (Ex French Congo), Tel 242 662 1683, Fax 242 682 0293, Email ejeej2003@yahoo.fr

A.B. Dambazau, General, Nigerian Army, Nigeria, Tel 234 80 35012743, Fax 234 70 36359118, Email adambazau@yahoo.com

IPES Institutional Supporters

1. Dubai Police Department, (Dr. Mohammed Murad Abdulla, Director), Decision- Making Support Center, P.O. Box 1493, Dubai, United Arab Emirates, Tel 971 4 269 3790, Fax 971 4 262 3233, E-mail: dxbpolrs@emirates.net.ae

2. Bahrain Police, (Lt. General Shaikh Rashed Bin Abdulla Al Khalifa, Minister of the Interior), P.O. Box 13, Manama, Kingdom of Bahrain, Tel 973 17 270800, Fax 973 17 253 266, E-mail: Colonel Tariq Hassan AL Hassan, Ropac@batelco.com.bh

3. Fayetteville State University, (Dr. David E. Barlow, Professor and Dean), College of Basic and Applied Sciences, 130 Chick Building, 1200 Murchison Road, Fayetteville, North Carolina, 28301 USA Tel 910-672-1659, Fax 910-672-1083, E-mail: dbarlow@uncfsu.edu

4. University of Hull, (Dr Bankole Cole, Director of Undergraduate Programmes, Department of Criminology and Sociological Studies), Cottingham Road, Hull HU6 7RX, UK, Tel 01482 465669 E-mail: B.Cole@hull.ac.uk

5. National Institute of Criminology and Forensic Science, (Mr. D M Mitra, Inspector General of Police) MHA, Outer Ring Road, Sector 3, Rohini, Delhi 110085, India, Tel 91 996 826 2008, Fax 91 11 275 10586, E-mail: Johndm_mitra@yahoo.co.in

6. Birmingham City University, (Mike King) Center for Criminal Justice Policy and Research, Perry Barr, Birmingham B42 2SU, UK, Tel 0121 3315163 Fax 0121 3316938, E-mail: Mike.King@bcu.ac.uk-. In the 2008 brochure you have the name wrong.

7. Defendology Center for Security, Sociology and Criminology Research, (Valibor Lalic), Srpska Street 63,78000 Banja Luka, Bosnia and Herzegovina, Tel and Fax, 387 51 308 914 E-mail: lalicv@teol. net

8. University of Maribor, (Dr. Gorazd Mesko), The Faculty of Criminal Justice and Security, University of Maribor, Kotnikova 8, 1000 Ljubljana, Slovenia, Tel 386 1 300 83 39, Fax 386 1 2302 687, E-mail: gorazd.mesko@fpvv.uni-mb.si

9. Florida Gulf Coast University, (Charlie Mesloh, Ph.D., Director), Weapons and Equipment Research Institute, 10501 FGCU Blvd S., Fort Myers, Fl 33965, USA, Tel 239-590-7761 (office), Fax 239-229-3462 (cellular), E-mail: cmesloh@fgcu.edu

10. Ohio Association of Chiefs of Police (Chief Michael Laage), 6277 Riverside Drive, #2N, Dublin, Ohio 43017, USA, Tel. 614 761 0330, Fax 614 718 3216. E-mail MLaage@springdale.org

11. Kent State Univ. Police Services (John A. Peach, Chief of Police), P. O. Box 5190, Stockdale Safety Building, Kent, Ohio USA 44242-0001, Tel 330 672 3111, E-mail: jpeach@kent.edu

12. Abbotsford Police Department, (Ian Mackenzie, Chief Constable), 2838 Justice Way, Abbotsford, British Columbia V2 T3 P5, Canada, Tel 604-864-4809, Fax 604-864-4725, E-mail: bobrich@abbypd.ca, swillms@abbypd.ca

13. Department of Criminal Justice, North Carolina Central University, 301 Whiting Criminal Justice Bldg., Durham, NC 27707 USA (Dr. Harvey L. McMurray, Chair) 919-530-5204, Fax 919-530-5195, E-mail: hmcmurray@nccu.edu

14. University of the Fraser Valley, (Dr. Darryl Plecas), Department of Criminology & Criminal Justice, 33844 King Road, Abbotsford, British Columbia V2 S7 M9, Canada, Tel 604-853-7441, Fax 604-853-9990, E-mail: Darryl.plecas@ucfv.ca

15. National Police Academy, Japan, Koichi Kurokawa, Assistant Director, Police Policy Research Center, Zip 183-8558: 3-12-1 Asahi-cho Fuchu-city, Tokyo, Tel 81 42 354 3550, Fax 81 42 330 1308, E-mail: tcr01@npac.jp

16. Canterbury Christ Church University (Claire Shrubsall), Department of Crime and Policing Studies, Northwood Road, Broadstairs, Kent CT 10 2 WA, UK, Tel 44 (0) 1843 609115, Fax 44 (0) 1843 280700, E-mail: Claire.shrubsall@canterbury.ac.uk

17. Police Standards Unit, Home Office (Stephen Cahill), 4th Floor Fry Building, 2 Marsham Street, London SW1P 4 DF, UK, Tel 44 20 7035 0922, Fax 44 870 336 9015, E-mail: Stephen.Cahill@homeoffice.gsi.gov.uk

18. Royal Canadian Mounted Police (Gary Bass, Deputy Commissioner, Pacific Region) 657 West 37th Avenue, Vancouver, BC V5Z. 1K6, Canada Tel 604 264 2003, Fax 604 264 3547, E-mail: gary.bass@rcmp-grc.gc.ca

19. Eastern Kentucky University (Dr. Robin Haarr), Stratton Building 412A, Stratton Building, 521 Lancaster Avenue, Richmond, KY 40475 USA, Tel 859-622-8152, E-mail: robin.haarr@eku.edu

20. The Faculty of Law, University of Kragujevac, Serbia, (Prof. Branislav Simonovic) Str. Jovanba Cvijica 1, Kragujevac, Serbia 34000 Tel 381 34 306 580, Fax 381 34 306 546, E-mail: simonov@EUnet.yu

21. Marc Dann, Attorney General, State of Ohio, (Jessica Utovich) State Office Tower, 30 E. Broad Street, 17th Floor, Columbus, OH 43215-3428, Tel (614) 466-4320, E-mail: mdann@ag.state.oh.us, JUtovich@ag.state.oh.us

22. The Ministry of Interior, PO Box 13320, Doha. Qatar, (Contact Brigadier Al Kaabi Nasser Rashid) Tel 250 552 6009. email: nasser55@windowslive.com

23. The Cyber Defense & Research Initiatives, LLC, PO Box 86, Leslie, MI 49251, (Contact James Lewis), Tel 517 242 6730, Email: lewisja@cyberdefenseresearch.com

24. Audiolex (Contact Kate J. Storey-Whyte, Ph.D.), 9-10 Old Police Station, Kington, Hereford, Herefordshire HR53DP, England, Fax 44 154 423 1965, Mobile, 44 7833 378 379.

25. The Department of Criminal Justice, Molloy College, 1000 Hempstead Avenue, PO Box 5002, Rockville Center, NY 11571-5002, USA (Contact Dr. John A. Eterno, NYPD Captain-Retired), Tel 516 678 5000, Ext. 6135, Fax 516 256 2289, email: jeterno@molloy.edu

26. The Senlis Council, Center of Excellence on Public Safety (George Howell) Rua Maria Queteria, 121/305, Ipanema, Rio de Janeiro, RJ 22410040, Brazil, Tel 55 21 3903 9495, Cel 55 21 8156 6485, howell@senlicouncil.net

27. The Department of Applied Social Studies, City University of Hong Kong (Li, Chi-mei, Jessica, Ph.D., Lecturer), Tat Chee Avenue, Kowloon Tong, Hong Kong, Tel: 2788 8839, Fax: 2788 8960, jessica@cityu.edu.hk

28. University of Maine at Augusta, College of Natural and Social Sciences (Professor Richard Mears), 46 University Drive. Augusta, ME 04330-9410, USA, Tel/Fax?, Rmears@maine.edu

Index